JOHN RUSKIN

SESAME AND LILIES

AND THE QUEEN OF THE AIR

By JOHN RUSKIN, M.A., LL.D.

Author of "THE STONES OF VENICE," "MODERN
PAINTERS," "THE CROWN OF WILD OLIVE,"
"THE SEVEN LAMPS OF ARCHITECTURE," etc.

A. L. BURT COMPANY, PUBLISHERS,
52-58 DUANE STREET, NEW YORK ❧ ❧

PREFACE.

BEING now fifty-one years old, and little likely to
change my mind hereafter on any important subject of
thought (unless through weakness of age), I wish to
publish a connected series of such parts of my works
as now seem to me right, and likely to be of permanent
use. In doing so I shall omit much, but not attempt
to mend what I think worth reprinting. A young
man necessarily writes otherwise than an old one, and
it would be worse than wasted time to try to recast
the juvenile language : nor is it to be thought that I
am ashamed even of what I cancel; for great part of
my earlier work was rapidly written for temporary
purposes, and is now unnecessary, though true, even to
truism. What I wrote about religion, was, on the
contrary, pains-taking, and, I think, forcible, as compared with most religious writing ; especially in its
frankness and fearlessness : but it was wholly mistaken; for I had been educated in the doctrines of a
narrow sect, and had read history as obliquely as
sectarians necessarily must.

Mingled among these either unnecessary or erroneous

995

statements, I find, indeed, some that might be still of value; but these, in my earlier books, disfigured by affected language, partly through the desire to be thought a fine writer, and partly, as in the second volume of *Modern Painters*, in the notion of returning as far as I could to what I thought the better style of old English literature, especially to that of my then favorite, in prose, Richard Hooker.

For these reasons, though, as respects either art, policy, or morality as distinct from religion, I not only still hold, but would even wish strongly to reaffirm the substance of what I said in my earliest books, I shall reprint scarcely anything in this series out of the first and second volumes of *Modern Painters ;* and shall omit much of the *Seven Lamps* and *Stones of Venice ;* but all my books written within the last fifteen years will be republished without change, as new editions of them are called for, with here and there perhaps an additional note, and having their text divided, for convenient reference, into paragraphs consecutive through each volume. I shall also throw together the shorter fragments that bear on each other, and fill in with such uprinted lectures or studies as seem to me worth preserving, so as to keep the volumes, on an average, composed of about a hundred leaves each.

The first book of which a new edition is required chances to be *Sesame and Lilies*, from

which I now detach the old preface, about the
Alps, for use elsewhere; and to which I add a
lecture given in Ireland on a subject closely connected with that of the book itself. I am glad
that it should be the first of the complete series,
for many reasons; though in now looking over
these two lectures, I am painfully struck by the
waste of good work in them. They cost me much
thought, and much strong emotion; but it was foolish to suppose that I could rouse my audiences in
a little while to any sympathy with the temper
into which I had brought myself by years of
thinking over subjects full of pain; while, if I
missed my purpose at the time, it was little to
be hoped I could attain it afterward; since phrases
written for oral delivery become ineffective when
quietly read. Yet I should only take away what
good is in them if I tried to translate them into
the language of books; nor, indeed, could I at all
have done so at the time of their delivery, my
thoughts then habitually and impatiently putting
themselves into forms fit only for emphatic speech:
and thus I am startled, in my review of them,
to find that, though there is much (forgive me the
impertinence) which seems to me accurately and en-
ergetically said, there is scarcely anything put in
a form to be generally convincing, or even easily
intelligible: and I can well imagine a reader lay-

ing down the book without being at all moved
by it, still less guided, to any definite course of
action.

I think, however, if I now say briefly and clearly
what I meant my hearers to understand, and what I
wanted, and still would fain have, them to do, there
may afterward be found some better service in the
passionately written text.

The first Lecture says, or tries to say, that, life
being very short, and the quiet hours of it few,
we ought to waste none of them in reading valueless books; and that valuable books should, in a
civilized country, be within the reach of every one,
printed in excellent form, for a just price: but not
in any vile, vulgar, or, by reason of smallness of type,
physically injurious form, at a vile price. For we
none of us need many books, and those which we
need ought to be clearly printed, on the best paper,
and strongly bound. And though we are, indeed,
now, a wretched and poverty-struck nation, and
hardly able to keep soul and body together, still,
as no person in decent circumstances would put
on his table confessedly bad wine, or bad meat
without being ashamed, so he need not have on
his shelves ill printed or loosely and wretchedly-
stitched books; for, though few can be rich, yet
every man who honestly exerts himself may, I
think, still provide, for himself and his family,

good shoes, good gloves, strong harness for his cart or carriage horses, and stout leather binding for his books. And I would urge upon every young man, as the beginning of his due and wise provision for his household, to obtain as soon as he can, by the severest economy, a restricted, serviceable, and steadily—however slowly—increasing, series of books, for use through life; making his little library, of all the furniture in his room, the most studied and decorative piece; every volume having its assigned place, like a little statue in its niche, and one of the earliest and strictest lessons to the children of the house being how to turn the pages of their own literary possessions lightly and deliberately, with no chance of tearing or dogs' ears.

That is my notion of the founding of Kings' Treasuries; and the first Lecture is intended to show somewhat the use and preciousness of their treasures: but the two following ones have wider scope, being written in the hope of awakening the youth of England, so far as my poor words might have any power with them, to take some thought of the purposes of the life into which they are entering, and the nature of the world they have to conquer.

These two lectures are fragmentary and ill-arranged, but not, I think, diffuse or much compressible. The entire gist and conclusion of them, however, is in the last six paragraphs, 135 to the end, of the third lecture, which I would beg the reader to look over not once nor twice (rather than any other part of the book), for they contain the best expression I have yet been able to put in words of what, so far as is within my power, I mean henceforward both to do myself, and to plead with all over whom I have any influence, to do also according to their means: the letters begun on the first day of this year, to the workmen of England, having the object of originating, if possible, this movement among them, in true alliance with whatever trustworthy element of help they can find in the higher classes. After these paragraphs, let me ask you to read, by the fiery light of recent events, the fable at p. 293 (§ 117), and then §§ 129–131; and observe, my statement respecting the famine at Orissa is not rhetorical, but certified by official documents as within the truth. Five hundred thousand persons, *at least*, died by starvation in our British dominions, wholly in consequence of carelessness and want of forethought. Keep that well in your memory; and note it as the best possible illustration of modern political economy in true practice, and of the relations it has accomplished between Supply and Demand. Then begin the second lecture, and all will read clear enough, I think, to the end; only, since that second lecture was written, questions have arisen respecting the education and claims of women which have greatly troubled simple minds and excited restless ones. I am sometimes asked my thoughts on this matter, and I suppose that some girl readers of the second lecture may at the end of it desire to be told summarily what I would have them do and desire in the present state of things. This, then, is what I would say to any girl who had confidence enough in me to believe what I told her, or do what I ask her.

First, be quite sure of one thing, that, however much you may know, and whatever advantages you may possess, and however good you may be, you have not been singled out, by the God who made you, from all the other girls in the world, to be especially informed respecting His own nature and character. You have not been born in a luminous point upon the surface of the globe, where a perfect theology might be expounded to you from your youth up, and where everything you were taught would be true, and everything that was enforced upon you, right. Of all the insolent, all the foolish persuasions that by any chance could enter and hold your empty little heart, this is the proudest and foolishest—that you have been so much the darling of the Heavens, and favorite of the Fates as to be born in the very nick of time, and in the punctual place, when and where pure Divine truth had been sifted from the errors of the Nations; and that your papa had been providentially disposed to buy a house in the convenient neighborhood of the steeple under which that Immaculate and final verity would be beautifully proclaimed. Do not think it, child; it is not so. This, on the contrary, is the fact—unpleasant you may think it; pleasant, it seems to *me*—that you, with all your pretty dresses, and dainty looks and kindly thoughts, and saintly aspirations, are not one whit more thought of or loved by the great Maker and Master than any poor little red, black, or blue savage, running wild in the pestilent woods, or naked on the hot sands of the earth: and that, of the two, you probably know less about God than she does; the only difference being that she thinks little of Him that is right, and you much that is wrong.

That, then, is the first thing to make sure of—that you are not yet perfectly well informed on the most abstruse of all possible subjects, and that, if you care to behave with modesty or propriety, you had better be silent about it.

The second thing which you may make sure of is, that however good you may be, you have faults; that however dull you may be, you can find out what some of them are; and that however slight they may be, you had better make some—not too painful, but patient—effort to get quit of them. And so far as you have confidence in me at all, trust me for this, that how many soever you may find or fancy your faults to be, there are only two that are of real consequence—Idleness and Cruelty. Perhaps you may be proud. Well, we can get much good out of pride, if only it be not religious. Perhaps you may be vain: it is highly probable; and very pleasant for the people who like to praise you. Perhaps you are a little envious: that is really very shocking; but then—so is everybody else. Perhaps, also, you are a little malicious, which I am truly concerned to hear, but should probably only the more, if I knew you, enjoy your conversation. But whatever else you may be, you must not be useless, and you must not be cruel. If there is any one point which, in six thousand years of thinking about right and wrong, wise and good men have agreed upon, or successively by experience discovered, it is that God dislikes idle and cruel people more than any others; that His first order is, "Work while you have light;" and His second, "Be merciful while you have mercy."

"Work while you have light," especially while you have the light of morning. There are few things more wonderful to me than that old people never tell young ones how precious their youth is. They some-times sentimentally regret their own earlier days; sometimes prudently forget them; often foolishly re-buke the young, often more foolishly indulge, often most foolishly thwart and restrain, but scarcely ever warn or watch them. Remember, then, that I, at least, have warned *you*, that the happiness of your life, and its power, and its part and rank in earth or in heaven, depend on the way you pass your days now. They are not to be sad days; far from that, the first

duty of young people is to be delighted and delightful:
but they are to be in the deepest sense solemn days.
There is no solemnity so deep, to a rightly-thinking
creature, as that of dawn. But not only in that
beautiful sense, but in all their character and method,
they are to be solemn days. Take your Latin dictionary, and look out "sollennis," and fix the sense of the
word well in your mind, and remember that every day
of your early life is ordaining irrevocably, for good or
evil, the custom and practice of your soul; ordaining
either sacred customs of dear and lovely recurrence, or
trenching deeper and deeper the furrows for seed of
sorrow. Now, therefore, see that no day passes in
which you do not make yourself a somewhat better
creature: and in order to do that, find out, first, what
you are now. Do not think vaguely about it; take
pen and paper, and write down as accurate a description of yourself as you can, with the date to it. If
you dare not do so, find out why you dare not, and try
to get strength of heart enough to look yourself fairly
in the face, in mind as well as body. I do not doubt
but that the mind is a less pleasant thing to look at
than the face, and for that very reason it needs more
looking at; so always have two mirrors on your toilet-
table, and see that with proper care you dress body
and mind before them daily. After the dressing is
once over for the day, think no more about it: as your
hair will blow about your ears, so your temper and

thoughts will get ruffled with the day's work, and may need, sometimes, twice dressing; but I don't want you to carry about a mental pocket-comb; only to be smooth-braided always in the morning.

Write down then, frankly, what you are, or, at least, what you think yourself, not dwelling upon those inevitable faults which I have just told you are of little consequence, and which the action of a right life will shake or smooth away; but that you may determine to the best of your intelligence what you are good for, and can be made into. You will find that the mere resolve not to be useless, and the honest desire to help other people, will, in the quickest and delicatest ways, improve yourself. Thus, from the beginning, consider all your accomplishments as means of assistance to others; read attentively, in this volume, paragraphs 74, 75, 19, and 79, and you will understand what I mean, with respect to languages and music. In music especially you will soon find what personal benefit there is in being serviceable: it is probable that, however limited your powers, you have voice and ear enough to sustain a note of moderate compass in a concerted piece—that, then, is the first thing to make sure you can do. Get your voice disciplined and clear, and think only of accuracy; never of effect or expression: if you have any soul worth expressing it will show itself in your singing; but most likely there are very few feelings in you, at present, needing any particular expression; and the one thing you have to do is to make a clear-voiced little instrument of yourself, which other people can entirely depend upon for the note wanted. So, in drawing, as soon as you can set down the right shape of anything, and thereby explain its character to another person, or make the look of it clear and interesting to a child, you will begin to enjoy the art vividly for its own sake, and all your habits of mind and powers of memory will gain precision: but if you only try to make showy drawings for praise, or pretty ones for amusement, your drawing will have little or no real interest for you, and no educational power whatever.

Then, besides this more delicate work, resolve to do every day some that is useful in the vulgar sense. Learn first thoroughly the economy of the kitchen; the good and bad qualities of every common article of food, and the simplest and best modes of their preparation: when you have time, go and help in the cooking of poorer families, and show them how to make as much of everything as possible, and how to make little, nice: coaxing and tempting them into tidy and pretty ways, and pleading for well-folded table-cloths, however coarse, and for a flower or two out of the garden to strew on them. If you manage to get a clean table-cloth, bright plates on it, and a good dish in the middle, of your own cooking, you may ask leave to say a short grace; and let your religious ministries be confined to that much for the present.

Again, let a certain part of your day (as little as you choose, but not to be broken in upon) be set apart for making strong and pretty dresses for the poor. Learn the sound qualities of all useful stuffs, and make everything of the best you can get, whatever its price. I have many reasons for desiring you to do this—too many to be told just now—trust me, and be sure you get everything as good as can be: and if, in the villainous state of modern trade, you cannot get it good at any price, buy its raw material, and set some of the poor women about you to spin and weave, till you have got stuff that can be trusted: and then, every day, make some little piece of useful clothing, sewn with your own fingers as strongly as it can be stitched; and embroider it or otherwise beautify it moderately with fine needlework, such as a girl may be proud of having done. And accumulate these things by you until you hear of some honest persons in need of clothing, which may often too sorrowfully be; and, even though you should be deceived, and give them to the dishonest, and hear of their being at once taken to the pawnbroker's, never mind that, for the pawnbroker must sell them to some one who has need of them. That is no business of yours; what concerns you is only that when you see a half-naked child, you should have good and fresh clothes to give it, if its parents will let it be taught to wear them. If they will not, consider how they came to be of such a mind, which it will be wholesome for you beyond most subjects of inquiry to ascertain. And after you have gone on doing this a little while, you will begin to understand the meaning of at least one chapter of your Bible, Proverbs xxxi., without need of any labored comment, sermon, or meditation.

In these, then (and of course in all minor ways, besides, that you can discover in your own household), you must be to the best of your strength usefully employed during the greater part of the day, so that you may be able at the end of it to say, as proudly as any peasant, that you have not eaten the bread of idleness. Then, secondly, I said, you are not to be cruel. Perhaps you think there is no chance of your being so; and indeed I hope it is not likely that you should be deliberately unkind to any creature; but unless you are deliberately kind to every creature, you will often be cruel to many. Cruel, partly through want of imagination (a far rarer and weaker faculty in women than men), and yet more, at the present day, through the subtle encouragement of your selfishness by the religious doctrine that all which we now suppose to be evil will be brought to a good end; doctrine practically issuing, not in less earnest efforts that the immediate unpleasantness may be averted from ourselves, but in our remaining satisfied in the contemplation of its ultimate objects, when it is inflicted on others.

It is not likely that the more accurate methods of

recent mental education will now long permit young people to grow up in the persuasion that, in any danger or distress, they may expect to be themselves saved by the providence of God, while those around them are lost by His Improvidence : but they may be yet long restrained from rightly kind action, and long accustomed to endure both their own pain occasionally, and the pain of others always, with an unwise patience, by misconception of the eternal and incurable nature of real evil. Observe, therefore, carefully in this matter: there are degrees of pain, as degrees of faultfulness, which are altogether conquerable, and which seem to be merely forms of wholesome trial or discipline. Your fingers tingle when you go out on a frosty morning, and are all the warmer afterward ; your limbs are weary with wholesome work, and lie down in the pleasanter rest; you are tried for a little while by having to wait for some promised good, and it is all the sweeter when it comes. But you cannot carry the trial past a certain point. Let the cold fasten on your hand in an extreme degree, and your fingers will molder from their sockets. Fatigue yourself, but once, to utter exhaustion, and to the end of life you shall not recover the former vigor of your frame. Let heart-sickness pass beyond a certain bitter point, and the heart loses its life forever.

Now, the very definition of evil is in this irremediableness. It means sorrow, or sin, which end in

death; and assuredly, as far as we know, or can conceive, there are many conditions both of pain and sin
which cannot but so end. Of course we are ignorant
and blind creatures, and we cannot know what seeds
of good may be in present suffering, or present crime;
but with what we cannot know, we are not concerned.
It is conceivable that murderers and liars may in some
distant world be exalted into a higher humanity than
they could have reached without homicide or falsehood; but the contingency is not one by which our
actions should be guided. There is, indeed, a better
hope that the beggar, who lies at our gates in misery,
may, within gates of pearl, be comforted, but the
Master, whose words are our only authority for thinking so, never Himself inflicted disease as a blessing,
nor sent away the hungry unfed, or the wounded un-
healed.

Believe me, then, the only right principle of action
here, is to consider good and evil as defined by our
natural sense of both; and to strive to promote the
one, and to conquer the other, with as hearty endeavor
as if there were, indeed, no other world than this.
Above all, get quit of the absurd idea that Heaven will
interfere to correct great errors, while allowing its
laws to take their course in punishing small ones. If
you prepare a dish of food carelessly, you do not expect Providence to make it palatable; neither if,
through years of folly, you misguide your own life,

need you expect Divine interference to bring round everything at last for the best. I tell you, positively, the world is not so constituted : the consequences of great mistakes are just as sure as those of small ones, and the happiness of your whole life, and of all the lives over which you have power, depends as literally on your own common sense and discretion as the excellence and order of the feast of a day.

Think carefully and bravely over these things, and you will find them true : having found them so, think also carefully over your own position in life. I assume that you belong to the middle or upper classes, and that you would shrink from descending into a lower sphere. You may fancy you would not : nay, if you are very good, strong-hearted, and romantic, perhaps you really would not ; but it is not wrong that you should. You have then, I suppose, good food, pretty rooms to live in, pretty dresses to wear, power of obtaining every rational and wholesome pleasure ; you are, moreover, probably gentle and grateful, and in the habit of every day thanking God for these things. But why do you thank Him ? Is it because, in these matters, as well as in your religious knowledge, you think He has made a favorite of you. Is the essential meaning of your thanksgiving, "Lord, I thank thee that I am not as other girls are, not in that I fast twice in the week while they feast, but in that I feast seven times a week, while they fast," and are you quite sure this

is a pleasing form of thanksgiving to your Heavenly
Father? Suppose you saw one of your own true
earthly sisters, Lucy or Emily, cast out of your mortal
father's house, starving, helpless, heart-broken; and
that every morning when you went into your father's
room, you said to him, "How good you are, father,
to give me what you don't give Lucy," are you sure
that, whatever anger your parent might have just cause
for, against your sister, he would be pleased by that
thanksgiving, or flattered by that praise? Nay, are
you even sure that you *are* so much the favorite: suppose that, all this while, he loves poor Lucy just as
well as you, and is only trying you through her pain,
and perhaps not angry with her in anywise, but deeply
angry with you, and all the more for your thanks-
givings? Would it not be well that you should think,
and earnestly too, over this standing of yours; and all
the more if you wish to believe that text, which clergymen so much dislike preaching on, "How hardly shall
they that have riches enter into the Kingdom of God?"
You do not believe it now, or you would be less complacent in your state; and you cannot believe it at all,
until you know that the Kingdom of God means—
"not meat and drink, but justice, peace, and joy in the
Holy Ghost," nor until you know also that such joy is
not by any means, necessarily, in going to church, or
in singing hymns; but may be joy in a dance, or joy in
a jest, or joy in anything you have deserved to possess,

or that you are willing to give; but joy in nothing that separates you, as by any strange favor, from your fellow-creatures, that exalts you through their degradation—exempts you from their toil—or indulges you in time of their distress.

Think, then, and some day, I believe, you will feel also—no morbid passion of pity such as would turn you into a black Sister of Charity, but the steady fire of perpetual kindness which will make you a bright one. I speak in no disparagement of them; I know well how good the Sisters of Charity are, and how much we owe to them; but all these professional pieties (except so far as distinction or association may be necessary for effectiveness of work), are in their spirit wrong, and in practice merely plaster the sores of disease that ought never have been permitted to exist; encouraging at the same time the herd of less excellent women in frivolity, by leading them to think that they must either be good up to the black standard, or cannot be good for anything. Wear a costume, by all means, if you like; but let it be a cheerful and becoming one; and be in your heart a Sister of Charity always, without either veiled or voluble declaration of it.

As I pause, before ending my preface—thinking of one or two more points that are difficult to write of— I find a letter in *The Times*, from a French lady, which says all I want so beautifully, that I will print it just as it stands:

Sir—It is often said that one example is worth many sermons. Shall I be judged presumptuous if I point out one, which seems to me so striking just now, that, however painful, I cannot help dwelling upon it?

It is the share, the sad and large share, that French society and its recent habits of luxury, of expenses, of dress, of indulgence in every kind of extravagant dissipation, has to lay to its own door in its actual crisis of ruin, misery, and humiliation. If our *ménagères* can be cited as an example to English housewives, so, alas! can other classes of our society be set up as an example—*not* to be followed.

Bitter must be the feelings of many a French woman whose days of luxury and expensive habits are at an end, and whose bills of by-gone splendor lie with a heavy weight on her conscience, if not on her purse!

With us the evil has spread high and low. Everywhere have the examples given by the highest ladies in the land been followed but too successfully.

Every year did dress become more extravagant, entertainments more costly, expenses of every kind more considerable. Lower and lower became the tone of society, its good breeding, its delicacy. More and more were *monde* and *demi-monde* associated in newspaper accounts of fashionable doings, in scandalous gossip, on race-courses, in *premières représentations*, in imitation of each other's costumes, *mobiliers* and slang.

Living beyond one's means became habitual—almost necessary—for every one to keep up with, if not to go beyond, every one else.

What the result of all this has been we now see in the wreck of our prosperity, in the downfall of all that seemed brightest and highest.

Deeply and fearfully impressed by what my own country has incurred and is suffering, I cannot help feeling sorrowful when I see in England signs of our besetting sins appearing also. Paint and chignons, slang and vaudevilles, knowing "Anonymas" by name, and reading doubtfully moral novels, are in themselves small offenses, although not many years ago they would have appeared very heinous ones, yet they are quick and tempting conveyances on a very dangerous high-road.

I would that all Englishwomen knew how they are looked up to from abroad—what a high opinion, what honor and reverence we foreigners have for their principles, their truthfulness, the fresh and pure innocence of their daughters, the healthy youthfulness of their lovely children.

May I illustrate this by a short example which happened very near me? During the days of the *émeutes* of 1848, all the houses in Paris were being searched for fire-arms by the mob. The one I was living in contained none, as the master of the house repeatedly assured the furious and incredulous Republicans. They were going to lay violent hands on him, when his wife, an English lady, hearing the loud discussion, came bravely forward and assured them that no arms were concealed. "Vous êtes anglaise, nous vous croyons; les anglaises disent toujours la vérité," was the immediate answer, and the rioters quietly left.

Now, sir, shall I be accused of unjust criticism if loving and admiring your country, as these lines will prove, certain new features strike me as painful discrepancies in English life?

Far be it from me to preach the contempt of all that can make life lovable and wholesomely pleasant. I love nothing better than to see a woman nice, neat, elegant, looking her best in the prettiest dress that her taste and purse can afford, or your bright, fresh young girls fearlessly and perfectly sitting their horses, or adorning their houses as pretty [*sic;* it is not quite grammar, but it is better than if it were;] as care, trouble, and refinement can make them.

It is the degree *beyond* that which to us has proved so fatal, and that I would our example could warn you from, as a small repayment for your hospitality and friendliness to us in our days of trouble.

May Englishwomen accept this in a kindly spirit as a new-year's wish from

A FRENCH LADY.

December 29.

That, then, is the substance of what I would fain say convincingly, if it might be, to my girl friends; at all events with certainty in my own mind that I was thus far a safe guide to them.

For other and older readers it is needful I should write a few words more, respecting what opportunity I have had to judge, or right I have to speak, of such things; for, indeed, too much of what I have said about women has been said in faith only. A wise and lovely English lady told me, when *Sesame and Lilies* first appeared, that she was sure the *Sesame* would be useful, but that in the *Lilies* I had been writing of what I knew nothing about. Which was in a measure too true, and also that it is more partial than my writings are usually: for as Ellesmere spoke his speech on the —— intervention, not indeed otherwise than he felt, but yet altogether for the sake of Gretchen, so I wrote the *Lilies* to please one girl; and were it not for what I remember of her, and of few besides, should now perhaps recast some of the sentences in the *Lilies* in a very different tone: for as years have gone by, it has chanced to me, untowardly in some respects, fortunately in others (because it enables me to read history more clearly), to see the utmost evil that is in women, while I have had but to believe the utmost good. The best women are indeed necessarily the most difficult to know; they are recognized chiefly in the happiness of their husbands and the nobleness of their children; they are only to be divined, not discerned, by the stranger; and, sometimes, seem almost helpless except in their homes; yet without the help of one of them, to whom this book is dedicated, the day would probably have come before now, when I should have written and thought no more.

On the other hand, the fashion of the time renders whatever is forward, coarse, or senseless, in feminine nature, too palpable to all men—the weak picturesqueness of my earlier writings brought me acquainted with much of their emptiest enthusiasm; and the chances of later life gave me opportunities of watching women in states of degradation and vindictiveness which opened to me the gloomiest secrets of Greek and Syrian tragedy. I have seen them betray their household charities to lust, their pledged love to devotion; I have seen mothers dutiful to their children, as Medea; and children dutiful to their parents, as the daughter of Herodias; but my trust is still unmoved in the preciousness of the natures that are so fatal in their error, and I leave the words of the *Lilies* unchanged; believing, yet, that no man ever lived a right life who had not been chastened by a woman's love, strengthened by her courage, and guided by her discretion.

What I might myself have been so helped, I rarely indulge in the idleness of thinking; but what I am since I take on me the function of a teacher, it is well that the reader should know, as far as I can tell him.

Not an unjust person; not an unkind one; not a false one; a lover of order, labor, and peace. That, it seems to me, is enough to give me right to say all I care to say on ethical subjects : more, I could only tell definitely through details of autobiography such as none but prosperous and (in the simple sense of the word) faultless, lives could justify—and mine has been neither. Yet, if any one, skilled in reading the torn manuscripts of the human soul, cares for more intimate knowledge of me, he may have it by knowing with what persons in past history I have most sympathy.

I will name three.

In all that is strongest and deepest in me—that fits me for my work, and gives light or shadow to my being, I have sympathy with Guido Guinicelli.

In my constant natural temper, and thoughts of things and of people, with Marmontel.

In my enforced and accidental temper, and thoughts of things and of people, with Dean Swift.

Any one who can understand the natures of those three men, can understand mine; and having said so much, I am content to leave both life and work to be remembered or forgotten, as their uses may deserve.

Denmark Hill,

   1st January, 1871.

PREFACE—FIRST EDITION.

A PASSAGE in page 49 of this book, referring to Alpine travelers, will fall somewhat harshly on the reader's ear since it has been sorrowfully enforced by the deaths on Mont Cervin. I leave it, nevertheless, as it stood, for I do not now write unadvisedly, and think it wrong to cancel what has once been thoughtfully said: but it must not so remain without a few added words.

No blame ought to attach to the Alpine tourist for incurring danger. There is usually sufficient cause, and real reward, for all difficult work; and even were it otherwise, some experience of distinct peril, and the acquirement of habits of quick and calm action in its presence, are necessary elements, at some period of life, in the formation of manly character. The blame of bribing guides into danger is a singular accusation, in behalf of a people who have made mercenary soldiers of themselves for centuries, without any one's thinking of giving their fidelity better employment: though, indeed, the piece of work they did at the gate of the Tuileries, however useless, was no unwise one;

and their lion of flawed molasse at Lucerne, worthless
in point of art though it be, is nevertheless a better
reward than much pay; and a better ornament to the
old town than the Schweizer Hof, or flat new quay,
for the promenade of those travelers who do *not* take
guides into danger. The British public are however,
at home, so innocent of ever buying their fellow-creatures' lives, that we may justly expect them to be
punctilious abroad! They do not, perhaps, often
calculate how many souls flit annually, choked in fire-
damp and sea-sand, from economically watched shafts,
and economically manned ships; nor see the fiery
ghosts writhe up out of every scuttleful of cheap
coals: nor count how many threads of girlish life are
cut off and woven annually by painted Fates, into
breadths of ball-dresses; or soaked away, like rotten
hemp-fiber, in the inlet of Cocytus which overflows
the Grassmarket where flesh is as grass. We need
not, it seems to me, loudly blame any one for paying a
guide to take a brave walk with him. Therefore,
gentlemen of the Alpine Club, as much danger as you
care to face, by all means; but, if it please you, not so
much talk of it. The real ground for reprehension of
Alpine climbing is that, with less cause, it excites
more vanity than any other athletic skill. A good
horseman knows what it has cost to make him one;
everybody else knows it too, and knows that he is one;
he need not ride at a fence merely to show his seat. But

credit for practice in climbing can only be claimed after success, which though perhaps accidental and un-merited, must yet be attained at all risks, or the shame of defeat borne with no evidence of the diffi-culties encountered. At this particular period, also, the distinction obtainable by first conquest of a peak is as tempting to a traveler as the discovery of a new element to a chemist, or of a new species to a natural-ist. Vanity is never so keenly excited as by competi-tions which involve chance; the course of science is continually arrested, and its nomenclature fatally con-fused, by the eagerness of even wise and able men to establish their priority in an unimportant discovery, or obtain vested right to a syllable in a deformed word; and many an otherwise sensible person will risk his life for the sake of a line in future guide-books, to the fact that "——horn was first ascended by Mr. X. in the year ——;" never reflecting that of all the lines in the page, the one he has thus wrought for will be pre-cisely the least interesting to the reader.

It is not therefore strange, however much to be re-gretted, that while no gentleman boasts in other cases of his sagacity or his courage—while no good soldier talks of the charge he led, nor any good sailor of the helm he held—every man among the Alps seems to lose his senses and modesty with the fall of the barometer, and returns from his Nephelo-coccygia brandishing his ice-ax in everybody's face. Whatever

the Alpine Club have done, or may yet accomplish, in
a sincere thirst for mountain knowledge, and in happy
sense of youthful strength and play of animal spirit,
they have done, and will do, wisely and well; but
whatever they are urged to by mere sting of competition and itch of praise, they will do, as all vain
things must be done forever, foolishly and ill. It is a
strange proof of that absence of any real national love
of science, of which I have had occasion to speak in
the text, that no entire survey of the Alps has yet
been made by properly qualified men; and that, except
of the chain of Chamouni, no accurate maps exist, nor
any complete geological section even of that. But
Mr. Reilly's survey of that central group, and the
generally accurate information collected in the guide-
book published by the Club, are honorable results of
English adventure; and it is to be hoped that the continuance of such work will gradually put an end to the
vulgar excitement which looked upon the granite of
the Alps only as an unoccupied advertisement wall for
chalking names upon.

Respecting the means of accomplishing such work
with least risk, there was a sentence in the article of
our leading public journal, which deserves, and requires
expansion.

" Their " (the Alpine club's) " ropes must not break."

Certainly not! nor any one else's ropes, if they may
be rendered unbreakable by honesty of make; seeing

that more lives hang by them on moving than on motionless seas. The records of the last gale at the Cape
may teach us that economy in the manufacture of
cables is not always a matter for exultation ; and, on
the whole, it might even be well in an honest country,
sending out, and up and down, various lines east and
west, that *nothing* should break ; banks—words—nor
dredging tackle.

Granting, however, such praise and such sphere of
exertion as we thus justly may, to the spirit of adventure, there is one consequence of it, coming directly under my own cognizance, of which I cannot but speak
with utter regret—the loss, namely, of all real understanding of the character and beauty of Switzerland,
by the country's being now regarded as half watering-
place, half gymnasium. It is indeed true that under
the influence of the pride which gives poignancy to
the sensations which others cannot share with us (and
a not unjustifiable zest to the pleasure which we have
worked for), an ordinary traveler will usually observe
and enjoy more on a difficult excursion than on an
easy one ; and more in objects to which he is unaccus-
tomed than in those with which he is familiar. He
will notice with extreme interest that snow is white
on the top of a hill in June, though he would have
attached little importance to the same peculiarity
in a wreath at the bottom of a hill in January. He
will generally find more to admire in a cloud under his

feet, than in one over his head ; and, oppressed by the
monotony of a sky which is prevalently blue, will de-
rive extraordinary satisfaction from its approximation
to black.   Add to such grounds of delight the aid given
to the effect of whatever is impressive in the scenery of
the high Alps, by the absence of ludicrous or degrading concomitants ; and it ceases to be surprising that
Alpine excursionists should be greatly pleased, or
that they should attribute their pleasure to some
true and increased apprehension of the nobleness
of natural scenery.   But no impression can be more
false.   The real beauty of the Alps is to be seen,
and seen only, where all may see it, the child, the
cripple, and the man of gray hairs.   There is more
true loveliness in a single glade of pasture shadowed by
pine, or gleam of rocky brook, or inlet of unsullied lake,
among the lower Bernese and Savoyard hills, than in
the entire field of jagged gneiss which crests the
central ridge from the Shreckhorn to the Viso.   The
valley of Cluse, through which unhappy travelers consent now to be invoiced, packed in baskets like fish, so
only that they may cheaply reach, in the feverous
haste which has become the law of their being, the
glen of Chamouni whose every lovely foreground rock
has now been broken up to build hotels for them, contains more beauty in half a league of it, than the entire valley they have devastated, and turned into a
casino, did in its uninjured pride; and that passage of

the Jura by Olten (between Basle and Lucerne), which is by the modern tourist triumphantly effected through a tunnel in ten minutes, between two piggish trumpet grunts proclamatory of the ecstatic transit, used to show from every turn and sweep of its winding ascent, up which one sauntered, gathering wild-flowers, for half a happy day, diviner aspects of the distant Alps than ever were achieved by toil of limb, or won by risk of life.

There is indeed a healthy enjoyment both in engineers' work, and in school-boys' play; the making and mending of roads has its true enthusiasms, and I have still pleasure enough in mere scrambling to wonder not a little at the supreme gravity with which apes exercise their superior powers in that kind, as if profitless to them. But neither macadamization, nor tunneling, nor rope-ladders, will ever enable one human creature to understand the pleasure in natural scenery felt by Theocritus or Virgil; and I believe the athletic health of our school-boys might be made perfectly consistent with a spirit of more courtesy and reverence, both for men and things, than is recognizable in the behavior of modern youth.

Some year or two back, I was staying at the Montanvert to paint Alpine roses, and went every day to watch the budding of a favorite bed, which was rounding into faultless bloom beneath a cirque of rock, high enough, as I hoped, and close enough,

to guard it from rude eyes and plucking hands.
But,

" Tra erto e piano era un sentiero ghembo,
Che ne condusse in fianco della lacca,"

and on the day it reached the fullness of its rubied fire,
I was standing near when it was discovered by a
forager on the flanks of a traveling school of English
and German lads. He shouted to his companions, and
they swooped down upon it ; threw themselves into it,
rolled over and over in it, shrieked, hallooed, and
fought in it, trampled it down, and tore it up by the
roots ; breathless at last with rapture of ravage, they
fixed the brightest of the remnant blossoms of it in
their caps, and went on their way rejoicing.

They left me much to think upon ; partly respecting
the essential power of the beauty which could so excite them, and partly respecting the character of the
youth which could only be excited to destroy. But
the incident was a perfect type of that irreverence for
natural beauty with respect to which I said in the text,
at the place already indicated, " You make railroads of
the aisles of the cathedrals of the earth, and eat off
their altars." For indeed all true lovers of natural
beauty hold it in reverence so deep, that they would
as soon think of climbing the pillars of the choir of
Beauvais for a gymnastic exercise, as of making a
play-ground of Alpine snow : and they would not risk

one hour of their joy among the hill meadows on a
May morning, for the fame or fortune of having stood
on every pinnacle of the silver temple, and beheld the
kingdoms of the world from it.   Love of excitement is
so far from being love of beauty, that it ends always in
a joy in its exact reverse; joy in destruction—as of my
poor roses—or in actual details of death; until, in the
literature of the day "nothing is too dreadful, or too
trivial, for the greed of the public."*   And in politics,
apathy, irreverence, and lust of luxury go hand in
hand, until the best solemnization which can be conceived for the greatest event in modern European history, the crowning of Florence capital of Italy, is the
accursed and ill-omened folly of casting down her old
walls, and surrounding her with a "boulevard:" and
this at the very time when every stone of her ancient
cities is more precious to her than the gems of a Urim
breast-plate, and when every nerve of her heart and
brain should have been strained to redeem her guilt
and fulfill her freedom.   It is not by making roads
round Florence, but through Calabria, that she should
begin her Roman causeway work again; and her fate
points her march, not on boulevards by Arno, but
waist-deep in the lagoons at Venice.   Not yet, indeed,
but five years of patience and discipline of her youth
would accomplish her power, and sweep the martello
towers from the cliffs of Verona, and the ramparts

---

* *Pall Mall Gazette*, August 15th, article on the Forward murders.

from the marsh of Mestre.   But she will not teach her
youth that discipline on boulevards.

Strange, that while we both, French and English,
can give lessons in war, we only corrupt other nations
when they imitate either our pleasures or our indus-
tries.   We English, had we loved Switzerland indeed,
should have striven to elevate, but not to disturb, the
simplicity of her people by teaching them the sacred-
ness of their fields and waters, the honor of their
pastoral and burgher life, and the fellowship in glory
of the gray turreted walls round their ancient cities,
with their cottages in their fair groups by the forest
and lake.   Beautiful, indeed, upon the mountains, had
been the feet of any who had spoken peace to their
children; who had taught those princely peasants to
remember their lineage, and their league with the
rocks of the field; that so they might keep their
mountain waters pure, and their mountain paths
peaceful, and their traditions of domestic life holy.
We have taught them (incapable by circumstances and
position of ever becoming a great commercial nation),
all the foulness of the modern lust of wealth, without
its practical intelligences; and we have developed
exactly the weakness of their temperament by which
they are liable to meanest ruin.   Of the ancient architecture and most expressive beauty of their country
there is now little vestige left; and it is one of the few
reasons which console me for the advance of life, that

I am old enough to remember the time when the sweet waves of the Reuss and Limmat (now foul with the refuse of manufacture) were as crystalline as the heaven above them when her pictured bridges and embattled towers ran unbroken round Lucerne; when the Rhone flowed in deep green, softly dividing currents round the wooded ramparts of Geneva; and when from the marble roof of the western vault of Milan, I could watch the Rose of Italy flush in the first morning light, before a human foot had sullied its summit, or the reddening dawn on its rocks taken shadow of sadness from the crimson which long ago stained the ripples of Otterburn.

CONTENTS.

SESAME AND LILIES.

LECTURE I.

PAGE

OF KINGS' TREASURIES.... 1

LECTURE II.

OF QUEENS' GARDENS. 68

LECTURE III.

THE MYSTERY OF LIFE AND ITS ARTS.. 114

THE QUEEN OF THE AIR.

LECTURE I.

ATHENA IN THE HEAVENS............................... 173

LECTURE II.

ATHENA IN THE EARTH................................· 236

LECTURE III.

ATHENA IN THE HEART................................. 264

LECTURE IV.

THE HERCULES OF CAMARINA........................... 350

SESAME AND LILIES.

LECTURE I.—SESAME.

OF KINGS' TREASURIES.

> "You shall each have a cake of sesame—and ten pound."
> —LUCIAN: *The Fisherman.*

I BELIEVE, ladies and gentlemen, that my first duty this evening is to ask your pardon for the ambiguity of title under which the subject of lecture has been announced; and for having endeavored, as you may ultimately think, to obtain your audience under false pretenses. For indeed I am not going to talk of kings, known as regnant, nor of treasuries, understood to contain wealth; but of quite another order of royalty, and material of riches, than those usually acknowledged. And I had even intended to ask your attention for a little while on trust, and (as sometimes one contrives in taking a friend to see a favorite piece of scenery) to hide what I wanted most to show, with such imperfect cunning as I might, until we had unexpectedly reached the best point of view by winding paths. But since my good plain-spoken friend, Canon

Anson, has already partly anticipated my reserved "trot for the avenue" in his first advertised title of subject, "How and What to Read"—and as also I have heard it said, by men practiced in public address, that hearers are never so much fatigued as by the endeavor to follow a speaker who gives them no clew to his purpose, I will take the slight mask off at once, and tell you plainly that I want to speak to you about books; and about the way we read them, and could. or should read them. A grave subject, you will say; and a wide one! Yes; so wide that I shall make no effort to touch the compass of it. I will try only to bring before you a few simple thoughts about reading, which press themselves upon me every day more deeply, as I watch the course of the public mind with respect to our daily enlarging means of education, and the answeringly wider spreading, on the levels, of the irrigation of literature. It happens that I have practically some connection with schools for different classes of youth; and I receive many letters from parents respecting the education of their children. In the mass of these letters, I am always struck by the precedence which the idea of a "position in life" takes above all other thoughts in the parents'—more especially in the mothers'—minds. "The education befitting such and such a *station in life*"—this is the phrase, this the object, always. They never seek, as far as I can make out, an education good in itself; the conception of abstract rightness in training rarely seems reached by the writers. But an education " which shall keep a good coat on my son's back—an education which shall enable him to ring with confidence the visitors' bell at double-belled doors—education which shall result ultimately in establishment of a double-belled door to his own house; in a word, which shall lead to advancement in life." It never seems to occur to the parents that there may be an education which, in itself *is* advancement in Life—that any other than that may perhaps be advancement in Death ; and that this essential education might be more easily got, or given, than they fancy if they set about it in the right way ; while it is for no price, and by no favor, to be got, if they set about it in the wrong.

Indeed, among the ideas most prevalent and effective in the mind of this busiest of countries, I suppose the first—at least that which is confessed with the greatest frankness, and put forward as the fittest stimulus to youthful exertion—is this of " Advancement in life." My main purpose this evening is to determine, with you, what this idea practically includes, and what it should include.

Practically, then, at present, "advancement in life " means becoming conspicuous in life—obtaining a position which shall be acknowledged by others to be respectable or honorable. We do not understand, by this advancement, in general, the mere making of money, but the being known to have made it; not the accomplishment of any great aim, but the being seen to have accomplished it. In a word, we mean the gratification of our thirst for applause. That thirst, if the last infirmity of noble minds, is also the first infirmity of weak ones; and on the whole, the strongest impulsive influence of average humanity : the greatest efforts of the race have always been traceable to the love of praise, as its greatest catastrophes to the love of pleasure.

I am not about to attack or defend this impulse. I want you only to feel how it lies at the root of effort; especially of all modern effort. It is the gratification of vanity which is, with us, the stimulus of toil, and balm of repose; so closely does it touch the very springs of life, that the wounding of our vanity is always spoken of (and truly) as in its measure *mortal;* we call it " mortification," using the same expression which we should apply to a gangrenous and incurable bodily hurt. And although few of us may be physicians enough to recognize the various effect of this passion upon health and energy, I believe most honest men know and would at once acknowledge, its leading power with them as a motive. The seaman does not commonly desire to be made captain only because he knows he can manage the ship better than any other sailor on board. He wants to be made captain that he may be *called* captain. The clergyman does not usually want to be made a bishop only because he believes that no other hand can, as firmly as his, direct the diocese through its difficulties. He wants to be made bishop primarily that he may be called "My Lord." And a prince does not usually desire to enlarge, or a subject to gain, a kingdom because he believes that no one else can as well serve the state upon the throne; but, briefly, because he wishes to be addressed as " Your Majesty," by as many lips as may be brought to such utterance.

This, then, being the main idea of advancement in life, the force of it applies, for all of us, according to our station, particularly to that secondary result of such advancement which we call " getting into good society." We want to get into good society, not that we may have it, but that we may be seen in it; and our notion of its goodness depends primarily on its conspicuousness.

Will you pardon me if I pause for a moment to put what I fear you may think an impertinent question? I never can go on with an address unless I feel, or know, that my audience are either with me or against me (I do not much care which, in beginning); but I must know where they are; and I would fain find out, at this instant, whether you think I am putting the motives of popular action too low. I am resolved to-night, to state them low enough to be admitted as probable; for whenever in my writings on Political

Economy, I assume that a little honesty, or generosity
—or what used to be called "virtue"—may be calculated upon as a human motive of action, people always
answer me, saying, "You must not calculate on that;
that is not in human nature: you must not assume
anything to be common to men but acquisitiveness
and jealousy; no other feeling ever has influence on
them, except accidentally, and in matters out of the
way of business." I begin accordingly to-night low
down in the scale of motives; but I must know if you
think me right in doing so. Therefore, let me ask
those who admit the love of praise to be usually
the strongest motive in men's minds in seeking advancement, and the honest desire of doing any kind of
duty to be an entirely secondary one, to hold up their
hands. (*About a dozen of hands held up—the audience
partly not being sure the lecturer is serious, and partly
shy of expressing opinion.*) I am quite serious—I
really do want to know what you think; however, I
can judge by putting the reverse question. Will those
who think that duty is generally the first, and love of
praise the second motive, hold up their hands? (*One
hand reported to have been held up, behind the lecturer.*)
Very good: I see you are with me, and that you think
I have not begun too near the ground. Now, without
teasing you by putting further question, I venture to
assume that you will admit duty as at least a secondary or tertiary motive. You think that the desire of

doing something useful, or obtaining some real good, is indeed an existent collateral idea, though a secondary one, in most men's desire of advancement. You will grant that moderately honest men desire place and office, at least in some measure for the sake of their beneficent power; and would wish to associate rather with sensible and well-informed persons than with fools and ignorant persons, whether they are seen in the company of the sensible ones or not. And finally, without being troubled by repetition of any common truisms about the preciousness of friends, and the influence of companions, you will admit, doubtless, that according to the sincerity of our desire that our friends may be true, and our companions wise—and in proportion to the earnestness and discretion with which we choose both, will be the general chances of our happiness and usefulness.

But, granting that we had both the will and the sense to choose our friends well, how few of us have the power! or, at least, how limited, for most, is the sphere of choice! Nearly all our associations are determined by chance or necessity; and restricted within a narrow circle. We cannot know whom we would; and those whom we know, we cannot have at our side when we most need them. All the higher circles of human intelligence are, to those beneath, only momentarily and partially open. We may, by good fortune, obtain a glimpse of a great poet, and hear the sound of his voice; or put a question to a man of science, and be answered good-humoredly. We may intrude ten minutes' talk on a cabinet minister, answered probably with words worse than silence, being deceptive; or snatch, once or twice in our lives, the privilege of throwing a bouquet in the path of a Princess, or arresting the kind glance of a Queen. And yet these momentary chances we covet; and spend our years, and passions, and powers in pursuit of little more than these; while, meantime, there is a society continually open to us, of people who will talk to us as long as we like, whatever our rank or occupation—talk to us in the best words they can choose, and with thanks if we listen to them. And this society, because it is so numerous and so gentle—and can be kept waiting round us all day long, not to grant audience, but to gain it—kings and statesmen lingering patiently in those plainly furnished and narrow anterooms, our book-case shelves—we make no account of that company—perhaps never listen to a word they would say, all day long!

You may tell me, perhaps, or think within yourselves, that the apathy with which we regard this company of the noble, who are praying us to listen to them, and the passion with which we pursue the company, probably of the ignoble, who despise us, or who have nothing to teach us, are grounded in this—that we can see the faces of the living men, and it is themselves, and not their sayings, with which we desire to become familiar. But it is not so. Suppose you never were to see their faces—suppose you could be put behind a screen in the statesman's cabinet, or the prince's chamber, would you not be glad to listen to their words, though you were forbidden to advance beyond the screen? And when the screen is only a little less, folded in two, instead of four, and you can be hidden behind the cover of the two boards that bind a book, and listen, all day long, not to the casual talk, but to the studied, determined, chosen addresses of the wisest of men—this station of audience, and honorable privy council, you despise!

But perhaps you will say that it is because the living people talk of things that are passing, and are of immediate interest to you, that you desire to hear them. Nay; that cannot be so, for the living people will themselves tell you about passing matters, much better in their writings than in their careless talk. But I admit that this motive does influence you, so far as you prefer those rapid and ephemeral writings to slow and enduring writings—books, properly so called. For all books are divisible into two classes, the books of the hour, and the books of all time. Mark this distinction—it is not one of quality only. It is not merely the bad book that does not last, and the good one that does. It is a distinction of species. There are good books for the hour, and good ones for all time; bad books for the hour, and bad ones for all time. I must define the two kinds before I go further.

The good book of the hour, then—I do not speak of the bad ones—is simply the useful or pleasant talk of some person whom you cannot otherwise converse with, printed for you. Very useful often, telling you what you need to know; very pleasant often, as a sensible friend's present talk would be. These bright accounts of travels; good-humored and witty discussions of question; lively or pathetic story-telling in the form of novel; firm fact-telling, by the real agents concerned in the events of passing history—all these books of the hour, multiplying among us as education becomes more general, are a peculiar characteristic and possession of the present age; we ought to be entirely thankful for them, and entirely ashamed of ourselves if we make no good use of them. But we make the worst possible use, if we allow them to usurp the place of true books: for, strictly speaking, they are not books at all, but merely letters or newspapers in good print. Our friend's letter may be delightful, or necessary, to-day: whether worth keeping or not, is to be considered. The newspaper may be entirely proper at breakfast-time, but assuredly it is not reading for all day. So, though bound up in a volume, the long letter which gives you so pleasant an account of the inns, and roads, and weather last year at such a place, or which tells you that amusing story, or gives you the real circumstances of such and such events, however valuable for occasional reference, may not be, in the real sense of the word, a "book" at all, nor, in the real sense, to be "read." A book is essentially not a talked thing, but a written thing; and written, not with the view of mere communication, but of permanence. The book of talk is printed only because its author cannot speak to thousands of people at once; if he could, he would—the volume is mere *multiplication* of his voice. You cannot talk to your friend in India; if you could, you would; you write instead: that is mere *conveyance* of voice. But a book is written, not to multiply the voice merely, not to carry it merely, but to preserve it. The author has something to say which he perceives to be true and useful, or helpfully beautiful. So far as he knows, no one has yet said it; so far as he knows, no one else can say it. He is bound to say it, clearly and melodiously if he may; clearly, at all events. In the sum of his life he finds this to be the thing, or group of things, manifest to him; this the piece of true knowledge, or sight which his share of sunshine and earth has permitted him to seize. He would fain set it down forever; engrave it on rock, if he could; saying, "This is the best of me; for the rest, I ate, and drank, and slept, loved, and hated, like another; my life was as the vapor, and is not; but this I saw and knew: this, if anything of mine, is worth your memory." That is his "writing;"

it is, in his small human way, and with whatever degree of true inspiration is in him, his inscription, or
scripture.   That is a "Book."

Perhaps you think no books were ever so written?

But, again, I ask you, do you at all believe in
honesty, or at all in kindness? or do you think there is
never any honesty or benevolence in wise people?
None of us, I hope, are so unhappy as to think that.
Well, whatever bit of a wise man's work is honestly
and benevolently done, that bit is his book, or his
piece of art.   It is mixed always with evil fragments
—ill-done, redundant, affected work.   But if you read
rightly, you will easily discover the true bits, and
those *are* the book.

Now books of this kind have been written in all
ages by their greatest men; by great leaders, great
statesmen, and great thinkers.   These are all at your
choice; and life is short.   You have heard as much before; yet have you measured and mapped out this
short life and its possibilities?   Do you know, if you
read this, that you cannot read that—that what you
lose to-day you cannot gain to-morrow?   Will you go
and gossip with your housemaid, or your stable-boy,
when you may talk with queens and kings; or flatter
yourselves that it is with any worthy consciousness of
your own claims to respect that you jostle with the
common crowd for *entrée* here, and audience there,
when all the while this eternal court is open to you,

with its society wide as the world, multitudinous as its days, the chosen, and the mighty, of every place and time? Into that you may enter always; in that you may take fellowship and rank according to your wish; from that, once entered into it, you can never be outcast but by your own fault; by your aristocracy of companionship there, your own inherent aristocracy will be assuredly tested, and the motives with which you strive to take high place in the society of the living, measured, as to all the truth and sincerity that are in them, by the place you desire to take in this company of the Dead.

"The place you desire," and the place you *fit yourself for*, I must also say; because, observe, this court of the past differs from all living aristocracy in this—it is open to labor and to merit, but to nothing else. No wealth will bribe, no name overawe, no artifice deceive, the guardian of those Elysian gates. In the deep sense, no vile or vulgar person ever enters there. At the portières of that silent Faubourg St. Germain, there is but brief question, "Do you deserve to enter?" "Pass. Do you ask to be the companion of nobles? Make yourself noble, and you shall be. Do you long for the conversation of the wise? Learn to understand it, and you shall hear it. But on other terms?—no. If you will not rise to us, we cannot stoop to you. The living lord may assume courtesy, the living philosopher explains his thought to you with considerable pain; but here we neither feign nor interpret; you must rise to the level of our thoughts if you would be gladdened by them, and share our feelings, if you would recognize our presence."

This, then, is what you have to do, and I admit that it is much. You must in a word, love these people, if you are to be among them. No ambition is of any use. They scorn your ambition. You must love them, and show your love in these two following ways.

I.—First, by a true desire to be taught by them, and to enter into their thoughts. To enter into theirs, observe; not to find your own expressed by them. If the person who wrote the book is not wiser than you, yon need not read it; if he be, he will think differently from you in many respects.

Very ready we are to say of a book, "How good this is—that's exactly what I think!" But the right feeling is, "How strange that is! I never thought of that before, and yet I see it is true; or if I do not now, I hope I shall, some day." But whether thus submissively or not, at least be sure that you go to the author to get at *his* meaning, not to find yours. Judge it afterward, if you think yourself qualified to do so, but ascertain it first. And be sure also, if the author is worth anything, that you will not get at his meaning all at once—nay, that at his whole meaning you will not for a long time arrive in any wise. Not that he does not say what he means and in strong words too; but he cannot say it all; and what is more strange, will not, but in a hidden way and in parables, in order that he may be sure you want it. I cannot quite see the reason of this, nor analyze that cruel reticence in the breasts of wise men which makes them always hide their deeper thought. They do not give it you by way of help, but of reward, and will make themselves sure that you deserve it before they allow you to reach it. But it is the same with the physical type of wisdom, gold. There seems, to you and me, no reason why the electric forces of the earth should not carry whatever there is of gold within it at once to the mountain tops, so that kings and people might know that all the gold they could get was there; and without any trouble of digging, or anxiety, or chance, or waste of time, cut it away, and coin as much as they needed. But Nature does not manage it so. She puts it in little fissures in the earth, nobody knows where: you may dig long and find none; you must dig painfully to find any.

And it is just the same with men's best wisdom. When you come to a good book, you must ask yourself, "Am I inclined to work as an Australian miner would? Are my pickaxes and shovels in good order, and am I in good trim myself, my sleeves well up to

the elbow, and my breath good, and my temper?"
And, keeping the figure a little longer, even at cost of
tiresomeness, for it is a thoroughly useful one, the
metal you are in search of being the author's mind or
meaning, his words are as the rock which you have to
crush and smelt in order to get at it. And your pickaxes are your own care, wit, and learning; your smelt-
ing-furnace is your own thoughtful soul. Do not hope
to get at any good author's meaning without those
tools and that fire; often you will need sharpest, finest
chiseling, and patientest fusing, before you can gather
one grain of the metal.

And, therefore, first of all, I tell you, earnestly and
authoritatively (I *know* I am right in this), you must get
into the habit of looking intensely at words, and assur-
ing yourself of their meaning, syllable by syllable—
nay, letter by letter. For though it is only by reason
of the opposition of letters in the function of signs,
to sounds in function of signs, that the study of books
is called "literature," and that a man versed in it
is called, by the consent of nations, a man of letters
instead of a man of books, or of words, you may yet
connect with that accidental nomenclature this real
principle—that you might read all the books in
the British Museum (if you could live long enough),
and remain an utterly "illiterate," uneducated person; but that if you read ten pages of a good
book, letter by letter—that is to say, with real

accuracy—you are forevermore in some measure an educated person. The entire difference between education and non-education (as regards the merely intellectual part of it), consists in this accuracy. A well-educated gentleman may not know many languages— may not be able to speak any but his own—may have read very few books. But whatever language he knows, he knows precisely; whatever word he pronounces he pronounces rightly; above all, he is learned in the *peerage* of words; knows the words of true descent and ancient blood, at a glance, from words of modern canaille; remembers all their ancestry—their intermarriages, distantest relationships, and the extent to which they were admitted, and offices they held, among the national noblesse of words at any time, and in any country. But an uneducated person may know by memory any number of languages, and talk them all, and yet truly know not a word of any—not a word even of his own. An ordinarily clever and sensible seaman will be able to make his way ashore at most ports; yet he has only to speak a sentence of any language to be known for an illiterate person: so also the accent, or turn of expression of a single sentence will at once mark a scholar. And this is so strongly felt, so conclusively admitted by educated persons, that a false accent or a mistaken syllable is enough, in the parliament of any civilized nation, to assign to a man a certain degree of inferior standing forever. And this is right; but it is a pity that the accuracy insisted on is not greater, and required to a serious purpose. It is right that a false Latin quantity should excite a smile in the House of Commons; but it is wrong that a false English meaning should *not* excite a frown there. Let the accent of words be watched, by all means, but let their meaning be watched more closely still, and fewer will do the work. A few words well chosen and well distinguished, will do work that a thousand cannot, when every one is acting, equivocally, in the function of another. Yes; and words, if they are not watched, will do deadly work sometimes. There are masked words droning and skulking about us in Europe just now—(there never were so many, owing to the spread of a shallow, blotching, blundering, infectious " information," or rather deformation, everywhere, and to the teaching of catechisms and phrases at schools instead of human meanings)—there are masked words abroad, I say, which nobody understands, but which everybody uses, and most people will also fight for, live for, or even die for, fancying they mean this or that, or the other, of things dear to them: for such words wear chameleon cloaks— "ground-lion" cloaks, of the color of the ground of any man's fancy: on that ground they lie in wait, and rend him with a spring from it. There were never creatures of prey so mischievous, never diplomatists so cunning, never poisoners so deadly, as these masked words;

they are the unjust stewards of all men's ideas: whatever fancy or favorite instinct a man most cherishes,
he gives to his favorite masked word to take care of for
him; the word at last comes to have an infinite power
over him—you cannot get at him but by its ministry.
And in languages so mongrel in breed as the English,
there is a fatal power of equivocation put into men's
hands, almost whether they will or no, in being able to
use Greek or Latin forms for a word when they want
it to be respectable, and Saxon or otherwise common
forms when they want to discredit it. What a singular and salutary effect, for instance, would be produced
on the minds of people who are in the habit of taking
the Form of the words they live by, for the Power of
which those words tell them, if we always either retained, or refused, the Greek form "biblos," or "bib-
lion," as the right expression for "book"—instead of
employing it only in the one instance in which we
wish to give dignity to the idea, and translating it
everywhere else. How wholesome it would be for the
many simple persons who worship the Letter of God's
Word instead of its Spirit (just as other idolators worship His picture instead of His presence), if, in such
places (for instance) as Acts xix. 19 we retained the
Greek expression, instead of translating it, and they
had to read—"Many of them also which used curious
arts, brought their bibles together, and burnt them before all men; and they counted the price of them, and

found it fifty thousand pieces of silver!" Or if, on the other hand, we translated instead of retaining it, and always spoke of "The Holy Book," instead of "Holy Bible," it might come into more heads than it does at present that the Word of God, by which the heavens were, of old, and by which they are now kept in store,* cannot be made a present of to any. body in morocco binding; nor sown on any wayside by help either of steam-plow or steam-press; but is nevertheless being offered to us daily, and by us with contumely refused; and sown in us daily, and by us as instantly as may be, choked.

So, again, consider what effect has been produced on the English vulgar mind by the use of the sonorous Latin form "damno," in translating the Greek κατακρίνω, when people charitably wish to make it forcible; and the substitution of the temperate "con-demn" for it, when they choose to keep it gentle. And what notable sermons have been preached by illiterate clergymen on—"He that believeth not shall be damned;" though they would shrink with horror from translating Heb. xi. 7, "The saving of his house, by which he damned the world," or John viii. 12, "Woman, hath no man damned thee? She saith, No man, Lord. Jesus answered her, Neither do I damn thee; go and sin no more." And divisions in the mind

* Peter iii. 5-7.

of Europe, which have cost seas of blood, and in the defense of which the noblest souls of men have been cast
away in frantic desolation, countless as forest leaves—
though, in the heart of them, founded on deeper
causes—have nevertheless been rendered practicably
possible, mainly, by the European adoption of the
Greek word for a public meeting, to give peculiar re-
spectability to such meetings, when held for religious
purposes : and other collateral equivocations, such as
the vulgar English one of using the word "priest" as
a contraction for "presbyter."

Now, in order to deal with words rightly, this
is the habit you must form. Nearly every word
in your language has been first a word of some
other language—of Saxon, German, French, Latin,
or Greek (not to speak of eastern and primitive
dialects). And many words have been all these—
that is to say, have been Greek first, Latin next,
French or German next, and English last: under-
going a certain change of sense and use on the
lips of each nation ; but retaining a deep vital meaning which all good scholars feel in employing them,
even at this day. If you do not know the Greek
alphabet, learn it; young or old—girl or boy—
whoever you may be, if you think of reading seri-
ously (which, of course, implies that you have
some leisure at command), learn your Greek alphabet; then get good dictionaries of all these lan-

guages, and whenever you are in doubt about a word, hunt it down patiently. Read Max Müller's lectures thoroughly, to begin with; and, after that, never let a word escape you that looks suspicious. It is severe work; but you will find it, even at first, interesting, and at last, endlessly amusing. And the general gain to your character, in power and precision, will be quite incalculable.

Mind, this does not imply knowing, or trying to know, Greek, or Latin, or French. It takes a whole life to learn any language perfectly. But you can easily ascertain the meanings through which the English word has passed; and those which in a good writer's work it must still bear.

And now, merely for example's sake, I will, with your permission, read a few lines of a true book with you, carefully; and see what will come out of them. I will take a book perfectly known to you all; no English words are more familiar to us, yet nothing perhaps has been less read with sincerity. I will take these few following lines of Lycidas.

> " Last came, and last did go,
>   The pilot of the Galilean lake;
>   Two massy keys he bore of metals twain
>   (The golden opes, the iron shuts amain),
>   He shook his mitred locks, and stern bespake,
>   How well could I have spar'd for thee, young swain,

Enow of such as for their bellies' sake
Creep and intrude, and climb into the fold!
Of other care they little reckoning make,
Than how to scramble at the shearers' feast,
And shove away the worthy bidden guest;
Blind mouths! that scarce themselves know how to hold
A sheep-hook, or have learn'd aught else, the least
That to the faithful herdsman's art belongs!
What recks it them? What need they? They are sped;
And when they list, their lean and flashy songs
Grate on their scrannel pipes of wretched straw;
The hungry sheep look up, and are not fed,
But swoln with wind, and the rank mist they draw,
Rot inwardly, and foul contagion spread;
Besides what the grim wolf with privy paw
Daily devours apace, and nothing said."

Let us think over this passage, and examine its words.

First, is it not singular to find Milton assigning to St. Peter, not only his full episcopal function, but the very types of it which Protestants usually refuse most passionately? His "mitered" locks! Milton was no Bishop-lover; how comes St. Peter to be "mitered?" "Two massy keys he bore." Is this, then, the power of the keys claimed by the Bishops of Rome, and is it acknowledged here by Milton only in a poetical license, for the sake of its picturesqueness, that he may get the gleam of the golden keys to help his effect? Do not think it. Great men do not play stage tricks with doctrines of life and death: only little men do that.

Milton means what he says; and means it with his might too—is going to put the whole strength of his spirit presently into the saying of it. For though not a lover of false bishops, he *was* a lover of true ones; and the Lake pilot is here, in his thoughts, the type and head of true episcopal power. For Milton reads that text, "I will give unto thee the keys of the kingdom of Heaven" quite honestly. Puritan though he be, he would not blot it out of the book because there have been bad bishops; nay, in order to understand him, we must understand that verse first; it will not do to eye it askance, or whisper it under our breath, as if it were a weapon of an adverse sect. It is a solemn, universal assertion, deeply to be kept in mind by all sects. But perhaps we shall be better able to reason on it if we go on a little further, and come back to it. For clearly, this marked insistance on the power of the true episcopate is to make us feel more weightily what is to be charged against the false claimants of episcopate; or generally against false claimants of power and rank in the body of the clergy; they who, "for their bellies' sake, creep, and intrude, and climb into the fold."

Do not think Milton uses those three words to fill up his verse, as a loose writer would. He needs all the three; specially those three, and no more than those—"creep," and "intrude," and "climb;" no other words would or could serve the turn, and no

more could be added. For they exhaustively compre-
hend the three classes, correspondent to the three
characters, of men who dishonestly seek ecclesiastical
power. First, those who "*creep*" into the fold; who
do not care for office, nor name, but for secret influence, and do all things occultly and cunningly, con-
senting to any servility of office or conduct, so only
that they may intimately discern, and unawares direct,
the minds of men. Then those who "intrude" (thrust,
that is) themselves into the fold, who by natural in-
solence of heart, and stout eloquence of tongue, and
fearlessly perseverant self-assertion, obtain hearing
and authority with the common crowd. Lastly, those
who "climb," who, by labor and learning, both stout
and sound, but selfishly exerted in the cause of their
own ambition, gain high dignities and authorities, and
become "lords over the heritage," though not "en-
samples to the flock."

Now go on:

> " Of other care they little reckoning make
> Than how to scramble at the shearers' feast.
> *Blind mouths—*"

I pause again, for this is a strange expression; a
broken metaphor, one might think, careless and un-
scholarly.

Not so: its very audacity and pithiness are intended
to make us look close at the phrase and remember it.
These two monosyllables express the precisely accurate

contraries of right character, in the two great offices of the Church—those of bishop and pastor.

A Bishop means a person who sees.

A Pastor means one who feeds.

The most unbishoply character a man can have is therefore to be Blind.

The most unpastoral is, instead of feeding, to want to be fed—to be a Mouth.

Take the two reverses together, and you have "blind mouths." We may advisably follow out this idea a little. Nearly all the evils in the Church have arisen from bishops desiring *power* more than *light*. They want authority, not outlook. Whereas their real office is not to rule; though it may be vigorously to exhort and rebuke; it is the king's office to rule; the bishop's office is to *oversee* the flock; to number it, sheep by sheep; to be ready always to give full account of it. Now it is clear he cannot give account of the souls, if he has not so much as numbered the bodies of his flock. The first thing, therefore, that a bishop has to do is at least to put himself in a position in which, at any moment, he can obtain the history from childhood of every living soul in his diocese, and of its present state. Down in that back street, Bill, and Nancy, knocking each other's teeth out!— does the bishop know all about it? Has he his eye upon them? Has he *had* his eye upon them? Can he circumstantially explain to us how Bill got into the habit of beating Nancy about the head? If he cannot, he is no bishop though he had a miter as high as Salisbury steeple; he is no bishop—he has sought to be at the helm instead of the masthead; he has no sight of things. "Nay," you say, it is not his duty to look after Bill in the back street. What! the fat sheep that have full fleeces—you think it is only those he should look after, while (go back to your Milton) "the hungry sheep look up, and are not fed, besides what the grim wolf, with privy paw" (bishops knowing nothing about it) "daily devours apace, and nothing said?"

"But that's not our idea of a bishop." Perhaps not; but it was St. Paul's; and it was Milton's. They may be right, or we may be; but we must not think we are reading either one or the other by putting our meaning into their words. I go on.

"But swollen with wind, and the rank mist they draw."

This is to meet the vulgar answer that "if the poor are not looked after in their bodies, they are in their souls; they have spiritual food."

And Milton says, "They have no such thing as spiritual food; they are only swollen with wind." At first you may think that is a coarse type, and an obscure one. But again, it is a quite literally accurate one. Take up your Latin and Greek dictionaries, and find out the meaning of "Spirit." It is only a con-traction of the Latin word " breath," and an indistinct translation of the Greek word for " wind." The same word is used in writing, " The wind bloweth where it listeth;" and in writing, " So is every one that is born of the Spirit;" born of the *breath*, that is ; for it means the breath of God, in soul and body. We have the true sense of it in our words " inspiration" and " expire." Now, there are two kinds of breath with which the flock may be filled; God's breath, and man's. The breath of God is health, and life, and peace to them, as the air of heaven is to the flocks on the hills; but man's breath—the word which *he* calls spiritual—is disease and contagion to them, as the fog of the fen. They rot inwardly with it; they are puffed up by it, as a dead body by the vapors of its own decomposition. This is literally true of all false religious teaching; the first, and last, and fatalest sign of it is that "puffing up." Your converted children, who teach their parents; your converted convicts, who teach honest men ; your converted dunces who, having lived in cretinous stupefaction half their lives, suddenly awaking to the fact of there being a God, fancy them-selves therefore His peculiar people and messengers; your sectarians of every species, small and great, Catholic or Protestant, of high church or low, in so far as they think themselves exclusively in the right and others wrong ; and pre-eminently, in every sect, those who hold that men can be saved by thinking rightly instead of doing rightly, by word instead of act, and wish instead of work—these are the true fog children—clouds, these, without water; bodies, these, of putrescent vapor and skin, without blood or flesh: blown bag-pipes for the fiends to pipe with—corrupt and corrupt-ing—"Swollen with wind, and the rank mist they draw."

Lastly, let us return to the lines respecting the power of the keys, for now we can understand them. Note the difference between Milton and Dante in their interpretation of this power: for once, the latter is weaker in thought; he supposes *both* the keys to be of the gate of heaven; one is of gold, the other of silver: they are given by St. Peter to the sentinel angel; and it is not easy to determine the meaning either of the substances of the three steps of the gate, or of the two keys. But Milton makes one, of gold, the key of heaven; the other, of iron, the key of the prison, in which the wicked teachers are to be bound who "have taken away the key of knowledge, yet entered not in themselves."

We have seen that the duties of bishop and pastor are to see, and feed; and, of all who do so, it is said, "He that watereth, shall be watered also himself." But the reverse is truth also. He that watereth not, shall be *withered* himself, and he that seeth not, shall himself be shut out of sight—shut into the perpetual pris-

on-house.   And that prison opens here, as well as hereafter : he who is to be bound in heaven must first be
bound on earth.   That command to the strong angels,
of which the rock-apostle is the image, "Take him, and
bind him hand and foot, and cast him out," issues, in
its measure, against the teacher, for every help withheld, and for every truth refused, and for every falsehood enforced; so that he is more strictly fettered the
more he fetters, and further outcast, as he more and
more misleads, till at last the bars of the iron cage
close upon him, and as "the golden opes, the iron
shuts amain."

We have got something out of the lines, I think,
and much more is yet to be found in them; but we
have done enough by way of example of the kind of
word-by-word examination of your author which is
rightly called "reading;" watching every accent
and expression, and putting ourselves always in the
author's place, annihilating our own personality,
and seeking to enter into his, so as to be able assuredly
to say, " Thus Milton thought," not " Thus I thought,
in misreading Milton."   And by this process you
will gradually come to attach less weight to your
own " Thus I thought " at other times.   You will
begin to perceive that what *you* thought was a
matter of no serious importance—that your thoughts
on any subject are not perhaps the clearest and
wisest that could be arrived at thereupon in fact,

that unless you are a very singular person, you cannot be said to have any "thoughts" at all; that you have no materials for them, in any serious matters; *
—no right to "think," but only to try to learn more of the facts. Nay, most probably all your life (unless, as I said, you are a singular person) you will have no legitimate right to an "opinion" an any business, except that instantly under your hand. What must of necessity be done, you can always find out, beyond question, how to do. Have you a house to keep in order, a commodity to sell, a field to plow, a ditch to cleanse? There need be no two opinions about these proceedings; it is at your peril if you have not much more than an "opinion" on the way to manage such matters. And also, outside of your own business, there are one or two subjects on which you are bound to have but one opinion. That roguery and lying are objectionable, and are instantly to be flogged out of the way whenever discovered—that covetousness and love of quarreling are dangerous dispositions even in children, and deadly dispositions in men and nations—that in the end, the God of heaven and earth loves active, modest, and kind people, and hates idle, proud, greedy, and cruel ones—on these general facts you are bound to have but one, and

---

* Modern "Education" for the most part signifies giving people the faculty of thinking wrong on every conceivable subject of importance to them.

that a very strong opinion. For the rest, respecting religions, governments, sciences, arts, you will find that, on the whole, you can know NOTHING—judge nothing; that the best you can do, even though you may be a well-educated person, is to be silent, and strive to be wiser every day, and to understand a little more of the thoughts of others, which so soon as you try to do honestly, you will discover that the thoughts even of the wisest are very little more than pertinent questions. To put the difficulty into a clear shape, and exhibit to you the grounds for *in*decision, that is all they can generally do for you!—and well for them and for us, if indeed they are able "to mix the music with our thoughts, and sadden us with heavenly doubts." This writer, from whom I have been reading to you, is not among the first or wisest: he sees shrewdly as far as he sees, and therefore it is easy to find out his full meaning, but with the greater men, you cannot fathom their meaning; they do not even wholly measure it themselves—it is so wide. Suppose I had asked you, for instance, to seek for Shakespeare's opinion, instead of Milton's, on this matter of Church authority?—or for Dante's? Have any of you, at this instant, the least idea what either thought about it? Have you ever balanced the scene with the bishops in Richard III against the character of Cranmer? the description of St. Francis and St. Dominic against that of him who made Virgil wonder to gaze upon him—

"disteso, tanto vilmente, nell' eterno esilio ; " or of him whom Dante stood beside, "come 'l frate che confessa lo perfido assassin ? "* Shakespeare and Alighieri knew men better than most of us, I presume? They were both in the midst of the main struggle between the temporal and spiritual powers. They had an opinion, we may guess? But where is it? Bring it into court! Put Shakespeare's or Dante's creed into articles, and send *that* up into the Ecclesiastical Courts !

You will not be able, I tell you again, for many and many a day, to come at the real purposes and teaching of these great men; but a very little honest study of them will enable you to perceive that what you took for your own "judgment" was mere chance prejudice, and drifted, helpless, entangled weed of castaway thought: nay, you will see that most men's minds are indeed little better than rough heath wilderness, neglected and stubborn, partly barren, partly overgrown with pestilent brakes and venomous wind-sown herbage of evil surmise; that the first thing you have to do for them, and yourself, is eagerly and scornfully to set fire to *this ;* burn all the jungle into wholesome ash-heaps, and then plow and sow. All the true literary work before you, for life, must begin with obedience to that order. "Break up your fallow-ground, and *sow not among thorns.*"

II.—Having then faithfully listened to the great

---

* Inf. xix. 71 ; xxiii. 117.

teachers, that you may enter into their Thoughts, you have yet this higher advance to make—you have to enter into their Hearts. As you go to them first for clear sight, so you must stay with them that you may share at last their just and mighty Passion. Passion, or "sensation." I am not afraid of the word; still less of the thing. You have heard many outcries against sensation lately; but, I can tell you, it is not less sensation we want, but more. The ennobling difference between one man and another—between one animal and another—is precisely in this, that one feels more than another. If we were sponges, perhaps sensation might not be easily got for us; if we were earth-worms, liable at every instant to be cut in two by the spade, perhaps too much sensation might not be good for us. But, being human creatures, *it is* good for us; nay, we are only human in so far as we are sensitive, and our honor is precisely in proportion to our passion.

You know I said of that great and pure society of the dead, that it would allow "no vain or vulgar person to enter there." What do you think I meant by a "vulgar" person? What do you yourselves mean by "vulgarity?" You will find it a fruitful subject of thought; but, briefly, the essence of all vulgarity lies in want of sensation. Simple and innocent vulgarity is merely an untrained and undeveloped bluntness of body and mind; but in true inbred vulgarity, there is a deathful callousness, which, in extremity. becomes capable of every sort of bestial habit and crime, without fear, without pleasure, without horror, and without pity. It is in the blunt hand and the dead heart, in the diseased habit, in the hardened conscience that men become vulgar; they are forever vulgar, precisely in proportion as they are incapable of sympathy—of quick understanding—of all that, in deep insistance on the common, but most accurate term, may be called the "tact" or touch-faculty of body and soul: that tact which the Mimosa has in trees, which the pure woman has above all creatures—fineness and fullness of sensation, beyond reason—the guide and sanctifier of reason itself. Reason can but determine what is true—it is the God-given passion of humanity which alone can recognize what God has made good.

We come then to that great concourse of the Dead, not merely to know from them what is True, but chiefly to feel with them what is Righteous. Now, to feel with them, we must be like them; and none of us can become that without pains. As the true knowledge is disciplined and tested knowledge—not the first thought that comes—so the true passion is disciplined and tested passion—not the first passion that comes. The first that come are the vain, the false, the treacherous; if you yield to them they will lead you wildly and far, in vain pursuit, in hollow enthusiasm, till you have no true purpose and no true passion left. Not that any feeling possible to humanity is in itself,

wrong, but only wrong when undisciplined. Its nobility
is in its force and justice ; it is wrong when it is weak,
and felt for paltry cause.   There is a mean wonder as
of a child who sees a juggler tossing golden balls, and
this is base, if you will.   But do you think that the
wonder is ignoble, or the sensation less, with which
every human soul is called to watch the golden balls
of heaven tossed through the night by the Hand that
made them?   There is a mean curiosity, as of a child
opening a forbidden door, or a servant prying into her
master's business—and a noble curiosity, questioning,
in the front of danger, the source of the great river
beyond the sand—the place of the great continents
beyond the sea—a nobler curiosity still, which questions of the source of the River of Life, and of the
space of the Continent of Heaven—things which "the
angels desire to look into."   So the anxiety is ignoble,
with which you linger over the course and catastrophe
of an idle tale ; but do you think the anxiety is less,
or greater, with which you watch, or *ought* to watch,
the dealings of fate and destiny with the life of an
agonized nation?   Alas! it is the narrowness, selfishness, minuteness, of your sensation that you have to
deplore in England at this day—sensation which
spends itself in bouquets and speeches; in revelings
and junketings ; in sham fights and gay puppet
shows, while you can look on and see noble nations
murdered, man by man, woman by woman, child by
child, without an effort. or a tear.

I said, "minuteness" and "selfishness" of sensation, but in a word, I ought to have said "injustice" or "unrighteousness" of sensation. For as in nothing is a gentleman better to be discerned from a vulgar person, so in nothing is a gentle nation (such nations have been) better to be discerned from a mob, than in this—that their feelings are constant and just, results of due contemplation, and of equal thought. You can talk a mob into anything; its feelings may be—usually are—on the whole generous and right; but it has no foundation for them, no hold of them; you may tease or tickle it into any, at your pleasure; it thinks by infection, for the most part, catching a passion like a cold, and there is nothing so little that it will not roar itself wild about, when the fit is on; nothing so great but it will forget in an hour, when the fit is past. But a gentleman's, or a gentle nation's, passions are just, measured, and continuous. A great nation, for instance, does not spend its entire national wits for a couple of months in weighing evidence of a single ruffian's having done a single murder; and for a couple of years, see its own children murder each other by their thousands or tens of thousands a day, considering only what the effect is likely to be on the price of cotton, and caring nowise to determine which side of battle is in the wrong. Neither does a great nation send its poor little boys to jail for stealing six walnuts, and allow its bankrupts to steal their hundreds of thousands with a bow, and its bankers, rich with poor men's savings, to close their doors "under circumstances over which they have no control," with a "by your leave;" and large landed estates to be bought by men who have made their money by going with armed steamers up and down the China Seas, selling opium at the cannon's mouth, and altering, for the benefit of the foreign nation, the common highwayman's demand of "your money *or* your life," into that of "your money *and* your life." Neither does a great nation allow the lives of its innocent poor to be parched out. of them by fog fever, and rotted out of them by dunghill plague, for the sake of sixpence a life extra per week to its landlords;* and then debate, with driveling

---

* See the evidence in the Medical officer's report to the Privy Council, just published. There are suggestions in its preface which will make some stir among us, I fancy, respecting which let me note these points following: There are two theories on the subject of land now abroad, and in contention; both false. The first is that by Heavenly law, there have always existed, and must continue to exist, a certain number of hereditarily sacred persons, to whom the earth, air, and water of the world belong, as personal property; of which earth, air, and water these persons may, at their pleasure, permit, or forbid, the rest of the human race to eat, to breathe, or to drink. This theory is not for many years longer tenable. The adverse theory is that a division of the land of the world among the mob of the world would immediately elevate the said mob into sacred personages; that houses would then build themselves, and corn grow of itself; and that everybody would be able to live, without doing any work for his living. This theory would also be found highly untenable in practice. It will, however, require some rough experiments, and rougher catastrophes, even in this magnesium-

tears, and diabolical sympathies, whether it ought not piously to save, and nursingly cherish, the lives of its murderers. Also, a great nation having made up its mind that hanging is quite the wholesomest process for its homicides in general, can yet with mercy distinguish between the degrees of guilt in homicides; and does not yelp like a pack of frost-pinched wolf-cubs on the blood track of an unhappy crazed boy, or gray-haired clod-pate Othello, "perplexed i' the extreme," at the very moment that it is sending a Minister of the Crown to make polite speeches to a man who is bayoneting young girls in their father's sight,

---

lighted epoch, before the generality of persons will be convinced that no law concerning anything, least of all concerning land, for either holding or dividing it, or renting it high, or renting it low, would be of the smallest ultimate use to the people, so long as the general contest for life, and for the means of life, remains one of mere brutal competition. That contest, in an unprincipled nation, will take one deadly form or another, whatever laws you make for it. For instance, it would be an entirely wholesome law for England, if it could be carried, that maximum limits should be assigned to incomes, according to classes; and that every nobleman's income should be paid to him as a fixed salary or pension by the nation; and not squeezed by him in a variable sum, at discretion, out of the tenants of his land. But if you could get such a law passed to-morrow; and if, which would be further necessary, you could fix the value of the assigned incomes by making a given weight of pure wheat-flour legal tender for a given sum, a twelvemonth would not pass before another currency would have been tacitly established, and the power of accumulative wealth would have reasserted itself in some other article, or some imaginary sign. Forbid men to buy each other's lives for sovereigns, and they will for shells, or slates. There is only one cure for public distress—and that is public education, directed to make men thoughtful, merciful, and just. There are, indeed, many

and killing noble youths in cold blood, faster than a country butcher kills lambs in spring. And, lastly, a great nation does not mock Heaven and its Powers, by pretending belief in a revelation which asserts the love of money to be the root of *all* evil, and declaring, at the same time, that it is actuated, and intends to be actuated, in all chief national deeds and measures, by no other love.

My friends, I do not know why any of us should talk about reading. We want some sharper discipline than that of reading; but, at all events, be assured, we cannot read. No reading is possible for a people

laws conceivable which would gradually better and strengthen the national temper; but, for the most part, they are such as the national temper must be much bettered before it would bear. A nation in its youth may be helped by laws, as a weak child by backboards, but when it is old, it cannot that way straighten its crooked spine. And besides, the problem of land, at its worst, is a by one; distribute the earth as you will, the principal question remains inexorable—Who is to dig it? Which of us, in brief words, is to do the hard and dirty work for the rest—and for what pay? Who is to do the pleasant and clean work, and for what pay? Who is to do no work, and for what pay? And there are curious moral and religious questions connected with these. How far is it lawful to suck a portion of the soul out of a great many persons, in order to put the abstracted psychical quantities together, and make one very beautiful or ideal soul? If we had to deal with mere blood, instead of spirit, and the thing might literally be done (as it has been done with infants before now) so that it were possible, by taking a certain quantity of blood from the arms of a given number of the mob, and putting it all into one person, to make a more azure-blooded gentleman of him, the thing would of course be managed; but secretly, I should conceive. But now because it is brain and soul that we abstract, not visible blood, it can be done quite openly; and we live, we gentlemen, on delicatest prey,

with its mind in this state. No sentence of any great writer is intelligible to them. It is simply and sternly impossible for the English public, at this moment, to understand any thoughtful writing—so incapable of thought has it become in its insanity of avarice. Happily, our disease is, as yet, little worse than this incapacity of thought; it is not corruption of the inner nature; we ring true still, when anything strikes home to us; and though the idea that everything should "pay" has infected our every purpose so deeply, that even when we would play the good Samaritan, we never take out our twopence and give them to the host, without saying, "When I come again, thou shalt give me fourpence," there is a capacity of noble passion left in our hearts' core. We show it in our work—in our war—even in those unjust domestic affections which make

---

after the manner of weasels; that is to say, we keep a certain number of clowns digging and ditching, and generally stupefied, in order that we, being fed gratis, may have all the thinking and feeling to ourselves. Yet there is a great deal to be said for this. A highly-bred and trained English, French, Austrian, or Italian gentleman (much more a lady) is a great production; a better production than most statues; being beautifully colored as well as shaped, and plus all the brains; a glorious thing to look at, a wonderful thing to talk to; and you cannot have it, any more than a pyramid or a church, but by sacrifice of much contributed life. And it is, perhaps, better to build a beautiful human creature than a beautiful dome or steeple, and more delightful to look up reverently to a creature far above us, than to a wall; only the beautiful human creature will have some duties to do in return—duties of living belfry and rampart—of which presently.

us furious at a small private wrong, while we are
polite to a boundless public one; we are still industrious to the last hour of the day, though we add the
gambler's fury to the laborer's patience: we are still
brave to the death, though incapable of discerning true
cause for battle, and are still true in affection to our
own flesh, to the death, as the sea-monsters are, and
the rock-eagles. And there is hope for a nation while
this can be still said of it. As long as it holds its life
in its hand, ready to give it for its honor (though a
foolish honor), for its love (though a selfish love), and
for its business (though a base business), there is hope
for it. But hope only; for this instinctive, reckless
virtue cannot last. No nation can last, which has
made a mob of itself, however generous at heart. It
must discipline its passions, and direct them, or they
will discipline it, one day, with scorpion whips. Above
all, a nation cannot last as a money-making mob: it
cannot with impunity—it cannot with existence—go
on despising literature, despising science, despising art,
despising nature, despising compassion, and concentrating its soul on Pence. Do you think these are
harsh or wild words? Have patience with me but a
little longer. I will prove their truth to you, clause
by clause.

I.—I say first we have despised literature. What do
we, as a nation, care about books? How much do you
think we spend altogether on our libraries, public or

private, as compared with what we spend on our horses? If a man spends lavishly on his library, you call him mad—a biblio-maniac. But you never call any one a horse-maniac, though men ruin themselves every day by their horses, and you do not hear of people ruining themselves by their books. Or, to go lower still, how much do you think the contents of the book-shelves of the United Kingdom, public and private, would fetch, as compared with the contents of its wine-cellars? What position would its expenditure on literature take, as compared with its expenditure on luxurious eating? We talk of food for the mind, as of food for the body: now a good book contains such food inexhaustibly; it is a provision for life, and for the best part of us; yet how long most people would look at the best book before they would give the price of a large turbot for it! Though there have been men who have pinched their stomachs and bared their backs to buy a book, whose libraries were cheaper to them, I think, in the end, than most men's dinners are. We are few of us put to such trial, and more the pity; for, indeed, a precious thing is all the more precious to us if it has been won by work or economy; and if public libraries were half as costly as public dinners, or books cost the tenth part of what bracelets do, even foolish men and women might sometimes sus-pect there was good in reading, as well as in munching and sparkling; whereas the very cheapness of literature is making even wise people forget that if a book is worth reading, it is worth buying. No book is worth anything which is not worth *much;* nor is it serviceable, until it has been read, and reread, and loved, and loved again; and marked, so that you can refer to the passages you want in it, as a soldier can seize the weapon he needs in an armory, or a housewife bring the spice she needs from her store. Bread of flour is good; but there is bread, sweet as honey, if we would eat it, in a good book; and the family must be poor indeed which, once in their lives, cannot, for such multipliable barley-loaves, pay their baker's bill. We call ourselves a rich nation, and we are filthy and foolish enough to thumb each other's books out of circulating libraries!

II.—I say we have despised science. "What!" (you exclaim) "are we not foremost in all discovery, and is not the whole world giddy by reason, or unreason, of our inventions?" Yes; but do you suppose that is national work? That work is all done in spite of the nation; by private people's zeal and money. We are glad enough, indeed, to make our profit of science; we snap up anything in the way of a scientific bone that has meat on it, eagerly enough; but if the scientific man comes for a bone or a crust to *us*, that is another story. What have we publicly done for science? We are obliged to know what o'clock it is, for the safety of our ships, and therefore we pay for

an observatory; and we allow ourselves, in the person
of our Parliament, to be annually tormented into doing something, in a slovenly way, for the British
Museum; sullenly apprehending that to be a place for
keeping stuffed birds in, to amuse our children. If
anybody will pay for their own telescope, and resolve
another nebula, we cackle over the discernment as if it
were our own; if one in ten thousand of our hunting
squires suddenly perceives that the earth was indeed
made to be something else than a portion for foxes,
and burrows in it himself, and tells us where the gold
is, and where the coals, we understand that there is
some use in that; and very properly knight him : but
is the accident of his having found out how to employ
himself usefully any credit to *us?* (The negation of
such discovery among his brother squires may perhaps be some *dis*credit to us, if we would consider of
it.) But if you doubt these generalities, here is one
fact for us all to meditate upon, illustrative of our love
of science. Two years ago there was a collection of
the fossils of Solenhofen to be sold in Bavaria; the
best in existence, containing many specimens unique
for perfectness, and one, unique as an example of a
species (a whole kingdom of unknown living creatures
being announced by that fossil). This collection, of
which the mere market worth, among private buyers,
would probably have been some thousand or twelve
hundred pounds, was offered to the English nation for

seven hundred: but we would not give seven hundred,
and the whole series would have been in the Munich
museum at this moment, if Professor Owen * had
not with loss of his own time, and patient tormenting of the British public in person of its representatives, got leave to give four hundred pounds at
once, and himself become answerable for the other
three! which the said public will doubtless pay him
eventually, but sulkily, and caring nothing about the
matter all the while; only always ready to cackle if
any credit comes of it.   Consider, I beg of you, arith-
metically, what this fact means.   Your annual expenditure for public purposes (a third of it for military
apparatus) is at least 50 millions.   Now £700 is to
£50,000,000 roughly, as seven pence to two thousand
pounds.   Suppose then, a gentleman of unknown income, but whose wealth was to be conjectured from
the fact that he spent two thousand a year on his park
walls and footmen only, professes himself fond of science; and that one of his servants comes eagerly to
tell him that a unique collection of fossils, giving
clew to a new era of creation, is to be had for the sum
of seven pence sterling; and that the gentleman, who
is fond of science, and spends two thousand a year on
his park, answers, after keeping his servant waiting

---

* I state this fact without Professor Owen's permission: which of
course he could not with propriety have granted, had I asked it; but
I consider it so important that the public should be aware of the fact,
that I do what seems to me right, though rude.

several months, "Well! I'll give you four pence for them, if you will be answerable for the extra three pence yourself, till next year!"

III.—I say you have despised art! "What!" you again answer, "have we not art exhibitions, miles long? and do we not pay thousands of pounds for single pictures? and have we not art schools and institutions, more than ever nation had before?" Yes, truly, but all that is for the sake of the shop. You would fain sell canvas as well as coals, and crockery as well as iron; you would take every other nation's bread out of its mouth if you could;* not being able to do that, your ideal of life is to stand in the thoroughfares of the world, like Ludgate apprentices, screaming to every passer-by, "What d'ye lack?" You know nothing of your own faculties or circumstances; you fancy that, among your damp, flat, fat fields of clay, you can have as quick art-fancy as the Frenchman among his bronzed vines, or the Italian under his volcanic cliffs—that art may be learned as book-keeping is, and when learned, will give you more books to keep. You care for pictures, absolutely, no more than you do for the bills pasted on your dead-walls. There is always room on the wall for the bills to be read—never for the pictures to be seen. You do not know what pict-

---

*That was our real idea of "Free Trade." "All the trade to myself." You find now that by "competition" other people can manage to sell something as well as you—and now we call for Protection again. Wretches!

ures you have (by repute) in the country, nor whether they are false or true, nor whether they are taken care of or not; in foreign countries, you calmly see the noblest existing pictures in the world rotting in abandoned wreck—(and, in Venice, with the Austrian guns deliberately pointed at the palaces containing them), and if you heard that all the Titians in Europe were made sand-bags to-morrow on the Austrian forts, it would not trouble you so much as the chance of a brace or two of game less in your own bags in a day's shooting. That is your national love of art.

IV.—You have despised nature; that is to say, all the deep and sacred sensations of natural scenery. The French revolutionists made stables of the cathedrals of France; you have made race-courses of the cathedrals of the earth. Your *one* conception of pleasure is to drive in railroad carriages round their aisles, and eat off their altars.* You have put a railroad bridge over the fall of Schaffhausen. You have tunneled the cliffs of Lucerne by Tell's chapel; you have destroyed the Clarens shore of the Lake of Geneva; there is not a quiet valley in England that you have not filled with bellowing fire; there is no particle left of English land which you have not trampled coal

---

* I meant that the beautiful places of the world—Switzerland, Italy, South Germany, and so on—are, indeed, the truest cathedrals—places to be reverent in, and to worship in; and that we only care to drive through them: and to eat and drink at their most sacred places.

ashes into—nor any foreign city in which the spread of your presence is not marked among its fair old streets and happy gardens by a consuming white leprosy of new hotels and perfumers' shops: the Alps themselves, which your own poets used to love so reverently, you look upon as soaped poles in a bear-garden, which you set yourselves to climb, and slide down again, with " shrieks of delight." When you are past shrieking, having no human articulate voice to say you are glad with, you fill the quietude of their valleys with gunpowder blasts, and rush home, red with cutaneous eruption of conceit, and voluble with convulsive hiccough of self-satisfaction. I think nearly the two sorrowfullest spectacles I have ever seen in humanity, taking the deep inner significance of them, are the English mobs in the valley of Chamouni, amusing themselves with firing rusty howitzers; and the Swiss vintagers of Zurich expressing their Christian thanks for the gift of the vine, by assembling in knots in the "towers of the vineyards," and slowly loading and firing horse-pistols from morning till evening. It is pitiful to have dim conceptions of duty ; more pitiful, it seems to me, to have conceptions like these, of mirth.

Lastly. You despise compassion. There is no need of words of mine for proof of this. I will merely print one of the newspaper paragraphs which I am in the habit of cutting out and throwing into my store-drawer; here is one from a *Daily Telegraph* of an early date this year; date which though by me carelessly left unmarked, is easily discoverable, for on the back of the slip, there is the announcement that " yesterday the seventh of the special services of this year was performed by the Bishop of Ripon in St. Paul's ; " and there is a pretty piece of modern political economy besides, worth preserving note of, I think, so I print it in the note below.* But my business is with the main paragraph, relating one of such facts as happen now daily, which, by chance, has taken a form in which it came before the coroner. I will print the paragraph in red.† Be sure, the facts themselves are written in that color, in a book which we shall all of us, literate or illiterate, have to read our page of, some day.

" An inquiry was held on Friday by Mr. Richards, deputy coroner, at the White Horse Tavern, Christ Church, Spitalfields, respecting the death of Michael Collins, aged 58 years. Mary Collins, a miserable-looking woman, said that she lived with the deceased

---

* It is announced that an arrangement has been concluded between the Ministry of Finance and the Bank of Credit for the payment of the eleven millions which the State has to pay to the National Bank by the 14th inst. This sum will be raised as follows: The eleven commercial members of the committee of the Bank of Credit will each borrow a million of florins for three months of this bank, which will accept their bills, which again will be discounted by the National Bank. By this arrangement *the National Bank will itself furnish the funds with which it will be paid.*

† The following extract was printed in *red* in the English edition.

and his son in a room at 2 Cobb's court, Christ Church.
Deceased was a 'translator' of boots. Witness went
out and bought old boots; deceased and his son made
them into good ones, and then witness sold them for
what she could get at the shops, which was very little
indeed. Deceased and his son used to work night and
day to try and get a little bread and tea, and pay for
the room (2s. a week), so as to keep the home together.
On Friday night week deceased got up from his bench
and began to shiver. He threw down the boots, saying, 'Somebody else must finish them when I am
gone, for I can do no more.' There was no fire, and
he said, 'I would be better if I was warm.' Witness
therefore took two pairs of translated boots* to sell at
the shop, but she could only get 14d. for the two pairs,
for the people at the shop said, 'We must have our
profit.' Witness got 14 pounds of coal, and a little tea
and bread. Her son sat up the whole night to make
the 'translations' to get money, but deceased died on
Saturday morning. The family never had enough to
eat. Coroner: 'It seems to me deplorable that you
did not go into the work-house.' Witness: 'We
wanted the comforts of our little home.' A juror
asked what the comforts were, for he only saw a little
straw in the corner of the room, the windows of which

---

* One of the things which we must very resolutely enforce, for
the good of all classes, in our future arrangements, must be that they
wear no "translated" articles of dress. See the preface.

were broken. The witness began to cry, and said that they had a quilt and other little things. The deceased said he never would go into the work-house. In summer, when the season was good, they sometimes made as much as 10s. profit in the week. They then always saved toward the next week, which was generally a bad one. In winter they made not half so much. For three years they had been getting from bad to worse. Cornelius Collins said that he had assisted his father since 1847. They used to work so far into the night that both nearly lost their eyesight. Witness now had a film over his eyes. Five years ago deceased applied to the parish for aid. The relieving officer gave him a four-pound loaf, and told him if he came again he should 'get the stones.'* That disgusted deceased, and he would have nothing to do with them since. They got worse and worse until last Friday week, when they had not even a half-penny to buy a candle.

---

* The abbreviation of the penalty of useless labor is curiously coincident in verbal form with a certain passage which some of us may remember. It may perhaps be well to preserve besides this paragraph another cutting out of my store-drawer, from the *Morning Post*, of about a parallel date, Friday, March 10th, 1865: "The *salons* of Mme. C——, who did the honors with clever imitative grace and elegance, were crowded with princes, dukes, marquises, and counts—in fact, with the same *male* company as one meets at the parties of the Princess Metternich and Madame Drouyn de Lhuys. Some English peers and members of Parliament were present, and appeared to enjoy the animated and dazzlingly improper scene. On the second floor the supper-tables were loaded with every delicacy of the season. That your readers may form some idea of the dainty fare of the Parisian demi-monde, I copy the menu of the supper, which

Deceased then lay down on the straw, and said he could not live till morning. A juror: You are dying of starvation yourself, and you ought to go into the house until the summer. Witness: If we went in we should die. When we come out in the summer we should be like people dropped from the sky. No one would know us, and we would not have even a room. I could work now if I had food, for my sight would get better. Dr. G. P. Walker said deceased died from syncope, from exhaustion from want of food. The deceased had had no bedclothes. For four months he had had nothing but bread to eat. There was not a particle of fat in the body. There was no disease, but if there had been medical attendance, he might have survived the syncope or fainting. The coroner having remarked upon the painful nature of the case, the jury returned the following verdict, 'That deceased died from exhaustion from want of

was served to all the guests (about 200) seated at four o'clock. Choice Yquem, Johannisberg, Laffitte, Tokay, and Champagne of the finest vintages were served most lavishly throughout the morning. After supper dancing was resumed with increased animation, and the ball terminated with a *chaîne diabolique* and a *cancan d'enfer* at seven in the morning. (Morning-service—' Ere the fresh lawns appeared, under the opening eyelids of the Morn.—') Here is the menu:— ' Consomme de volaille à la Bagration; 16 hors-d'œuvres variés. Bouchées à la Talleyrand. Saumons froids, sauce Ravigote. Filets de bœuf en Bellevue, timbales milanaises chaudfroid de gibier. Dindes truffées. Pâtés de foies gras, buissons d'écrevisses, salades vénétiennes, gelées blanches aux fruits, gateaux mancini, parisiens et parisiennes. Fromages glacés Ananas. Dessert.' "

food and the common necessaries of life; also through want of medical aid.' "

"Why would witness not go into the work-house?" you ask. Well, the poor seem to have a prejudice against the work-house which the rich have not; for of course every one who takes a pension from Government goes into the work-house on a grand scale: only the work-houses for the rich do not involve the idea of work, and should be called play-houses. But the poor like to die independently, it appears; perhaps if we made the play-houses for them pretty and pleasant enough, or gave them their pensions at home, and allowed them a little introductory peculations with the public money, their minds might be reconciled to it. Meantime, here are the facts: we make our relief either so insulting to them, or so painful, that they rather die than take it at our hands; or, for third alternative, we leave them so untaught and foolish that they starve like brute creatures, wild and dumb, not knowing what to do, or what to ask. I say, you despise compassion; if you did not, such a newspaper paragraph would be as impossible in a Christian country as a deliberate assassination permitted in its public streets.* "Christian" did I say? Alas, if we were

---

* I am heartily glad to see such a paper as the *Pall Mall Gazette* established; for the power of the press in the hands of highly-educated men, in independent position, and of honest purpose, may indeed become all that it has been hitherto vainly vaunted to be. Its editor will therefore, I doubt not, pardon me, in that, by very reason

but wholesomely un-Christian, it would be impossible:
it is our imaginary Christianity that helps us to com-
mit these crimes, for we revel and luxuriate in our
faith, for the lewd sensation of it; dressing *it* up,
like everything else, in fiction. The dramatic Christianity of the organ and aisle, of dawn-service and twi-
light-revival—the Christianity which we do not fear to
mix the mockery of, pictorially, with our play about
the devil, in our Satanellas—Roberts—Fausts, chanting

---

of my respect for the journal, I do not let pass unnoticed an article in
its third number, page 5, which was wrong in every word of it, with
the intense wrongness which only an honest man can achieve who
has taken a false turn of thought in the outset, and is following it,
regardless of consequences. It contained at the end this notable passage: "The bread of affliction, and the water of affliction—ay, and
the bedsteads and blankets of affliction, are the very utmost that the
law ought to give to *outcasts merely as outcasts.*" I merely put beside this expression of the gentlemanly mind of England in 1865, a
part of the message which Isaiah was ordered to "lift up his voice
like a trumpet" in declaring to the gentlemen of his day: "Ye fast
for strife, and to smite with the fist of wickedness. Is not this the
fast that I have chosen, to deal thy bread to the hungry, and that
thou bring the poor *that are cast out* (margin 'afflicted') to *thy*
house." The falsehood on which the writer had mentally founded
himself, as previously stated by him, was this: "To confound the
functions of the dispensers of the poor-rates with those of the dispensers of a charitable institution is a great and pernicious error."
This sentence is so accurately and exquisitely wrong, that its substance must be thus reversed in our minds before we can deal with
any existing problem of national distress. "To understand that the
dispensers of the poor-rates are the almoners of the nation, and
should distribute its alms with a gentleness and freedom of hand as
much greater and franker than that possible to individual charity, as
the collective national wisdom and power may be supposed greater
than those of any single person, is the foundation of all law respecting pauperism."

hymns through traceried windows for background effect, and artistically modulating the " Dio" through variation on variation of mimicked prayer (while we distribute tracts, next day, for the benefit of uncultivated swearers, upon what we suppose to be the signification of the Third Commandment)—this gas-lighted, and gas-inspired, Christianity, we are triumphant in, and draw back the hem of our robes from the touch of the heretics who dispute it. But to do a piece of common Christian righteousness in a plain English word or deed ; to make Christian law any rule of life, and found one National act or hope thereon—we know too well what our faith comes to for that! You might sooner get lightning out of incense smoke than true action or passion out of your modern English religion. You had better get rid of the smoke, and the organ-pipes, both : leave them, and the Gothic windows, and the painted glass, to the property-man; give up your carbureted hydrogen ghost in one healthy expiration, and look after Lazarus at the door-step. For there is a true Church wherever one hand meets another helpfully, and that is the only holy or Mother Church which ever was, or ever shall be.

All these pleasures, then, and all these virtues, I repeat, you nationally despise. You have, indeed, men among you who do not; by whose work, by whose strength, by whose life, by whose death, you live, and never thank them. Your wealth, your amusement, your pride, would all be alike impossible, but for those whom you scorn or forget. The policeman, who is walking up and down the black lane all night to watch the guilt you have created there, and may have his brains beaten out and be maimed for life at any moment, and never be thanked; the sailor wrestling with the sea's rage; the quiet student poring over his book or his vial; the common worker, without praise, and nearly without bread, fulfilling his task as your horses drag your carts, hopeless, and spurned of all: these are the men by whom England lives; but they are not the nation; they are only the body and nervous force of it, acting still from old habit in a convulsive perseverance, while the mind is gone. Our National mind and purpose are to be amused; our National religion, the performance of church ceremonies, and preaching of soporific truths (or untruths) to keep the mob quietly at work, while we amuse ourselves; and the necessity for this amusement is fastening on us as a feverous disease of parched throat and wandering eyes— senseless, dissolute, merciless. When men are rightly occupied, their amusement grows out of their work, as the color-petals out of a fruitful flower; when they are faithfully helpful and compassionate, all their emotions become steady, deep, perpetual, and vivifying to the soul as the natural pulse to the body. But now, having no true business, we pour our whole masculine energy into the false business of money-making; and having no true emotion, we must have false emotions dressed up for us to play with, not innocently, as children with dolls, but guiltily and darkly, as the idolatrous Jews with their pictures on cavern walls, which men had to dig to detect. The justice we do not execute, we mimic in the novel and on the stage; for the beauty we destroy in nature, we substitute the metamorphosis of the pantomime, and (the human nature of us imperatively requiring awe and sorrow of *some* kind) for the noble grief we should have borne with our fellows, and the pure tears we should have wept with them, we gloat over the pathos of the police court, and gather the night-dew of the grave.

It is difficult to estimate the true significance of these things; the facts are frightful enough—the measure of national fault involved in them is perhaps not as great as it would at first seem. We permit, or cause, thousands of deaths daily, but we mean no harm; we set fire to houses, and ravage peasants' fields; yet we should be sorry to find we had injured anybody. We are still kind at heart; still capable of virtue, but only as children are. Chalmers, at the end of his long life, having had much power with the public, being plagued in some serious matter by a reference to "public opinion," uttered the impatient exclamation, "The public is just a great baby!" And the reason that I have allowed all these graver subjects of thought to mix themselves up with an inquiry into methods of reading, is that, the more I see of our national faults or miseries, the more they resolve themselves into conditions of childish illiterateness, and want of education in the most ordinary habits of thought. It is, I repeat, not vice, not selfishness, not dullness of brain, which we have to lament; but an unreachable school-boy's recklessness, only differing from the true school-boy's in its incapacity of being helped, because it acknowledges no master. There is a curious type of us given in one of the lovely, neglected works of the last of our great painters. It is a drawing of Kirby Lonsdale church-yard, and of its brook, and valley, and hills, and folded morning sky beyond. And unmindful alike of these, and of the dead who have left these for other valleys and for other skies, a group of school-boys have piled their little books upon a grave, to strike them off with stones. So do we play with the words of the dead that would teach us, and strike them far from us with our bitter, reckless will, little thinking that those leaves which the wind scatters had been piled, not only upon a grave-stone, but upon the seal of an enchanted vault—nay, the gate of a great city of sleeping kings, who would awake for us, and walk with us, if we knew but how to call them by their names. How often, even if we lift the marble entrance gate, do we but wander among those old kings in their repose, and finger the robes they lie in, and stir the crowns on their foreheads; and still they are silent to us, and seem but a dusty imagery; because we know not the incantation of the heart that would wake them—which, if they once heard, they would start up to meet us in their power of long ago, narrowly to look upon us, and consider us; and, as the fallen kings of Hades meet the newly fallen, saying, "Art thou also become weak as we—art thou also become one of us?" so would these kings, with their undimmed, unshaken diadems, meet us saying, "Art thou also become pure and mighty of heart as we? art thou also become one of us?"

Mighty of heart, mighty of mind—"magnanimous" —to be this, is indeed to be great in life; to become this increasingly, is, indeed, to "advance in life"—in life itself—not in the trappings of it. My friends, do you remember that old Scythian custom, when the head of a house died? How he was dressed in his finest dress, and set in his chariot, and carried about to his friends' houses; and each of them placed him at his table's head, and all feasted in his presence? Suppose it were offered to you, in plain words, as it *is* offered to you in dire facts, that you should gain this Scythian honor, gradually, while you yet thought yourself alive. Suppose the offer were this: "You shall die slowly; your blood shall daily grow cold, your flesh petrify, your heart beat at last only as a rusted group of iron valves. Your life shall fade from you, and sink through the earth into the ice of Caina; but, day by day, your body shall be dressed more gayly, and set in higher chariots, and have more orders on its breast—crowns on its head, if you will. Men shall bow before it, stare and shout round it, crowd after it up and down the streets; build palaces for it, feast with it at their tables' heads all the night long; your soul shall stay enough within it to know what they do, and feel the weight of the golden dress on its shoulders, and the furrow of the crown-edge on the skull—no more." Would you take the offer, verbally made by the death-angel? Would the meanest among us take it, think you? Yet practically and verily we grasp at it, every one of us, in a measure; many of us grasp at it in its fullness of horror. Every man accepts it, who desires to advance in life without knowing what life is; who means only that he is to get more horses, and more footmen, and more fortune, and more public honor, and—*not* more personal soul. He only is advancing in life, whose heart is getting softer, whose blood warmer, whose brain quicker, whose spirit is entering into Living peace. And the men who have this life in them are the true lords or kings of the earth—they, and they only. All other kingships, so far as they are true, are only the practical issue and expression of theirs; if less than this, they are either dramatic royalties—costly shows, with real jewels instead of tinsel—the toys of nations; or else, they are no royalties at all, but tyrannies, or the mere active and practical issue of national folly; for which reason I have said of them elsewhere, "Visible governments are the toys of some nations, the diseases of others, the harness of some, the burdens of more."

But I have no words for the wonder with which I hear Kinghood still spoken of, even among thoughtful men, as if governed nations were a personal property, and might be bought and sold, or otherwise acquired, as sheep, of whose flesh their king was to feed, and whose fleece he was to gather; as if Achilles' indignant epithet of base kings, "people-eating," were the constant and proper title of all monarchs; and enlargement of a king's dominion meant the same thing as the increase of a private man's estate! Kings who think so, however powerful, can no more be the true kings of the nation than gad-flies are the kings of a horse; they suck it, and may drive it wild, but do not guide it. They, are the courts, and their armies are, if one could see clearly, only a large species of marsh mosquito, with bayonet proboscis and melodious, band-mastered, trumpeting in the summer air; the twilight being, perhaps, sometimes fairer, but hardly more wholesome, for its glittering mists of midge companies. The true kings, meanwhile, rule quietly if at all, and hate ruling; too many of them make "il gran refiúto;" and if they do not, the mob, as soon as they are likely to become useful to it, is pretty sure to make *its* "gran refiúto" of *them*.

Yet the visible king may also be a true one, some day, if ever a day comes when he will estimate his dominion by the *force* of it—not the geographical boundaries. It matters very little whether Trent cuts you a cantel out here, or Rhine rounds you a castle less there.   But it does matter to you, king of men, whether you can verily say to this man, "Go," and he goeth; and to another, "Come," and he cometh.   Whether you can turn your people as you can Trent—and where it is that you bid them come, and where go.   It matters to you, king of men, whether your people hate you, nd die by you, or love you, and live by you. You may measure your dominion by multitudes better than by miles; and count degrees of love latitude, not from, but to, a wonderfully warm and infinite equator. Measure! nay you cannot measure.   Who shall measure the difference between the power of those who "do and teach," and who are greatest in the kingdoms of earth, as of heaven—and the power of those who undo, and consume—whose power, at the fullest, is only the power of the moth and the rust?   Strange! to think how the Moth-kings lay up treasures for the moth, and the Rust-kings, who are to their people's strength, as rust to armor, lay up treasures for the rust; and the Robber-kings, treasures for the robber;

but how few kings have ever laid up treasures that needed no guarding—treasures of which the more thieves there were, the better! Broidered robe, only to be rent—helm and sword, only to be dimmed; jewel and gold, only to be scattered—there have been three kinds of kings who have gathered these. Suppose there ever should arise a Fourth order of kings, who had read, in some obscure writing of long ago, that there was a Fourth kind of treasure, which the jewel and gold could not equal, neither should it be valued with pure gold. A web more fair in the weaving, by Athena's shuttle; an armor, forged in diviner fire by Vulcanian force—a gold only to be mined in the sun's red heart, where he sets over the Delphian cliffs—deep-pictured tissue, impenetrable armor, potable gold—the three great Angels of Conduct, Toil, and Thought, still calling to us, and waiting at the posts of our doors, to lead us, if we would, with their winged power, and guide us, with their inescapable eyes, by the path which no fowl knoweth, and which the vulture's eye has not seen! Suppose kings should ever arise, who heard and believed this word, and at last gathered and brought forth treasures of—Wisdom— for their people?

Think what an amazing business *that* would be! How inconceivable, in the state of our present national wisdom. That we should bring up our peasants to a book exercise instead of a bayonet exercise—organize, drill, maintain with pay, and good generalship, armies of thinkers, instead of armies of stabbers—find national amusement in reading-rooms as well as rifle-grounds; give prizes for a fair shot at a fact, as well as for a leaden splash on a target. What an absurd idea it seems, put fairly in words, that the wealth of the capitalists of civilized nations should ever come to support literature instead of war! Have yet patience with me, while I read you a single sentence out of the only book, properly to be called a book, that I have yet written myself, the one that will stand (if anything stand) surest and longest of all work of mine.

"It is one very awful form of the operation of wealth in Europe that it is entirely capitalists' wealth which supports unjust wars. Just wars do not need so much money to support them; for most of the men who wage such, wage them gratis; but for an unjust war, men's bodies and souls have both to be bought; and the best tools of war for them besides, which makes such war costly to the maximum; not to speak of the cost of base fear, and angry suspicion, between nations which have not grace nor honesty enough in all their multitudes to buy an hour's peace of mind with; as, at present France and England, purchasing of each other ten millions' sterling worth of consternation, annually (a remarkably light crop, half thorns and half aspen leaves, sown, reaped, and granaried by the 'science' of the modern political economist, teaching covetousness instead of truth). And, all unjust war being supportable, if not by pillage of the enemy, only by loans from capitalists, these loans are repaid by subsequent taxation of the people, who appear to have no will in the matter, the capitalists' will being the primary root of the war; but its real root is the covetousness of the whole nation, rendering it incapable of faith, frankness, or justice, and bringing about, therefore, in due time, his own separate loss and punishment to each person."

France and England literally, observe, buy *panic* or each other; they pay, each of them, for ten thousand thousand pounds' worth of terror, a year. Now suppose, instead of buying these ten millions' worth of panic annually, they made up their minds to be at peace with each other, and buy ten millions' worth of knowledge annually; and that each nation spent its ten thousand thousand pounds a year in founding royal libraries, royal art-galleries, royal museums, royal gardens, and places of rest. Might it not be better somewhat for both French and English?

It will be long, yet, before that comes to pass. Nevertheless, I hope it will not be long before royal or national libraries will be founded in every considerable city, with a royal series of books in them; the same series in every one of them, chosen books, the best in every kind, prepared for that national series in the most perfect way possible; their text printed all on leaves of equal size, broad of margin, and divided into pleasant volumes, light in the hand, beautiful, and strong, and thorough as examples of binders' work; and that these great libraries will be accessible to all clean and orderly persons at all times of the day and evening; strict law being enforced for this cleanliness and quietness.

I could shape for you other plans, for art-galleries, and for natural-history galleries, and for many precious, many, it seems to me, needful things; but this book plan is the easiest and needfullest, and would prove a considerable tonic to what we call our British constitution, which has fallen dropsical of late, and has an evil thirst, and evil hunger, and wants healthier feeding. You have got its corn laws repealed for it; try if you cannot get corn laws established for it, dealing in a better bread; bread made of that old enchanted Arabian grain, the Sesame, which opens doors; doors, not of robbers', but of Kings' Treasuries.

Friends, the treasuries of true kings are the streets of their cities; and the gold they gather, which for others is as the mire of the streets, changes itself, for them and their people, into a crystalline pavement forevermore.

LECTURE II.—LILIES.

OF QUEENS' GARDENS.

"Be thou glad, oh thirsting Desert; let the desert be made cheerful and bloom as the lily; and the barren places of Jordan shall run wild with wood."—ISAIAH 35, i. (Septuagint.)

IT will, perhaps, be well, as this Lecture is the sequel of one previously given, that I should shortly state to you my general intention in both. The questions specially proposed to you in the first, namely, How and What to Read, rose out of a far deeper one, which it was my endeavor to make you propose earnestly to yourselves, namely, *Why* to Read. I want you to feel, with me, that whatever advantages we possess in the present day in the diffusion of education and of literature, can only be rightly used by any of us when we have apprehended clearly what education is to lead to, and literature to teach. I wish you to see that both well-directed moral training and well-chosen reading lead to the possession of a power over the ill-guided and illiterate, which is, according to the measure of it, in the truest sense, *kingly;* conferring indeed the purest kingship that can exist among men : too many other kingships (however distinguished by visible insignia or material power) being either spectral, or tyrannous; special—that is to say, aspects and shadows only of royalty, hollow as death, and which only the "Likeness of a kingly crown have on;" or else tyrannous—that is to say, substituting their own will for the law of justice and love by which all true kings rule.

There is, then, I repeat—and as I want to leave this idea with you, I begin with it, and shall end with it— only one pure kind of kingship; an inevitable and eternal kind, crowned or not : the kingship, namely, which consists in a stronger moral state, and a truer thoughtful state, than that of others; enabling you, therefore, to guide, or to raise them. Observe that word "State;" we have got into a loose way of using it. It means literally the standing and stability of a thing; and you have the full force of it in the derived word "statue"—"the immovable thing." A king's majesty or "state," then, and the right of his kingdom to be called a state, depends on the movelessness of both : without tremor, without quiver of balance; established and enthroned upon a foundation of eternal law which nothing can alter nor overthrow.

Believing that all literature and all education are only useful so far as they tend to confirm this calm, beneficent, and *therefore* kingly, power—first, over ourselves, and, through ourselves, over all around us, I am

now going to ask you to consider with me further,
what special portion or kind of this royal authority,
arising out of noble education, may rightly be pos-
sessed by women; and how far they also are called
to a true queenly power. Not in their households
merely, but over all within their sphere. And in what
sense, if they rightly understood and exercised this
royal or gracious influence, the order and beauty in-
duced by such benignant power would justify us in
speaking of the territories over which each of them
reigned, as "Queens' Gardens."

And here, in the very outset, we are met by a far
deeper question, which—strange though this may seem
—remains among many of us yet quite undecided, in
spite of its infinite importance.

We cannot determine what the queenly power of
women should be, until we are agreed what their
ordinary power should be. We cannot consider how
education may fit them for any widely extending duty,
until we are agreed what is their true constant duty.
And there never was a time when wilder words were
spoken, or more vain imagination permitted, respecting this question—quite vital to all social happiness.
The relations of the womanly to the manly nature,
their different capacities of intellect or of virtue, seem
never to have been yet measured with entire consent.
We hear of the mission and of the rights of Woman,
as if these could ever be separate from the mission

and the rights of Man; as if she and her lord were creatures of independent kind and of irreconcilable claim. This, at least, is wrong. And not less wrong —perhaps even more foolishly wrong (for I will anticipate thus far what I hope to prove)—is the idea that woman is only the shadow and attendant image of her lord, owing him a thoughtless and servile obedience, and supported altogether in her weakness by the pre-eminence of his fortitude.

This, I say, is the most foolish of all errors respecting her who was made to be the helpmate of man. As if he could be helped effectively by a shadow, or worthily by a slave!

Let us try, then, whether we cannot get at some clear and harmonious idea (it must be harmonious if it is true) of what womanly mind and virtue are in power and office, with respect to man's; and how their relations, rightly accepted, aid, and increase, the vigor, and honor, and authority of both.

And now I must repeat one thing I said in the last lecture: namely, that the first use of education was to enable us to consult with the wisest and the greatest men on all points of earnest difficulty. That to use books rightly, was to go to them for help: to appeal to them, when our own knowledge and power of thought failed; to be led by them into wider sight, purer conception than our own, and receive from them the united sentence of the judges and councils of all time, against our solitary and unstable opinion.

Let us do this now. Let us see whether the greatest, the wisest, the purest-hearted of all ages are agreed in any wise on this point: let us hear the testimony they have left respecting what they held to be the true dignity of woman, and her mode of help to man.

And first let us take Shakespeare.

Note broadly in the outset, Shakespeare has no heroes—he has only heroines. There is not one entirely heroic figure in all his plays, except the slight sketch of Henry the Fifth, exaggerated for the purposes of the stage; and the still slighter Valentine in the Two Gentlemen of Verona. In his labored and perfect plays you have no hero. Othello would have been one, if his simplicity had not been so great as to leave him the prey of every base practice round him; but he is the only example even approximating to the heroic type. Coriolanus—Cæsar—Antony, stand in flawed strength, and fall by their vanities—Hamlet is indolent, and drowsily speculative; Romeo, an impatient boy; the Merchant of Venice languidly submissive to adverse fortune; Kent, in King Lear, is entirely noble at heart, but too rough and unpolished to be of true use at the critical time, and he sinks into the office of a servant only. Orlando, no less noble, is yet the despairing toy of chance, followed, comforted, saved, by Rosalind. Whereas there is hardly a play that has not a perfect woman in it, steadfast in grave hope, and errorless purpose; Cordelia, Desdemona, Isabella, Hermione, Imogen, Queen Katherine, Perditi, Sylvia, Viola, Rosalind, Helena, and last, and perhaps loveliest, Virgilia, are all faultless; conceived in the highest heroic type of humanity.

Then observe, secondly.

The catastrophe of every play is caused always by the folly or fault of a man; the redemption, if there be any, is by the wisdom and virtue of a woman, and, failing that, there is none. The catastrophe of King Lear is owing to his own want of judgment, his impatient vanity, his misunderstanding of his children; the virtue of his one true daughter would have saved him from all the injuries of the others, unless he had cast her away from him; as it is, she all but saves him.

Of Othello I need not trace the tale—nor the one weakness of his so mighty love; nor the inferiority of his perceptive intellect to that even of the second woman character in the play, the Emilia who dies in wild testimony against his error—"Oh, murderous coxcomb! What should such a fool do with so good a wife?"

In Romeo and Juliet, the wise and entirely brave stratagem of the wife is brought to ruinous issue by

the reckless impatience of her husband. In Winter's
Tale, and in Cymbeline, the happiness and existence of
two princely households, lost through long years, and
imperiled to the death by the folly and obstinacy of
the husbands, are redeemed at last by the queenly
patience and wisdom of the wives. In Measure for
Measure, the injustice of the judges, and the corrupt
cowardice of the brother, are opposed to the victorious
truth and adamantine purity of a woman. In Coriolanus,
the mother's counsel, acted upon in time, would have
saved her son from all evil; his momentary forgetful-
ness of it is his ruin; her prayer at last granted, saves
him—not, indeed, from death, but from the curse of
living as the destroyer of his country.

And what shall I say of Julia, constant against the
fickleness of a lover who is a mere wicked child?—of
Helena, against the petulance and insult of a careless
youth?—of the patience of Hero, the passion of Beat-
rice, and the calmly devoted wisdom of the "unles-
soned girl," who appears among the helplessness, the
blindness, and the vindictive passions of men, as a
gentle angel, to save merely by her presence, and defeat the worst intensities of crime by her smile?

Observe, further, among all the principal figures in
Shakespeare's plays, there is only one weak woman—
Ophelia; and it is because she fails Hamlet at the critical moment, and is not, and cannot in her nature be,
a guide to him when he needs her most, that all the

bitter catastrophe follows. Finally, though there are
three wicked women among the principal figures, Lady
Macbeth, Regan, and Goneril, they are felt at once to
be frightful exceptions to the ordinary laws of life;
fatal in their influence also in proportion to the power
for good which they have abandoned.

Such, in broad light, is Shakespeare's testimony to
the position and character of women in human life.
He represents them as infallibly faithful and wise
counselors—incorruptibly just and pure examples—
always strong to sanctify, even when they cannot save.

Not as in any wise comparable in knowledge of the
nature of man—still less in his understanding of the
causes and courses of fate—but only as the writer who
has given us the broadest view of the conditions and
modes of ordinary thought in modern society, I ask
you next to receive the witness of Walter Scott.

I put aside his merely romantic prose writings as of
no value: and though the early romantic poetry is
very beautiful, its testimony is of no weight, other
than that of a boy's ideal. But his true works,
studied from Scottish life, bear a true witness, and in
the whole range of these there are but three men who
reach the heroic type*—Dandie Dinmont, Rob Roy,

---

* I ought, in order to make this assertion fully understood, to
have noted the various weaknesses which lower the ideal of other
great characters of men in the Waverley Novels—the selfishness and
narrowness of thought in Redgauntlet, the weak religious enthusiasm
in Edward Glendenning, and the like; and I ought to have noticed

and Claverhouse: of these, one is a border farmer; another a freebooter; the third a soldier in a bad cause. And these touch the ideal of heroism only in their courage, and faith, together with a strong, but uncultivated, or mistakenly applied, intellectual power; while his younger men are the gentlemanly playthings of fantastic fortune, and only by aid (or accident) of that fortune, survive, not vanquish, the trials they involuntarily sustain. Of any disciplined, or consistent character, earnest in a purpose wisely conceived, or dealing with forms of hostile evil, definitely challenged, and resolutely subdued, there is no trace in his conceptions of men. Whereas in his imaginations of women—in the characters of Ellen Douglas, of Flora MacIvor, Rose Bradwardine, Catharine Seyton, Diana Vernon, Lilias Redgauntlet, Alice Bridgenorth, Alice Lee, and Jeanie Deans—with endless varieties of grace, tenderness, and intellectual power, we find in all a quite infallible and inevitable sense of dignity and justice; a fearless, instant, and untiring self-sacrifice to even the appearance of duty, much more to its real claims; and, finally, a patient wisdom of deeply restrained affection, which does infinitely more than protect its objects from a momentary error; it grad-

---

that there are several quite perfect characters sketched sometimes in the backgrounds; three—let us accept joyously this courtesy to England and her soldiers—are English officers: Colonel Gardiner, Colonel Talbot, and Colonel Mannering.

ually forms, animates and exalts the characters of the unworthy lovers, until, at the close of the tale, we are just able, and no more, to take patience, in hearing of their unmerited success.

So that in all cases, with Scott as with Shakespeare, it is the woman who watches over, teaches and guides the youth ; it is never, by any chance, the youth who watches over or educates his mistress.

Next, take, though more briefly, graver and deeper testimony—that of the great Italians and Greeks. You know well the plan of Dante's great poem— that it is a love-poem to his dead lady, a song of praise for her watch over his soul. Stooping only to pity, never to love, she yet saves him from destruction— saves him from hell. He is going eternally astray in despair ; she comes down from heaven to his help, and throughout the ascents of Paradise is his teacher, interpreting for him the most difficult truths, divine and human ; and leading him, with rebuke upon rebuke, from star to star.

I do not insist upon Dante's conception ; if I began I could not cease : besides, you might think this a wild imagination of one poet's heart. So I will rather read to you a few verses of the deliberate writing of a knight of Pisa to his living lady, wholly characteristic of the feeling of all the noblest men of the thirteenth century, preserved among many other such records of knightly honor

and love, which Dante Rossetti has gathered for us
from among the early Italian poets.

> For lo! thy law is passed
> That this my love should manifestly be
> To serve and honor thee:
> And so I do; and my delight is full,
> Accepted for the servant of thy rule.
>
> Without almost, I am all rapturous,
> Since thus my will was set
> To serve, thou flower of joy, thine excellence:
> Nor ever seems it anything could rouse
> A pain or regret,
> But on thee dwells mine every thought and sense:
> Considering that from thee all virtues spread
> As from a fountain head—
> *That in thy gift is wisdom's best avail,*
> *And honor without fail;*
> With whom each sovereign good dwells separate,
> Fulfilling the perfection of thy state.
>
> Lady, since I conceived
> Thy pleasurable aspect in my heart,
> *My life has been apart*
> *In shining brightness and the place of truth;*
> Which till that time, good sooth,
> Groped among shadows in a darken'd place,
> Where many hours and days
> It hardly ever had remember'd good.
> But now my servitude
> Is thine, and I am full of joy and rest.
> A man from a wild beast
> Thou madest me, since for thy love I lived.

You may think, perhaps, a Greek knight would have had a lower estimate of women than this Christian lover. His own spiritual subjection to them was indeed not so absolute; but as regards their own personal character, it was only because you could not have followed me so easily, that I did not take the Greek women instead of Shakespeare's; and instance, for chief ideal types of human beauty and faith, the simple mother's and wife's heart of Andromache; the divine, yet rejected wisdom of Cassandra; the playful kindness and simple princess-life of happy Nausicaa; the housewifely calm of that of Penelope, with its watch upon the sea; the ever patient, fearless, hopelessly devoted piety of the sister, and daughter, in Antigone; the bowing down of Iphigenia, lamb-like and silent; and, finally, the expectation of the resurrection, made clear to the soul of the Greeks in the return from her grave of that Alcestis, who, to save her husband, had passed calmly through the bitterness of death.

Now I could multiply witness upon witness of this kind upon you if I had time. I would take Chaucer, and show you why he wrote a Legend of Good Women; but no Legend of Good Men. I would take Spenser, and show you how all his fairy knights are sometimes deceived and sometimes vanquished; but the soul of Una is never darkened, and the spear of Britomart is never broken. Nay, I could go back into the mythical teaching of the most ancient times, and show you how the great people—by one of whose princesses it was appointed that the Law-giver of all the earth should be educated, rather than by his own kindred—how that great Egyptian people, wisest then of nations, gave to their Spirit of Wisdom the form of a woman; and into her hand, for a symbol, the weaver's shuttle: and how the name and the form of that spirit, adopted, believed, and obeyed by the Greeks, became that Athena of the olive-helm, and cloudy shield, to whose faith you owe, down to this date, whatever you hold most precious in art, in literature, or in types of national virtue.

But I will not wander into this distant and mythical element; I will only ask you to give its legitimate value to the testimony of these great poets and men of the world—consistent as you see it is on this head. I will ask you whether it can be supposed that these men, in the main work of their lives, are amusing themselves with a fictitious and idle view of the relations between man and woman—nay, worse than fictitious or idle; for a thing may be imaginary, yet desirable, if it were possible; but this, their ideal of women, is, according to our common idea of the marriage relation, wholly undesirable. The woman, we say, is not to guide, nor even to think, for herself. The man is always to be the wiser; he is to be the thinker, the ruler, the superior in knowledge and discretion, as in power. Is it not somewhat important to make up our minds on this matter? Are all these great men mistaken, or are we? Are Shakespeare and Æschylus, Dante and Homer, merely dressing dolls for us; or, worse than dolls, unnatural visions, the realization of which, were it possible, would bring anarchy into all households and ruin into all affections? Nay, if you could suppose this, take lastly the evidence of facts, given by the human heart itself.

In all Christian ages which have been remarkable for their purity or progress, there has been absolute yielding of obedient devotion, by the lover, to his mistress. I say *obedient*—not merely enthusiastic and worshiping in imagination, but entirely subject, receiving from the beloved woman, however young, not only the encouragement, the praise, and the reward of all toil, but, so far as any choice is open, or any question difficult of decision, the *direction* of all toil. That chivalry, to the abuse and dishonor of which are attributable primarily whatever is cruel in war, unjust in peace, or corrupt and ignoble in domestic relations; and to the original purity and power of which we owe the defense alike of faith, of law, and of love

—that chivalry, I say, in its very first conception of honorable life, assumes the subjection of the young knight to the command—should it even be the command in caprice—of his lady. It assumes this, because its masters knew that the first and necessary impulse of every truly taught and knightly heart is this of blind service to its lady; that where that true faith and captivity are not, all wayward and wicked passion must be; and that in this rapturous obedience to the single love of his youth, is the sanctification of all man's strength, and the continuance of all his purposes. And this not because such obedience would be safe, or honorable, were it ever rendered to the unworthy; but because it ought to be impossible for every noble youth—it *is* impossible for every one rightly trained—to love any one whose gentle counsel he cannot trust, or whose prayerful command he can hesitate to obey.

I do not insist by any further argument on this, for I think it should commend itself at once to your knowledge of what has been and to your feeling of what should be. You cannot think that the buckling on of the knight's armor by his lady's hand was a mere caprice of romantic fashion. It is the type of an eternal truth—that the soul's armor is never well set to the heart unless a woman's hand has braced it; and it is only when she braces it loosely that the honor of manhood fails. Know you not those lovely lines—I would they were learned by all youthful ladies of England :

> " Ah wasteful woman! she who may
> On her sweet self set her own price,
> Knowing he cannot choose but pay—
> How has she cheapen'd Paradise!
> How given for naught her priceless gift,
> How spoiled the bread and spill'd the wine,
> Which, spent with due, respective thrift,
> Had made brutes men, and men divine!" *

Thus much, then, respecting the relations of lovers I believe you will accept. But what we too often doubt is the fitness of the continuance of such a relation throughout the whole of human life. We think it right in the lover and mistress, not in the husband and wife. That is to say, we think that a reverent and tender duty is due to one whose affection we still doubt, and whose character we as yet do but partially and distantly discern ; and that this reverence and duty are to be withdrawn when the affection has become wholly and limitlessly our own, and the character has been so sifted and tried that we fear not to intrust it with the happiness of our lives. Do you not see how ignoble this is, as well as how unreasonable? Do you not feel that marriage—when it is marriage at all—is only the seal which marks the vowed transition of temporary into untiring service, and of fitful into eternal love?

---

* Coventry Patmore.

But how, you will ask, is the idea of this guiding function of the woman reconcilable with a true wifely subjection? Simply in that it is a *guiding*, not a determining, function. Let me try to show you briefly how these powers seem to be rightly distinguishable.

We are foolish, and without excuse foolish, in speaking of the "superiority" of one sex to the other, as if they could be compared in similar things. Each has what the other has not: each completes the other, and is completed by the other: they are in nothing alike, and the happiness and perfection of both depends on each asking and receiving from the other what the other only can give.

Now their separate characters are briefly these. The man's power is active, progressive, defensive. He is eminently the doer, the creator, the discoverer, the defender. His intellect is for speculation and invention; his energy for adventure, for war, and for conquest, wherever war is just, wherever conquest necessary. But the woman's power is for rule, not for battle—and her intellect is not for invention or creation, but for sweet ordering, arrangement, and decision. She sees the qualities of things, their claims and their places. Her great function is Praise; she enters into no contest, but infallibly judges the crown of contest. By her office, and place, she is protected from all danger and temptation. The man in his rough work in open world, must encounter all peril and trial: to him, therefore, the failure, the offense, the inevitable error: often he must be wounded, or subdued, often misled, and *always* hardened. But he guards the woman from all this; within his house, as ruled by her, unless she herself has sought it, need enter no danger, no temptation, no cause of error or offense. This is the true nature of home—it is the place of Peace; the shelter, not only from all injury, but from all terror, doubt, and division. In so far as it is not this, it is not home; so far as the anxieties of the outer life penetrate into it, and the inconsistently-minded, unknown, unloved, or hostile society of the outer world is allowed by either husband or wife to cross the threshold, it ceases to be home; it is then only a part of that outer world which you have roofed over, and lighted fire in. But so far as it is a sacred place, a vestal temple, a temple of the hearth watched over by Household Gods, before whose faces none may come but those whom they can receive with love—so far as it is this, and roof and fire are types only of a nobler shade and light—shade as of the rock in a weary land, and light as of the Pharos in the stormy sea—so far it vindicates the name, and fulfills the praise, of home.

And wherever a true wife comes, this home is always round her. The stars only may be over her head; the glow-worm in the night-cold grass may be the only fire at her foot: but home is yet wherever she is: and for a noble woman it stretches far round her, better than ceiled with cedar, or painted with vermilion, shedding its quiet light far, for those who else were homeless.

This, then, I believe to be—will you not admit it to be—the woman's true place and power? But do not you see that to fulfill this, she must—as far as one can use such terms of a human creature—be incapable of error? So far as she rules, all must be right, or nothing is. She must be enduringly, incorruptibly good; instinctively, infallibly wise—wise, not for self-development, but for self-renunciation: wise, not that she may set herself above her husband, but that she may never fail from his side: wise, not with the narrowness of insolent and loveless pride, but with the passionate gentleness of an infinitely variable, because infinitely applicable, modesty of service—the true changefulness of woman. In that great sense—" La donna e mobile," not " Qual piùm al vento;" no, nor yet "Variable as the shade, by the light quivering aspen made;" but variable as the *light*, manifold in fair and serene division, that it may take the color of all that it falls upon, and exalt it.

II.—I have been trying, thus far, to show you what should be the place, and what the power of woman. Now, secondly, we ask, What kind of education is to fit her for these?

And if you indeed think this a true conception of her office and dignity, it will not be difficult to trace the course of education which would fit her for the one, and raise her to the other.

The first of our duties to her—no thoughtful persons now doubt this—is to secure for her such physical training and exercise as may confirm her health, and perfect her beauty; the highest refinement of that beauty being unattainable without splendor of activity and of delicate strength. To perfect her beauty, I say, and increase its power; it cannot be too powerful, nor shed its sacred light too far; only remember that all physical freedom is vain to produce beauty without a corresponding freedom of heart. There are two passages of that poet who is distinguished, it seems to me, from all others—not by power, but by exquisite *right-*ness—which point you to the source, and describe to you, in a few syllables, the completion of womanly beauty. I will read the introductory stanzas, but the last is the one I wish you specially to notice:

> " Three years she grew in sun and shower,
> Then Nature said, a lovelier flower
>   On earth was never sown.
> This child I to myself will take;
> She shall be mine, and I will make
>   A lady of my own.
>
> " Myself will to my darling be
> Both law and impulse; and with me
>   The girl, in rock and plain,
> In earth and heaven, in glade and bower,
> Shall feel an overseeing power
>   To kindle, or restrain.

> " The floating clouds their state shall lend
>   To her, for her the willow bend;
>   Nor shall she fail to see
>   Even in the motions of the storm,
>   Grace that shall mold the maiden's form
>   By silent sympathy.

> " And *vital feelings of delight*
>   Shall rear her form to stately height—
>   Her virgin bosom swell.
>   Such *thoughts* to Lucy I will give,
>   While she and I together live,
>   Here in this happy dell."

" *Vital* feelings of delight," observe. There are deadly feelings of delight; but the natural ones are vital, necesary to very life.

And they must be feelings of delight, if they are to be vital. Do not think you can make a girl lovely, if you do not make her happy. There is not one restraint you put on a good girl's nature—there is not one check you give to her instincts of affection or of effort—which will not be indelibly written on her features, with a hardness which is all the more painful because it takes away the brightness from the eyes of innocence, and the charm from the brow of virtue.

This for the means: now note the end. Take from the same poet, in two lines, a perfect description of womanly beauty—

> " A countenance in which did meet
>   Sweet records, promises as sweet."

The perfect loveliness of a woman's countenance can only consist in that majestic peace, which is founded in the memory of happy and useful years—full of sweet records; and from the joining of this with that yet more majestic childishness, which is still full of change and promise—opening always—modest at once, and bright, with hope of better things to be won, and to be bestowed. There is no old age where there is still that promise—it is eternal youth.

Thus, then, you have first to mold your physical frame, and then, as the strength she gains will permit you, to fill and temper her mind with all knowledge and thoughts which tend to confirm its natural instincts of justice, and refine its natural tact of love.

All such knowledge should be given her as may enable her to understand, and even to aid, the work of men: and yet it should be given, not as knowledge—not as if it were, or could be, for her an object to know; but only to feel, and to judge. It is of no moment, as a matter of pride or perfectness in herself, whether she knows many languages or one; but it is of the utmost, that she should be able to show kindness to a stranger, and to understand the sweetness of a stranger's tongue. It is of no moment to her own worth or dignity that she should be acquainted with this science or that; but it is of the highest that she should be trained in habits of accurate thought; that she should understand the meaning, the inevitableness, and the loveliness of natural laws, and follow at least some one path of scientific attainment, as far as to the threshold of that bitter Valley of Humiliation, into which only the wisest and bravest of men can descend, owning themselves forever children, gathering pebbles on a boundless shore. It is of little consequence how many positions of cities she knows, or how many dates of events, or how many names of celebrated persons—it is not the object of education to turn a woman into a dictionary; but it is deeply necessary that she should be taught to enter with her whole personality into the history she reads; to picture the passages of it vitally in her own bright imagination; to apprehend, with her fine instincts, the pathetic circumstances and dramatic relations, which the historian too often only eclipses by his reasoning, and disconnects by his arrangement: it is for her to trace the hidden equities of divine reward, and catch sight, through the darkness, of the fateful threads of woven fire that connect error with its retribution. But, chiefly of all, she is to be taught to extend the limits of her sympathy with respect to that history which is being forever determined, as the moments pass in which she draws her peaceful breath; and to the contemporary calamity which, were it but rightly mourned by her, would recur no more hereafter. She is to exercise herself in imagining what would be the effects upon her mind and conduct, if she were daily brought into the presence of the suffering which is not the less real because shut from her sight. She is to be taught somewhat to understand the nothingness of the proportion which that little world in which she lives and loves, bears to the world in which God lives and loves; and solemnly she is to be taught to strive that her thoughts of piety may not be feeble in proportion to the number they embrace, nor her prayer more languid than it is for the momentary relief from pain of her husband or her child, when it is uttered for the multitudes of those who have none to love them—and is "for all who are desolate and oppressed."

Thus far, I think, I have had your concurrence; perhaps you will not be with me in what I believe is most needful for me to say. There *is* one dangerous science for women—one which let them indeed beware how they profanely touch—that of theology. Strange, and miserably strange, that while they are modest enough to doubt their powers, and pause at the threshold of sciences where every step is demonstrable and sure, they will plunge headlong, and without one thought of incompetency, into that science in which the greatest men have trembled, and the wiset erred. Strange, that they will complacently and pridefully bind up whatever vice or folly there is in them, whatever arrogance, petulance, or blind incomprehensiveness, into one bitter bundle of consecrated myrrh.

Strange, in creatures born to be Love visible, that where they can know least, they will condemn first, and think to recommend themselves to their Master by scrambling up the steps of His judgment-throne, to divide it with Him. Most strange, that they should think they were led by the Spirit of the Comforter into habits of mind which have become in them the unmixed elements of home discomfort; and that they dare to turn the Household Gods of Christianity into ugly idols of their own—spiritual dolls, for them to dress accordiug to their caprice; and from which their husbands must turn away in grieved contempt, lest they should be shrieked at for breaking them.

I believe, then, with this exception, that a girl's education should be nearly, in its course and material of study, the same as a boy's; but quite differently directed. A woman in any rank of life, ought to know whatever her husband is likely to know, but to know it in a different way. His command of it should be foundational and progressive, hers, general and accomplished for daily and helpful use. Not but that it would often be wiser in men to learn things in a womanly sort of way, for present use, and to seek for the discipline and training of their mental powers in such branches of study as will be afterward fittest for social service; but, speaking broadly, a man ought to know any language or science he learns, thoroughly, while a woman ought to know the same language, or science, only so far as may enable her to sympathize in her husband's pleasures, and in those of his best friends.

Yet, observe, with exquisite accuracy as far as she reaches. There is a wide difference between elementary knowledge and superficial knowledge— between a firm beginning, and a feeble smattering. A woman may always help her husband by what she knows, however little; by what she half-knows, or mis-knows, she will only teaze him.

And, indeed, if there were to be any difference between a girl's education and a boy's, I should say that of the two the girl should be earlier led, as her intellect ripens faster, into deep and serious subjects; and that her range of literature should be, not more, but less frivolous, calculated to add the qualities of patience and seriousness to her natural poignancy of thought and quickness of wit; and also to keep her in a lofty and pure element of thought. I enter not now into any question of choice of books; only be sure that her books are not heaped up in her lap as they fall out of the package of the circulatiug library, wet with the last and lightest spray of the fountain of folly.

Or even of the fountain of wit; for with respect to that sore temptation of novel-reading, it is not the badness of a novel that we should dread, but its overwrought interest. The weakest romance is not so stupefying as the lower forms of religious exciting literature, and the worst romance is not so corrupting as false history, false philosophy, or false political essays. But the best romance becomes dangerous, if, by its excitement, it renders the ordinary course of life uninteresting, and increases the morbid thirst for useless acquaintance with scenes in which we shall never be called upon to act.

I speak therefore of good novels only; and our modern literature is particularly rich in types of such. Well read, indeed, these books have serious use, being nothing less than treatises on moral anatomy and chemistry; studies of human nature in the elements of it. But I attach little weight to this function; they are hardly ever read with earnestness enough to permit them to fulfill it. The utmost they usually do is to enlarge somewhat the charity of a kind reader, or the bitterness of a malicious one; for each will gather, from the novel, food for her own disposition. Those who are naturally proud and envious will learn from Thackeray to despise humanity; those who are naturally gentle, to pity it; those who are naturally shallow, to laugh at it. So, also, there might be a serviceable power in novels to bring before us, in vividness, a human truth which we had before

dimly conceived; bnt the temptation to picturesqueness of statement is so great, that often the best
writers of fiction cannot resist it; and our views
are rendered so violent and one sided, that their vitality is rather a harm than good.

Without, however, venturing here on any attempt at
decision how much novel-reading should be allowed,
let me at least clearly assert this, that whether novels,
or poetry, or history be read, they should be chosen,
not for what is *out* of them, but for what is *in* them.
The chance and scattered evil that may here and there
haunt, or hide itself in, a powerful book, never does
any harm to a noble girl; but the emptiness of an
author oppresses her, and his amiable folly degrades
her.   And if she can have access to a good library of
old and classical books, there need be no choosing at
all.   Keep the modern magazine and novel out of your
girl's way : turn her loose into the old library every wet
day, and let her alone.   She will find what is good for
her; you cannot : for there is just this difference between the making of a girl's character and a boy's—
you may chisel a boy into shape, as you would a rock,
or hammer him into it, if he be of a better kind, as
you would a piece of bronze.   But you cannot hammer
a girl into anything.   She grows as a flower does—
she will wither without sun; she will decay in her
sheath, as the narcissus does, if you do not give her air
enough ; she may fall and defile her head in dust, if

you leave her without help at some moments of her life; but you cannot fetter her; she must take her own fair form and way, if she takes any, and in mind as in body, must have always

> " Her household motions light and free
> And steps of virgin liberty."

Let her loose in the library, I say, as you do a fawn in a field. It knows the bad weeds twenty times better than you; and the good ones too, and will eat some bitter and prickly ones, good for it, which you had not the slightest thought were good.

Then, in art, keep the finest models before her, and let her practice in all accomplishments be accurate and thorough, so as to enable her to understand more than she accomplishes. I say the finest models—that is to say, the truest, simplest, usefullest. Note those epithets; they will range through all the arts. Try them in music, where you might think them the least applicable. I say the truest, that in which the notes most closely and faithfully express the meaning of the words, or the character of intended emotion; again, the simplest, that in which the meaning and melody are attained with the fewest and most significant notes possible; and, finally, the usefullest, that music which makes the best words most beautiful, which enchants them in our memories each with its own glory of sound, and which applies them closest to the heart at the moment we need them.

And not only in the material and in the course, but yet more earnestly in the spirit of it, let a girl's education be as serious as a boy's. You bring up your girls as if they were meant for sideboard ornaments, and then complain of their frivolity. Give them the same advantages that you give their brothers—appeal to the same grand instincts of virtue in them ; teach *them* also that courage and truth are the pillars of their being : do you think that they would not answer that appeal, brave and true as they are even now, when you know that there is hardly a girl's school in this Christian kingdom where the children's courage or sincerity would be thought of half so much importance as their way of coming in at a door ; and when the whole system of society, as respects the mode of establishing them in life, is one rotten plague of cowardice and imposture—cowardice, in not daring to let them live, or love, except as their neighbors choose ; and imposture, in bringing, for the purpose of our own pride, the full glow of the world's worst vanity upon a girl's eye, at the very period when the whole happiness of her future existence depends upon her remaining undazzled?

And give them, lastly, not only noble teachings, but noble teachers. You consider somewhat, before you send your boy to school, what kind of a man the master is—whatsoever kind of man he is, you at least give him full authority over your son, and show some respect to him yourself; if he comes to dine with you, you do not put him at a side table; you know also that, at his college, your child's immediate tutor will be under the direction of some still higher tutor, for whom you have absolute reverence. You do not treat the Dean of Christ Church or the Master of Trinity as your inferiors.

But what teachers do you give your girls, and what reverence do you show to the teachers you have chosen? Is a girl likely to think her own conduct, or her own intellect, of much importance, when you trust the entire formation of her character, moral and intellectual, to a person whom you let your servants treat with less respect than they do your housekeeper (as if the soul of your child were a less charge than jams and groceries,) and whom you yourself think you confer an honor upon them by letting her sometimes sit in the drawing-room in the evening?

Thus, then, of literature as her help, and thus of art. There is one more help which she cannot do without —one which, alone, has sometimes done more than all other influences besides—the help of wild and fair nature. Hear this of the education of Joan of Arc:

" The education of this poor girl was meant according to the present standard; was ineffably grand, according to a purer philosophic standard, and only not good for our age, because for us it would be unattainable. . . .

" Next after her spiritual advantages, she owed most to the advantages of her situation. The fountain of Domrémy was on the brink of a boundless forest; and it was haunted to that degree by fairies, that the parish priest (*curé*) was obliged to read mass there once a year, in order to keep them in any decent bounds. . . .

"But the forests of Domrémy—those were the glories of the land, for in them abode mysterious powers and ancient secrets that towered into tragic strength. 'Abbeys there were, and abbey windows' —'like Moorish temples of the Hindoos,' that exercised even princely power both in Touraine and in the German Diets. These had their sweet bells that pierced the forests for many a league at matins or vespers, and each its own dreamy legend. Few enough, and scattered enough, were these abbeys, so as in no degree to disturb the deep solitude of the region; yet many enough to spread a net-work or awning of Christian sanctity over what else might have seemed a heathen wilderness." *

Now, you cannot, indeed, have here in England, woods eighteen miles deep to the center; but you can, perhaps, keep a fairy or two for your children yet, if you wish to keep them. But *do* you wish it? Suppose you had each, at the back of your house, a garden, large enough for your children to play in, with just as much lawn as would give them room to run—no more—and that you could not change your abode; but that, if you chose, you could double your income, or quadruple it, by digging a coal-shaft in the middle of the lawn, and turning the flower-beds into heaps of coke. Would you do it? I think not. I can tell you, you would be wrong if you did, though it gave you income sixtyfold instead of fourfold.

---

* "Joan of Arc: in reference to M. Michelet's History of France." De Quincey's Works. Vol. iii. p. 217.

Yet this is what you are doing with all England. The whole country is but a little garden, not more than enough for your children to run on the lawns of, if you would let them *all* run there. And this little garden you will turn into furnace-ground, and fill with heaps of cinders, if you can; and those children of yours, not you, will suffer for it. For the fairies will not be all banished; there are fairies of the furnace as of the wood, and their first gifts seem to be "sharp arrows of the mighty;" but their last gifts are "coals of juniper."

And yet I cannot—though there is no part of my subject that I feel more—press this upon you; for we made so little use of the power of nature while we had it that we shall hardly feel what we have lost. Just on the other side of the Mersey you have your Snowdon, and your Menai Straits, and that mighty granite rock beyond the moors of Anglesea, splendid in its heathery crest, and foot planted in the deep sea, once thought of as sacred —a divine promontory, looking westward; the Holy Head or Headland, still not without awe when its red light glares first through storm. These are the hills, and these the bays and blue inlets, which among the Greeks, would have been always loved, always fateful in influence on the national mind. That Snowdon is your Parnassus; but where are its

Muses? That Holyhead mountain is your Island of Ægina, but where is its Temple to Minerva?

Shall I read you what the Christian Minerva had achieved under the shadow of our Parnassus, up to the year 1848? Here is a little account of a Welsh school, from page 261 of the Report on Wales, published by the Committee of Council on Education. This is a school close to a town containing 5,000 persons:

"I then called up a larger class, most of whom had recently come to the school. Three girls repeatedly declared they had never heard of Christ, and two that they had never heard of God. Two out of six thought Christ was on earth now ('they might have had a worse thought, perhaps'), three knew nothing about the crucifixion. Four out of seven did not know the names of the months, nor the number of days in a year. They had no notion whatever of addition beyond two and two, or three and three; their minds were perfect blanks."

Oh ye women of England! from the Princess of that Wales to the simplest of you, do not think your own children can be brought into their true fold of rest while these are scattered on the hills, as sheep having no shepherd. And do not think your daughters can be trained to the truth of their own human beauty, while the pleasant places, which God made at once for their school-room and their play-ground, lie desolate and defiled. You cannot baptize them rightly in those inch-deep fonts of yours, unless you baptize them also in the sweet waters which the great Law-giver strikes forth forever from the rocks of your native land—waters which a Pagan would have worshiped in their purity, and you only worship with pollution. You cannot lead your children faith-fully to those narrow ax-hewn church altars of yours, while the dark azure altars in heaven—the mountains that sustain your island throne—mount-ains on which a Pagan would have seen the pow-ers of heaven rest in every wreathed cloud—remain for you without inscription; altars built, not to, but by, an Unknown God.

III.—Thus far, then, of the nature, thus far of the teaching, of woman, and thus of her household office, and queenliness. We come now to our last, our widest question: What is her queenly office with respect to the state?

Generally, we are under an impression that a man's duties are public, and a woman's private. But this is not altogether so. A man has a personal work or duty, relating to his own home, and a public work or duty, which is the expansion of the other, relat-ing to the state. So a woman has a personal work or duty, relating to her own home, and a public work and duty, which is also the expansion of that.

Now the man's work for his own home is, as has

been said, to secure its maintenance, progress, and defense ; the woman's to secure its order, comfort, and loveliness.

Expand both these functions. The man's duty as a member of a commonwealth, is to assist in the maintenance, in the advance, in the defense of the state. The woman's duty, as a member of the commonwealth, is to assist in the ordering, in the comforting, and in the beautiful adornment of the state.

What the man is at his own gate, defending it, if need be, against insult and spoil, that also, not in a less, but in a more devoted measure, he is to be at the gate of his country, leaving his home, if need be, even to the spoiler, to do his more incumbent work there.

And, in like manner, what the woman is to be within her gates, as the center of order, the balm of distress, and the mirror of beauty ; that she is also to be without her gates, where order is more difficult, distress more imminent, loveliness more rare.

And as within the human heart there is always set an instinct for all its real duties—an instinct which you cannot quench, but only warp and corrupt if you withdraw it from its true purpose ; as there is the intense instinct of love, which, rightly disciplined, maintains all the sanctities of life and, misdirected, undermines them ; and *must* do either the one or the other ; so there is in the human heart an inextinguishable instinct, the love of power, which, rightly directed, maintains all the majesty of law and life, and mis-directed, wrecks them.

Deep rooted in the innermost life of the heart of man, and of the heart of woman, God set it there, and God keeps it there. Vainly, as falsely, you blame or rebuke the desire of power! For Heaven's sake, and for Man's sake, desire it all you can. But *what* power? That is all the question. Power to destroy? the lion's limb, and the dragon's breath? Not so. Power to heal, to redeem, to guide and to guard. Power of the scepter and shield; the power of the royal hand that heals in touching—that binds the fiend and looses the captive; the throne that is founded on the rock of Justice, and descended from only by steps of mercy. Will you not covet such power as this, and seek such throne as this, and be no more house-wives, but queens?

It is now long since the women of England arro-gated universally, a title which once belonged to nobility only, and, having once been in the habit of accepting the simple title of gentlewoman, as corre-spondent to that of gentleman, insisted on the privilege of assuming the title of "Lady,"* which properly corresponds only to the title of "Lord."

---

*I wish there were a true order of chivalry instituted for our English youth of certain ranks, in which both boy and girl should receive, at a given age, their knighthood and ladyhood by true title; attainable only by certain probation and trial both of character and accomplishment; and to be forfeited, on conviction, by their peers, of

I do not blame them for this; but only for their narrow motive in this. I would have them desire and claim the title of Lady, provided they claim, not merely the title, but the office and duty signified by it. Lady means "bread-giver" or "loaf-giver," and Lord means "maintainer of laws," and both titles have reference, not to the law which is maintained in the house, nor to the bread which is given to the household; but to law maintained for the multitude, and to bread broken among the multitude. So that a Lord has legal claim only to his title in so far as he is the maintainer of the justice of the Lord of Lords; and a Lady has legal claim to her title, only so far as she communicates that help to the poor representatives of her Master, which women once, ministering to Him of their substance, were permitted to extend to that Master Himself; and when she is known, as He Himself once was, in breaking of bread.

And this beneficent and legal dominion, this power of the Dominus, or House Lord, and of the Domina, or House-Lady, is great and venerable, not in the number of those through whom it has lineally descended, but in the number of those whom it grasps within its sway; it is always regarded with reverent worship wherever its dynasty is founded on its duty, and its

___

any dishonorable act. Such an institution would be entirely, and with all noble results, possible, in a nation which loved honor. That it would not be possible among us is not to the discredit of the scheme.

ambition co-relative with its beneficence. Your fancy is pleased with the thought of being noble ladies, with a train of vassals. Be it so; you cannot be too noble, and your train cannot be too great; but see to it that your train is of vassals whom you serve and feed, not merely of slaves who serve and feed *you;* and that the multitude which obeys you is of those whom you have comforted, not oppressed—whom you have redeemed, not led into captivity.

And this, which is true of the lower or household dominion, is equally true of the queenly dominion; that highest dignity is open to you, if you will also accept that highest duty. Rex et Regina—Roi et Reine—" *Right*-doers;" they differ but from the Lady and Lord, in that their power is supreme, over the mind as over the person—that they not only feed and clothe, but direct and teach. And whether consciously or not, you must be, in many a heart enthroned: there is no putting by that crown; queens you must always be; queens to your lovers; queens to your husbands and your sons; queens of higher mystery to the world beyond, which bows itself, and will forever bow, before the myrtle crown, and the stainless scepter, of womanhood. But, alas! you are too often idle and careless queens, grasping at majesty in the least things, while you abdicate it in the greatest; and leaving misrule and violence to work their will among men, in defiance of the power, which, holding straight in gift from the Prince of all Peace, the wicked among you betray, and the good forget.

"Prince of Peace." Note that name. When kings rule in that name, and nobles, and the judges of the earth, they also, in their narrow place, and mortal measure, receive the power of it. There are no other rulers than they: other rule than theirs is but *misrule*; they who govern verily "Dei gratiâ" are all princes, yes, or princesses, of peace. There is not a war in the world, no, nor an injustice, but you women are answerable for it; not in that you have provoked, but in that you have not hindered. Men, by their nature, are prone to fight; they will fight for any cause, or for none. It is for you to choose their cause for them, and to forbid them when there is no cause. There is no suffering, no injustice, no misery in the earth, but the guilt of it lies lastly with you. Men can bear the sight of it, but you should not be able to bear it. Men may tread it down without sympathy in their own struggle; but men are feeble in sympathy, and contracted in hope; it is you only who can feel the depths of pain; and conceive the way of its healings. Instead of trying to do this, you turn away from it; you shut yourselves within your park walls and garden gates; and you are content to know that there is beyond them a whole world in wilderness—a world of secrets which you dare not penetrate; and of suffering which you dare not conceive.

I tell you that this is to me quite the most amazing among the phenomena of humanity. I am surprised at no depths to which, when once warped from its honor, that humanity can be degraded. I do not wonder at the miser's death, with his hands, as they relax, dropping gold. I do not wonder at the sensualist's life, with the shroud wrapped about his feet. I do not wonder at the single-handed murder of a single victim, done by the assassin in the darkness of the railway, or reed-shadow of the marsh. I do not even wonder at the myriad-handed murder of multitudes, done boastfully in the daylight, by the frenzy of nations, and the immeasurable, unimaginable guilt, heaped up from hell to heaven, of their priests and kings. But this is wonderful to me—oh, how wonderful!—to see the tender and delicate woman among you, with her child at her breast, and a power, if she would wield it, over it, and over its father, purer than the air of heaven, and stronger than the seas of earth—nay, a magnitude of blessing which her husband would not part with for all that earth itself, though it were made of one entire and perfect chrysolite—to see her abdicate this majesty to play at precedence with her next-door neighbor! This is wonderful—oh, wonderful!—to see her, with every innocent feeling fresh within her, go out in the morning into her garden to play with the fringes of its guarded flowers, and lift their heads when they are drooping, with her happy smile upon her face, and no cloud upon her brow, because there is a little wall around her place of peace: and yet she knows, in her heart, if she would only look for its knowledge, that, outside of that little rose-covered wall, the wild grass, to the horizon, is torn up by the agony of men, and beat level by the drift of their life-blood.

Have you ever considered what a deep under meaning there lies, or at least, may be read, if we choose, in our custom of strewing flowers before those whom we think most happy? Do you suppose it is merely to deceive them into the hope that happiness is always to fall thus in showers at their feet?—that wherever they pass they will tread on herbs of sweet scent, and that the rough ground will be made smooth for them by depth of roses? So surely as they believe that, they will have, instead, to walk on bitter herbs and thorns; and the only softness to their feet will be of snow. But it is not thus intended they should believe there is a better meaning in that old custom. The path of a good woman is indeed strewn with flowers; but they rise behind her steps, not before them. "Her feet have touched the meadows, and left the daises rosy." You think that only a lover's fancy; false and vain! How if it could be true? You think this also, perhaps, only a poet's fancy:

> "Even the light harebell raised its head
> Elastic from her airy tread."

But it is little to say of a woman, that she only does
not destroy where she passes. She should revive; the
harebells should bloom, not stoop, as she passes. You
think I am going into wild hyperbole? Pardon me,
not a whit—I mean what I say in calm English,
spoken in resolute truth. You have heard it said
—and I believe there is more than fancy even in that
saying, but let it pass for a fanciful one—that flowers
only flourish rightly in the garden of some one who
loves them. I know you would like that to be true;
you would think it a pleasant magic if you could flush
your flowers into brighter bloom by a kind look upon
them: nay, more, if your look had the power, not
only to cheer, but to guard them—if you could bid
the black blight turn away, and the knotted cater-
pillar spare—if you could bid the dew fall upon
them in the drought, and say to the south
wind, in frost—" Come, thou south, and breathe
upon my garden, that the spices of it may flow out."
This you would think a great thing? And do you
think it not a greater thing, that all this (and how
much more than this!) you *can* do, for fairer flowers
than these—flowers that could bless you for having
blessed them, and will love you for having loved them;
flowers that have eyes like yours, and thoughts like
yours, and lives like yours; which, once saved, you
save forever? Is this only a little power? Far among
the moorlands and the rocks—far in the darkness of

the terrible streets—these feeble florets are lying, with all their fresh leaves torn, and their stems broken— will you never go down to them, nor set them in order in their little fragrant beds, nor fence them in their shuddering from the fierce wind? Shall morning follow morning, for you, but not for them; and the dawn rise to watch, far away, those frantic Dances of Death;* but no dawn rise to breathe upon these living banks of wild violet, and woodbine, and rose; nor call to you, through your casement—call (not giving you the name of the English poet's lady, but the name of Dante's great Matilda, who, on the edge of happy Lethe, stood, wreathing flowers with flowers), saying:

> " Come into the garden, Maud,
> For the black bat, night, has flown,
> And the woodbine spices are wafted abroad
> And the musk of the roses blown?"

Will you not go down among them?—among those sweet living things, whose new courage, sprung from the earth with the deep color of heaven upon it, is starting up in strength of goodly spire; and whose purity, washed from the dust, is opening, bud by bud, into the flower of promise—and still they turn to you, and for you, "The Larkspur listens—I hear, I hear! And the Lily whispers—I wait."

Did you notice that I missed two lines when I

* See note, p. 210.

read you that first stanza; and think that I had
forgotten them? Hear them now:

> "Come into the garden, Maud,
>   For the black bat, night, has flown;
>   Come into the garden, Maud,
>   I am here at the gate, alone."

Who is it, think you, who stands at the gate
of this sweeter garden, alone, waiting for you?
Did you ever hear, not of a Maude, but of a Mad-
eleine, who went down to her garden in the dawn,
and found one waiting at the gate, whom she supposed to be the gardener? Have you not sought
Him often—sought Him in vain, all through the
night—sought Him in vain, at the gate of that old
garden where the fiery sword is set? He is never
there; but at the gate of *this* garden He is waiting always—waiting to take your hand—ready to go
down to see the fruits of the valley, to see whether the
vine has flourished, and the pomegranate budded.
There you shall see with Him the little tendrils
of the vines that His hand is guiding—there you
shall see the pomegranate springing where His hand
cast the sanguine seed—more: you shall see the
troops of the angel-keepers that, with their wings,
wave away the hungry birds from the pathsides
where He has sown, and call to each other between the vineyard rows, "Take us the foxes, the
little foxes, that spoil the vines, for our vines

have tender grapes." Oh—you queens—you queens! among the hills and happy greenwood of this land of yours, shall the foxes have holes, and the birds of the air have nests; and, in your cities, shall the stones cry out against you, that they are the only pillows where the Son of Man can lay His head?

LECTURE III.

THE MYSTERY OF LIFE AND ITS ARTS.

Lecture delivered in the theater of the Royal College of Science,
Dublin, 1868.

96. WHEN I accepted the privilege of addressing you to-day, I was not aware of a restriction with respect to the topics of discussion which may be brought before this Society *—a restriction which, though entirely wise and right under the circumstances contemplated in its introduction, would necessarily have disabled me, thinking as I think, from preparing any lecture for you on the subject of art in a form which might be permanently useful. Pardon me, therefore, in so far as I must transgress such limitation; for indeed my infringement will be of the letter—not of the spirit—of your commands. In whatever I may say touching the religion which has been the foundation of art, or the policy which has contributed to its power, if I offend one, I shall offend all; for I shall take no note of any separations in creeds, or antagonisms in

---

* That no reference should be made to religious questions.

parties: neither do I fear that ultimately I shall offend any, by proving—or at least stating as capable of positive proof—the connection of all that is best in the crafts and arts of man, with the simplicity of his faith, and the sincerity of his patriotism.

97. But I speak to you under another disadvantage, by which I am checked in frankness of utterance, not here only, but everywhere; namely, that I am never fully aware how far my audiences are disposed to give me credit for real knowledge of my subject, or how far they grant me attention only because I have been sometimes thought an ingenious or pleasant essayist upon it. For I have had what, in many respects, I boldly call the misfortune, to set my words sometimes prettily together; not without a foolish vanity in the poor knack that I had of doing so; until I was heavily punished for this pride, by finding that many people thought of the words only, and cared nothing for their meaning. Happily, therefore, the power of using such pleasant language—if indeed it ever were mine—is passing away from me; and whatever I am now able to say at all, I find myself forced to say with great plainness. For my thoughts have changed also, as my words have; and whereas in earlier life, what little influence I obtained was due perhaps chiefly to the enthusiasm with which I was able to dwell on the beauty of the physical clouds, and of their colors in

the sky; so all the influence I now desire to retain must be due to the earnestness with which I am endeavoring to trace the form and beauty of another kind of cloud than those; the bright cloud, of which it is written—

" What is your life? It is even as a vapor, that appeareth for a little time, and then vanisheth away."

98. I suppose few people reach the middle or latter period of their age, without having, at some moment of change or disappointment, felt the truth of those bitter words; and been startled by the fading of the sunshine from the cloud of their life, into the sudden agony of the knowledge that the fabric of it was as fragile as a dream, and the endurance of it as transient as the dew. But it is not always that, even at such times of melancholy surprise, we can enter into any true perception that this human life shares, in the nature of it, not only the evanescence, but the mystery of the cloud; that its avenues are wreathed in darkness, and its forms and courses no less fantastic, than spectral and obscure: so that not only in the vanity which we cannot grasp, but in the shadow which we cannot pierce, it is true of this cloudy life of ours, that "man walketh in a vain shadow, and disquieteth himself in vain."

99. And least of all, whatever may have been the eagerness of our passions, or the height of our pride, are we able to understand in its depths the

third and most solemn character in which our life is like those clouds of heaven ; that to it belongs not only their transience, not only their mystery, but also their power ; that in the cloud of the human soul there is a fire stronger than the lightning, and a grace more precious than the rain ; and that though of the good and evil it shall one day be said alike, that the place that knew them knows them no more, there is an infinite separation between those whose brief presence had there been a blessing, like the mist of Eden that went up from the earth to water the garden, and those whose place knew them only as a drifting and changeful shade, of whom the heavenly sentence is that they are " wells without water ; clouds that are carried with a tempest, to whom the mist of darkness is reserved forever ? "

100. To those among us, however, who have lived long enough to form some just estimate of the rate of the changes which are, hour by hour in accelerating catastrophe, manifesting themselves in the laws, the arts, and the creeds of men, it seems to me, that now at least, if never at any former time, the thoughts of the true nature of our life, and of its powers and responsibilities, should present themselves with absolute sadness and sternness.

And although I know that this feeling is much deepened in my own mind by disappointment, which, by chance, has attended the greater number of my cherished purposes, I do not for that reason distrust the feeling itself, though I am on my guard against an exaggerated degree of it : nay, I rather believe that in periods of new effort and violent change, disappointment is a wholesome medicine ; and that in the secret of it, as in the twilight so beloved by Titian, we may see the colors of things with deeper truth than in the most dazzling sunshine. And because these truths about the works of men, which I want to bring to-day before you, are most of them sad ones, though at the same time helpful ; and because also I believe that your kind Irish hearts will answer more gladly to the truthful expression of a personal feeling, than to the exposition of an abstract principle, I will permit myself so much unreserved speaking of my own causes of regret, as may enable you to make just allowance for what, according to your sympathies, you will call either the bitterness, or the insight, of a mind which has surrendered its best hopes, and been foiled in its favorite aims.

101. I spent the ten strongest years of my life (from twenty to thirty), in endeavoring to show the excellence of the work of the man whom I believed, and rightly believed, to be the greatest painter of the schools of England since Reynolds. I had then perfect faith in the power of every great truth or beauty to prevail ultimately, and take its right place in usefulness and

honor; and I strove to bring the painter's work into this due place, while the painter was yet alive. But he knew, better than I, the uselessness of talking about what people could not see for themselves. He always discouraged me scornfully, even when he thanked me—and he died before even the superficial effect of my work was visible. I went on, however, thinking I could at least be of use to the public, if not to him, in proving his power. My books got talked about a little. The prices of modern pictures, generally, rose, and I was beginning to take some pleasure in a sense of gradual victory, when, fortunately or unfortunately, an opportunity of perfect trial undeceived me at once, and forever. The Trustees of the National Gallery commissioned me to arrange the Turner drawings there, and permitted me to prepare three hundred examples of his studies from nature, for exhibition at Kensington. At Kensington they were and are, placed for exhibition; but they are not exhibited, for the room in which they hang is always empty.

102. Well—this showed me at once, that those ten years of my life had been, in their chief purpose, lost. For that, I did not so much care; I had, at least, learned my own business thoroughly, and should be able, as I fondly supposed, after such a lesson, now to use my knowledge with better effect. But what I did care for, was the—to me frightful—discovery, that the most splendid genius in the arts might be permitted by

Providence to labor and perish uselessly; that in the very fineness of it there might be something rendering it invisible to ordinary eyes; but, that with this strange excellence, faults might be mingled which would be as deadly as its virtues were vain; that the glory of it was perishable, as well as invisible, and the gift and grace of it might be to us, as snow in summer, and as rain in harvest.

103. That was the first mystery of life to me. But, while my best energy was given to the study of painting, I had put collateral effort, more prudent, if less enthusiastic, into that of architecture; and in this I could not complain of meeting with no sympathy. Among several personal reasons which caused me to desire that I might give this, my closing lecture on the subject of art here, in Ireland, one of the chief was, that in reading it, I should stand near the beautiful building—the engineers' school of your college— which was the first realization I had the joy to see, of the principles I had, until then, been endeavoring to teach; but which alas! is now, to me, no more than the richly canopied monument of one of the most earnest souls that ever gave itself to the arts, and one of my truest and most loving friends, Benjamin Woodward. Nor was it here in Ireland only that I received the help of Irish sympathy and genius. When, to another friend, Sir Thomas Deane, with Mr. Woodward, was intrusted the building of the

museum at Oxford, the best details of the work were executed by sculptors who had been born and trained here; and the first window of the façade of the building, in which was inaugurated the study of natural science in England, in true fellowship with literature, was carved from my design by an Irish sculptor.

104. You may perhaps think that no man ought to speak of disappointment, to whom, even in one branch of labor, so much success was granted. Had Mr. Woodward now been beside me, I had not so spoken; but his gentle and passionate spirit was cut off from the fulfillment of its purposes, and the work we did together is now become vain. It may not be so in future; but the architecture we endeavored to introduce is inconsistent alike with the reckless luxury, the deforming mechanism, and the squalid misery of modern cities; among the formative fashions of the day, aided, especially in England, by ecclesiastical sentiment, it indeed obtained notoriety; and sometimes behind an engine furnace, or a railroad bank, you may detect the pathetic discord of its momentary grace, and, with toil, decipher its floral carvings choked with soot. I felt answerable to the schools I loved, only for their injury. I perceived that this new portion of my strength had also been spent in vain; and from amid streets of iron, and pal-

aces of crystal, shrunk back at last to the carving of the mountain and color of the flower.

105. And still I could tell of failure, and failure repeated, as years went on; but I have trespassed enough on your patience to show you, in part, the causes of my discouragement. Now let me more deliberately tell you its results. You know there is a tendency in the minds of many men, when they are heavily disappointed in the main purposes of their life, to feel, and perhaps in warning, perhaps in mockery, to declare, that life itself is a vanity. Because it has disappointed them, they think its nature is of disappointment always, or at best, of pleasure that can be grasped by imagination only; that the cloud of it has no strength nor fire within; but is a painted cloud only, to be delighted in, yet despised. You know how beautifully Pope has expressed this particular phase of thought:

> " Meanwhile opinion gilds, with varying rays,
>   These painted clouds that beautify our days;
>   Each want of happiness by hope supplied,
>   And each vacuity of sense, by pride.
>   Hope builds as fast as Knowledge can destroy;
>   In Folly's cup, still laughs the bubble joy.
>   One pleasure past, another still we gain
>   And not a vanity is given in vain."

But the effect of failure upon my own mind has been

just the reverse of this. The more that my life disappointed me, the more solemn and wonderful it became to me. It seemed, contrarily to Pope's saying, that the vanity of it *was* indeed given in vain; but that there was something behind the veil of it, which was not vanity. It became to me not a painted cloud, but a terrible and impenetrable one : not a mirage, which vanished as I drew near, but a pillar of darkness, to which I was forbidden to draw near. For I saw that both my own failure, and such success in petty things as in its poor triumph seemed to me worse than failure, came from the want of sufficiently earnest effort to understand the whole law and meaning of existence, and to bring it to noble and due end; as, on the other hand, I saw more and more clearly that all enduring success in the arts, or in any other occupation, had come from the ruling of lower purposes, not by a conviction of their nothingness, but by a solemn faith in the advancing power of human nature, or in the promise, however dimly apprehended, that the mortal part of it would one day be swallowed up in immortality; and that, indeed, the arts themselves never had reached any vital strength or honor but in the effort to proclaim this immortality, and in the service either of great and just religion, or of some unselfish patriotism, and law of such national life as must be the foundation of religion.

106. Nothing that I have ever said is more true or

necessary—nothing has been more misunderstood or misapplied—than my strong assertion, that the arts can never be right themselves, unless their motive is right. It is misunderstood this way : weak painters, who have never learned their business, and cannot lay a true line, continually come to me, crying out—" Look at this picture of mine ; it *must* be good, I had such a lovely motive. I have put my whole heart into it, and taken years to think over its treatment." Well, the only answer for these people is—if one had the cruelty to make it—" Sir, you cannot think over *any*thing in any number of years—you haven't the head to do it ; and though you had fine motives, strong enough to make you burn yourself in a slow fire, if only first you could paint a picture, you can't paint one, nor half an inch of one ; and you haven't the hand to do it."

But, far more decisively we have to say to the men who *do* know their business, or may know it if they choose—" Sir, you have this gift, and a mighty one ; see that you serve your nation faithfully with it. It is a greater trust than ships and armies : you might cast *them* away, if you were their captain, with less treason to your people than in casting your own glorious power away, and serving the devil with it instead of men. Ships and armies you may replace if they are lost, but a great intellect, once abused, is a curse to the earth forever."

107. This, then, I meant by saying that the arts

must have noble motive. This also I said respecting them, that they never had prospered, nor could prosper, but when they had such true purpose, and were devoted to the proclamation of divine truth or law. And yet I said also that they had always failed in this proclamation—that poetry, and sculpture, and painting, though only great when they strove to teach us something about the gods, never had taught us anything trustworthy about the gods, but had always betrayed their trust in the crisis of it, and, with their powers at the full reach, became ministers to pride and to lust. And I felt also, with increasing amazement, the unconquerable apathy in ourselves and hearers, no less than in these the teachers; and that, while the wisdom and rightness of every act and art of life could only be consistent with a right understanding of the ends of life, we were all plunged as in a languid dream —our heart fat, and our eyes heavy, and our ears closed, lest the inspiration of hand and voice should reach us—lest we should see with our eyes, and understand with our hearts, and be healed.

108. This intense apathy in all of us is the first great mystery of life; it stands in the way of every perception, every virtue. There is no making ourselves feel enough astonishment at it. That the occupations or pastimes of life should have no motive, is understandable; but that life itself should have no motive— that we neither care to find out what it may lead to,

nor to guard against its being forever taken away from us—here is a mystery indeed. For, just suppose I were able to call at this moment to any one in this audience by name, and to tell him positively that I knew a large estate had been lately left to him on some curious conditions; but that, though I knew it was large, I did not know how large, nor even where it was—whether in the East Indies or the West, or in England, or at the Antipodes. I only knew it was a vast estate, and that there was a chance of his losing it altogether if he did not soon find out on what terms it had been left to him. Suppose I were able to say this positively to any single man in this audience, and he knew that I did not speak without warrant, do you think that he would rest content with that vague knowledge, if it were anywise possible to obtain more? Would he not give every energy to find some trace of the facts, and nevr rest till he had ascertained where this place was, and what it was like? And suppose he were a young man, and all he could discover by his best endeavor was, that the estate was never to be his at all, unless he persevered, during certain years of probation, in an orderly and industrious life; but that, according to the rightness of his conduct, the portion of the estate assigned to him would be greater or less, so that it literally depended on his behavior from day to day whether he got ten thousand a year, or thirty thousand a year, or nothing whatever—would you not think it strange if the youth never troubled himself to satisfy the conditions in any way, nor even to know what was required of him, but lived exactly as he chose, and never inquired whether his chances of the estate were increasing or passing away? Well, you know that this is actually and literally so with the greater number of the educated persons now living in Christian countries. Nearly every man and woman, in any company such as this, outwardly professes to believe—and a large number unquestionably think they believe—much more than this; not only that a quite unlimited estate is in prospect for them if they please the Holder of it, but that the infinite contrary of such a possession—an estate of perpetual misery, is in store for them if they displease this great Land-Holder, this great Heaven-Holder. And yet there is not one in a thousand of these human souls that cares to think, for ten minutes of the day, where this estate is, or how beautiful it is, or what kind of life they are to lead in it, or what kind of life they must lead to obtain it.

109. You fancy that you care to know this: so little do you care that, probably, at this moment many of you are displeased with me for talking of the matter! You came to hear about the Art of this world, not about the Life of the next, and you are provoked with me for talking of what you can hear any Sunday in church. But do not be afraid. I will

tell you something before you go about pictures, and carvings, and pottery, and what else you would like better to hear of than the other world. Nay, perhaps you say, "We want you to talk of pictures and pottery, because we are sure that you know something of them, and you know nothing of the other world." Well—I don't. That is quite true. But the very strangeness and mystery of which I urge you to take notice is in this—that I do not; nor you either. Can you answer a single bold question unflinchingly about that other world—Are you sure there is a heaven? Sure there is a hell? Sure that men are dropping before your faces through the pavements of these streets into eternal fire, or sure that they are not? Sure that at your own death you are going to be delivered from all sorrow, to be endowed with all virtue, to be gifted with all felicity, and raised into perpetual companionship with a King, compared to whom the kings of the earth are as grasshoppers, and the nations as the dust of His feet? Are you sure of this? or, if not sure, do any of us so much as care to make it sure? and, if not, how can anything that we do be right—how can anything we think be wise; what honor can there be in the arts that amuse us, or what profit in the possessions that please?

Is not this a mystery of life?

110. But further, you may, perhaps, think it a beneficent ordinance for the generality of men that they do not, with earnestness or anxiety, dwell on such questions of the future; because the business of the day could not be done if this kind of thought were taken by all of us for the morrow. Be it so: but at least we might anticipate that the greatest and wisest of us, who were evidently the appointed teachers of the rest, would set themselves apart to seek out whatever could be surely known of the future destines of their race; and to teach this in no rhetorical or ambiguous manner, but in the plainest and most severely earnest words.

Now, the highest representatives of men who have thus endeavored, during the Christian era, to search out these deep things, and relate them, are Dante and Milton. There is none who for earnestness of thought, for mastery of word, can be classed with these. I am not at present, mind you, speaking of persons set apart in any priestly or pastoral office, to deliver creeds to us, or doctrines; but of men who try to discover and set forth, as far as by human intellect is possible, the facts of the other world. Divines may perhaps teach us how to arrive there, but only these two poets have in any powerful manner striven to discover, or in any definite words professed to tell, what we shall

9

see and become there: or how these upper and
nether worlds are, and have been, inhabited.

111. And what have they told us? Milton's account of the most important event in his whole
system of the universe, the fall of the angels, is
evidently unbelievable to himself; and the more so,
that it is wholly founded on, and in a great part spoiled
and degraded from, Hesiod's account of the decisive
war of the younger Gods with the Titans. The rest
of his poem is a picturesque drama, in which every artifice of invention is visibly and consciously employed,
not a single fact being, for an instant, conceived as
tenable by any living faith. Dante's conception is far
more intense, and, by himself, for the time, not to be
escaped from; it is indeed a vision, but a vision only,
and that one of the wildest that ever entranced a soul
—a dream in which every grotesque type or phantasy
of heathen tradition is renewed, and adorned; and the
destinies of the Christian Church, under their most
sacred symbols, become literally subordinate to the
praise, and are only to be understood by the aid, of
one dear Florentine maiden.

112. I tell you truly that, as I strive more with this
strange lethargy and trance in myself, and awake to
the meaning and power of life, it seems daily more
amazing to me that men such as these should dare to
play with the most precious truths (or the most
deadly untruths), by which the whole human race

listening to them could be informed or deceived—all the world their audiences forever, with pleased ear, and passionate heart—and yet, to this submissive infinitude of souls, and evermore succeeding and succeeding multitude, hungry for bread of life, they do but play upon sweetly modulated pipes; with pompous nomenclature adorn the councils of hell; touch a troubadour's guitar to the courses of the suns; and fill the openings of eternity, before which prophets have veiled their faces, and which angels desire to look into, with idle puppets of their scholastic imagination, and melancholy lights of frantic faith in their lost mortal love.

Is not this a mystery of life?

113. But more. We have to remember that these two great teachers were both of them warped in their temper, and thwarted in their search for truth. They were men of intellectual war, unable, through darkness of controversy, or stress of personal grief, to discern where their own ambition modified their utterances of the moral law; or their own agony mingled with their anger at its violation. But greater men than these have been—innocent-hearted—too great for contest. Men, like Homer and Shakespeare, of so unrecognized personality, that it disappears in future ages, and becomes ghostly, like the tradition of a lost heathen god. Men, therefore, to whose unoffended, uncondemning sight, the whole of human

nature reveals itself in a pathetic weakness, with which they will not strive; or in mournful and transitory strength, which they dare not praise. And all Pagan and Christian civilization thus becomes subject to them. It does not matter how little, or how much, any of us have read, either of Homer or Shakespeare; everything round us, in substance, or in thought, has been molded by them. All Greek gentlemen were educated under Homer. All Roman gentlemen, by Greek literature. All Italian, and French, and English gentlemen, by Roman literature, and by its principles. Of the scope of Shakespeare, I will say only, that the intellectual measure of every man since born, in the domains of creative thought, may be assigned to him, according to the degree in which he has been taught by Shakespeare. Well, what do these two men, centers of moral intelligence, deliver to us of conviction respecting what it most behooves that intelligence to grasp? What is their hope; their crown of rejoicing? what manner of exhortation have they for us, or of rebuke? what lies next their own hearts, and dictates their undying words? Have they any peace to promise to our unrest—any redemption to our misery?

114. Take Homer first, and think if there is any sadder image of human fate than the great Homeric story. The main features in the character of Achilles are its intense desire of justice, and its tenderness of affection. And in that bit-

ter song of the Iliad, this man, though aided continually by the wisest of the gods, and burning with the desire of justice in his heart, becomes yet, through ill-governed passion, the most unjust of men: and, full of the deepest tenderness in his heart, becomes yet, through ill-governed passion, the most cruel of men. Intense alike in love and in friendship, he loses, first his mistress, and then his friend; for the sake of the one, he surrenders to death the armies of his own land; for the sake of the other, he surrenders all. Will a man lay down his life for his friend? Yea—even for his *dead* friend, this Achilles, though goddess-born, and goddess-taught, gives up his kingdom, his country, and his life—casts alike the innocent and guilty, with himself, into one gulf of slaughter, and dies at last by the hand of the basest of his adversaries. Is not this a mystery of life?

115. But what, then, is the message to us of our own poet, and searcher of hearts, after fifteen hundred years of Christian faith have been numbered over the graves of men? Are his words more cheerful than the heathen's—is his hope more near—his trust more sure—his reading of fate more happy? Ah, no! He differs from the Heathen poet chiefly in this—that he recognizes, for deliverance, no gods nigh at hand; and that, by petty chance—by momentary folly—by broken

is a pleasing form of thanksgiving to your Heavenly
Father?   Suppose you saw one of your own true
earthly sisters, Lucy or Emily, cast out of your mortal
father's house, starving, helpless, heart-broken; and
that every morning when you went into your father's
room, you said to him, "How good you are, father,
to give me what you don't give Lucy," are you sure
that, whatever anger your parent might have just cause
for, against your sister, he would be pleased by that
thanksgiving, or flattered by that praise?   Nay, are
you even sure that you *are* so much the favorite: suppose that, all this while, he loves poor Lucy just as
well as you, and is only trying you through her pain,
and perhaps not angry with her in anywise, but deeply
angry with you, and all the more for your thanks-
givings?   Would it not be well that you should think,
and earnestly too, over this standing of yours; and all
the more if you wish to believe that text, which clergymen so much dislike preaching on, "How hardly shall
they that have riches enter into the Kingdom of God?"
You do not believe it now, or you would be less complacent in your state; and you cannot believe it at all,
until you know that the Kingdom of God means—
"not meat and drink, but justice, peace, and joy in the
Holy Ghost," nor until you know also that such joy is
not by any means, necessarily, in going to church, or
in singing hymns; but may be joy in a dance, or joy in
a jest, or joy in anything you have deserved to possess,

116. Be it so then. About this human life that is to be, or that is, the wise religious men tell us nothing that we can trust; and the wise contemplative men, nothing that can give us peace. But there is yet a third class, to whom we may turn—the wise practical men. We have sat at the feet of the poets who sung of heaven, and they have told us their dreams. We have listened to the poets who sung of earth, and they have chanted to us dirges, and words of despair. But there is one class of men more—men, not capable of vision, nor sensitive to sorrow, but firm of purpose—practiced in business; learned in all that can be (by handling) known. Men, whose hearts and hopes are wholly in this present world, from whom, therefore, we may surely learn, at least, how, at present, conveniently to live in it. What will *they* say to us, or show us by example? These kings—these councilors—these statesmen and builders of kingdoms—these capitalists and men of business, who weigh the earth, and the dust of it, in a balance. They know the world, surely; and what is the mystery of life to us, is none to them. They can surely show us how to live, while we live, and to gather out of the present world what is best.

117. I think I can best tell you their answer, by telling you a dream I had once. For though

I am no poet, I have dreams sometimes : I dreamed I was at a child's May-day party, in which every means of entertainment had been provided for them, by a wise and kind host. It was in a stately house, with beautiful gardens attached to it ; and the children had been set free in the rooms and gardens, with no care whatever but how to pass their afternoon rejoicingly. They did not, indeed, know much about what was to happen next day ; and some of them, I thought, were a little frightened, because there was a chance of their being sent to a new school where there were examinations ; but they kept the thoughts of that out of their heads as well as they could, and resolved to enjoy themselves. The house, I said, was in a beautiful garden, and in the garden were all kinds of flowers ; sweet grassy banks for rest ; and smooth lawns for play ; and pleasant streams and woods ; and rocky places for climbing. And the children were happy for a little while, but presently they separated themselves into parties ; and then each party declared, it would have a piece of the garden for its own, and that none of the others should have anything to do with that piece. Next, they quarreled violently, which pieces they would have ; and at last the boys took up the thing, as boys should do, "practically," and fought in the flower-beds till there was hardly a flower left standing; then they trampled down each other's bits of the garden out of spite; and the girls cried till they could cry no more; and so they all lay down at last breathless in the ruin, and waited for the time when they were to be taken home in the evening.*

118. Meanwhile, the children in the house had been making themselves happy also in their manner. For them, there had been provided every kind of in-door pleasure: there was music for them to dance to; and the library was open, with all manner of amusing books; and there was a museum, full of the most curious shells, and animals, and birds; and there was a workshop, with lathes and carpenter's tools, for the ingenious boys; and there were pretty fantastic dresses, for the girls to dress in; and there were microscopes, and kaleidoscopes; and whatever toys a child could fancy; and a table, in the dining-room, loaded with everything nice to eat.

But, in the midst of all this, it struck two or three of the more "practical" children, that they would like some of the brass-headed nails that studded the chairs; and so they set to work to pull them out. Presently, the others, who were reading,

---

*I have sometimes been asked what this means. I intended it to set forth the wisdom of men in war contending for kingdoms, and what follows to set forth their wisdom in peace, contending for wealth.

or looking at shells, took a fancy to do the like;
and, in a little while, all the children, nearly,
were spraining their fingers, in pulling out brass-
headed nails. With all that they could pull out,
they were not satisfied; and then, everybody wanted
some of somebody else's. And at last, the really
practical and sensible ones declared, that nothing
was of any real consequence, that afternoon, except to get plenty of brass-headed nails; and that
the books, and the cakes, and the microscopes, were
of no use at all in themselves, but only, if they
could be exchanged for nail-heads. And, at last, they
began to fight for nail-heads, as the others fought for
the bits of garden. Only here and there, a despised
one shrunk away into a corner, and tried to get a little
quiet with a book, in the midst of the noise; but
all the practical ones thought of nothing else but
counting nail-heads all the afternoon—even though
they knew they would not be allowed to carry
so much as one brass knob away with them.
But no—it was—" who has most nails? I have a
hundred, and you have fifty; or, I have a thousand
and you have two. I must have as many as you
before I leave the house, or I cannot possibly go
home in peace." At last, they made so much
noise that I awoke, and thought to myself, "What
a false dream that is, of *children*." The child is
the father of the man; and wiser. Children never
do such foolish things. Only men do.

119. But there is yet one last class of persons to be interrogated. The wise religious men we have asked in vain; the wise contemplative men, in vain; the wise worldly men, in vain. But there is another group yet. In the midst of this vanity of empty religion—of tragic contemplation—of wrathful and wretched ambition, and dispute for dust, there is yet one great group of persons, by whom all these disputers live—the persons who have determined, or have had it by a beneficent Providence determined for them, that they will do something useful; that whatever may be prepared for them hereafter, or happens to them here, they will, at least, deserve the food that God gives them by winning it honorably; and that, however fallen from the purity, or far from the peace, of Eden, they will carry out the duty of human dominion, though they have lost its felicity; and dress and keep the wilderness, though they no more can dress or keep the garden.

These—hewers of wood, and drawers of water—these bent under burdens, or torn of scourges—these that dig and weave—that plant and build; workers in wood, and in marble, and in iron—by whom all food, clothing, habitation, furniture, and means of delight are produced, for themselves, and for all men besides; men, whose deeds are good, though their words may be few; men, whose lives are serviceable, be they never so short, and worthy of honor, be they never so humble—from these, surely at least, we may receive some clear message of teaching: and pierce, for an instant, into the mystery of life, and of its arts.

120. Yes; from these, at last, we do receive a lesson. But I grieve to say, or rather—for that is the deeper truth of the matter—I rejoice to say—this message of theirs can only be received by joining them—not by thinking about them.

You sent for me to talk to you of art; and I have obeyed you in coming. But the main thing I have to tell you is—that art must not be talked about. The fact that there is talk about it at all, signifies that it is ill done, or cannot be done. No true painter ever speaks, or ever has spoken, much of his art. The greatest speak nothing. Even Reynolds is no exception, for he wrote of all that he could not himself do, and was utterly silent respecting all that he himself did.

The moment a man can really do his work, he becomes speechless about it. All words become idle to him—all theories.

121. Does a bird need to theorize about building its nest, or boast of it when built? All good work is essentially done that way—without hesitation, without difficulty, without boasting; and in the doers of the best, there is an inner and involuntary power

which approximates literally to the instinct of an
animal—nay, I am certain that in the most perfect
human artists, reason does *not* supersede instinct,
but is added to an instinct as much more divine than
that of the lower animals as the human body is more
beautiful than theirs; that a great singer sings not
with less instinct than the nightingale, but with
more—only more various, applicable, and govern-
able; that a great architect does not build with less
instinct than the beaver or the bee, but with more
—with an innate cunning of proportion that em-
braces all beauty, and a divine ingenuity of skill
that improvises all construction. But be that as it
may—be the instinct less or more than that of inferior animals—like or unlike theirs, still the human
art is dependent on that first, and then upon an
amount of practice, of science—and of imagination
disciplined by thought, which the true possessor of
it knows to be incommunicable, and the true critic
of it, inexplicable, except through long process of
laborious years. The journey of life's conquest, in
which hills over hills, and Alps on Alps arose, and
sunk—do you think you can make another trace
it painlessly, by talking? Why, you cannot even
carry us up an Alp, by talking. You can guide
us up it, step by step, no otherwise—even so, best
silently. You girls, who have been among the
hills, know how the bad guide chatters and gestic-

ulates, and it is "put your foot here," and "mind how you balance yourself there;" but the good guide walks on quietly, without a word, only with his eyes on you when need is, and his arm like an iron bar, if need be.

122. In that slow way, also, art can be taught—if you have faith in your guide, and will let his arm be to you as an iron bar when need is. But in what teacher of art have you such faith? Certainly not in me; for, as I told you at first, I know well enough it is only because you think I can talk, not because you think I know my business, that you let me speak to you at all. If I were to tell you anything that seemed to you strange, you would not believe it, and yet it would only be in telling you strange things that I could be of use to you. I could be of great use to you—infinite use, with brief saying, if you would believe it; but you would not, just because the thing that would be of real use would displease you. You are all wild, for instance, with admiration of Gustave Doré. Well, suppose I were to tell you, in the strongest terms I could use, that Gustave Doré's art was bad—bad, not in weakness—not in failure—but bad with dreadful power—the power of the Furies and the Harpies mingled, enraging, and polluting; that so long as you looked at it, no perception of pure or beautiful art was possible

for you. Suppose I were to tell you that? What would be the use? Would you look at Gustave Doré less? Rather, more, I fancy. On the other hand, I could soon put you into good humor with me, if I chose. I know well enough what you like, and how to praise it to your better liking. I could talk to you about moonlight, and twilight, and spring flowers, and autumn leaves, and the Madonnas of Raphael—how motherly! and the Sibyls of Michael Angelo—how majestic! and the Saints of Angelico—how pious! and the Cherubs of Correggio—how delicious! Old as I am, I could play you a tune on the harp yet, that you would dance to. But neither you nor I should be a bit the better or wiser; or, if we were, our increased wisdom could be of no practical effect. For, indeed, the arts, as regards teachableness, differ from the sciences also in this, that their power is founded not merely on facts which can be communicated, but on dispositions which require to be created. Art is neither to be achieved by effort of thinking, nor explained by accuracy of speaking. It is the instinctive and necessary result of powers which can only be developed through the mind of successive generations, and which finally burst into life under social conditions as slow of growth as the faculties they regulate. Whole eras of mighty history are summed, and the passions

of dead myriads are concentrated, in the existence of a noble art; and if that noble art were
among us, we should feel it and rejoice; not caring
in the least to hear lectures on it; and since it is
not among us, be assured we have to go back to
the root of it, or, at least, to the place where
the stock of it is yet alive, and the branches began to die.

123. And now, may I have your pardon for
pointing out, partly with reference to matters
which are at this time of greater moment than
the arts—that if we undertook such recession to
the vital germ of national arts that have decayed,
we should find a more singular arrest of their
power in Ireland than in any other European
country. For in the eighth century, Ireland pos-
sessed a school of art in her manuscripts and
sculpture, which, in many of its qualities—apparently in all essential qualities of decorative invention—was quite without rival; seeming as if it
might have advanced to the highest triumphs in
architecture and in painting. But there was one
fatal flaw in its nature, by which it was stayed,
and stayed with a conspicuousness of pause to
which there is no parallel: so that, long ago, in
tracing the progress of European schools from infancy to strength, I chose for the students of
Kensington, in a lecture since published, two charac-

teristic examples of early art, of equal skill; but in the one case, skill which was progressive—in the other, skill which was at pause. In the one case, it was work receptive of correction—hungry for correction—and in the other, work which inherently rejected correction. I chose for them a corrigible Eve, and an incorrigible Angel, and I grieve to say that the incorrigible Angel was also an Irish Angel!

124. And the fatal difference lay wholly in this. In both pieces of art there was an equal falling short of the needs of fact; but the Lombardic Eve knew she was in the wrong, and the Irish Angel thought himself all right. The eager Lombardic sculptor, though firmly insisting on his childish idea, yet showed in the irregular broken touches of the features, and the imperfect struggle for softer lines in the form, a perception of beauty and law that he could not render; there was a strain of effort, uuder conscious imperfection, in every line. But the Irish missal-painter had drawn his angel with no sense of failure, in happy complacency, and put red dots into the palms of each hand, and rounded the eyes into perfect circles, and, I regret to say, left the mouth out altogether, with perfect satisfaction to himself.

125. May I without offense ask you to consider whether this mode of arrest in ancient Irish art

may not be indicative of points of character which even yet, in some measure, arrest your national power? I have seen much of Irish character, and have watched it closely, for I have also much loved it. And I think the form of failure to which it is most liable is this, that being gener-ous-hearted, and wholly intending always to do right, it does not attend to the external laws of right, but thinks it must necessarily do right be-cause it means to do so, and therefore does wrong without finding it out; and then when the con-sequences of its wrong come upon it, or upon others connected with it, it cannot conceive that the wrong is in anywise of its causing or of its doing, but flies into wrath, and a strange agony of desire for justice, as feeling itself wholly innocent, which leads it further astray, until there is noth-ing that it is not capable of doing with a good conscience.

126. But mind, I do not mean to say that, in past or present relations between Ireland and England, you have been wrong, and we right. Far from that, I believe that in all great ques-tions of principle, and in all details of adminis-tration of law, you have been usually right, and we wrong; sometimes in misunderstanding you, sometimes in resolute iniquity to you. Neverthe-less, in all disputes between states, though the

strongest is nearly always mainly in the wrong, the weaker is often so in a minor degree; and I think we sometimes admit the possibility of our being in error, and you never do.

127. And now, returning to the broader question, what these arts and labors of life have to teach us of its mystery, this is the first of their lessons —that the more beautiful the art, the more it is essentially the work of people who *feel themselves wrong*—who are striving for the fulfillment of a law, and the grasp of a loveliness, which they have not yet attained, which they feel even further and further from attaining, the more they strive for it. And yet, in still deeper sense, it is the work of people who know also that they are right. The very sense of inevitable error from their purpose marks the perfectness of that purpose, and the continued sense of failure arises from the continued opening of the eyes more clearly to all the sacredest laws of truth.

128. This is one lesson. The second is a very plain, and greatly precious one, namely: that whenever the arts and labors of life are fulfilled in this spirit of striving against misrule, and doing whatever we have to do, honorably and perfectly, they invariably bring happiness, as much as seems possible to the nature of man. In all other paths, by which that happiness is pursued, there is disap-

pointment, or destruction; for ambition and for passion there is no rest—no fruition; the fairest pleasures of youth perish in a darkness greater than their past light; and the loftiest and purest love too often does but inflame the cloud of life with endless fire of pain. But, ascending from lowest to highest, through every scale of human industry, that industry worthily followed, gives peace. Ask the laborer in the field, at the forge, or in the mine; ask the patient, delicate-fingered artisan, or the strong-armed, fiery-hearted worker in bronze, and in marble, and with the colors of light; and none of these, who are true workmen, will ever tell you, that they have found the law of heaven an unkind one—that in the sweat of their face they should eat bread, till they return to the ground; nor that they ever found it an unrewarded obedience, if, indeed, it was rendered faithfully to the command—"Whatsoever thy hand findeth to do—do it with thy might."

129. These are the two great and constant lessons which our laborers teach us of the mystery of life. But there is another, and a sadder one, which they cannot teach us, which we must read on their tombstones.

"Do it with thy might." There have been myriads upon myriads of human creatures who have obeyed this law—who have put every breath and nerve of their being into its toil—who have devoted every hour, and exhausted every faculty—who have bequeathed their unaccomplished thoughts at death— who being dead, have yet spoken, by majesty of memory, and strength of example. And, at last, what has all this "Might" of humanity accomplished, in six thousand years of labor and sorrow? What has it *done?* Take the three chief occupations and arts of men, one by one, and count their achievements. Begin with the first—the lord of them all— agriculture. Six thousand years have passed since we were set to till the ground, from which we were taken. How much of it is tilled? How much of that which is, wisely or well? In the very center and chief garden of Europe—where the two forms of parent Christianity have had their fortresses— where the noble Catholics of the Forest Cantons, and the noble Protestants of the Vaudois valleys, have maintained, for dateless ages, their faiths and liberties—there the unchecked Alpine rivers yet run wild in devastation; and the marshes, which a few hundred men could redeem with a year's labor, still blast their helpless inhabitants into fevered idiotism. That is so, in the center of Europe! While, on the near coast of Africa, once the Garden of the Hesperides, an Arab woman, but a few sunsets since, ate her child, for famine. And, with all the treasures of the East at our feet, we, in our own dominion, could not find a few grains of rice, for a people that asked of us no more; but stood by, and saw five hundred thousand of them perish of hunger.

130. Then, after agriculture, the art of kings, take the next head of human arts—weaving; the art of queens, honored of all noble Heathen women, in the person of their virgin goddess—honored of all Hebrew women, by the word of their wisest king— "She layeth her hands to the spindle, and her hands hold the distaff; she stretcheth out her hand to the poor. She is not afraid of the snow for her household, for all her household are clothed with scarlet. She maketh herself covering of tapestry, her clothing is silk and purple. She maketh fine linen, and selleth it, and delivereth girdles to the merchant." What have we done in all these thousands of years with this bright art of Greek maid and Christian matron? Six thousand years of weaving, and have we learned to weave? Might not every naked wall have been purple with tapestry, and every feeble breast fenced with sweet colors from the cold? What have we done? Our fingers are too few, it seems, to twist together some poor covering for our bodies. We set our streams to work for us, and choke the air with fire, to turn our spinning-wheels—and—*are we yet clothed?* Are not the streets of the capitals of Europe foul with sale of cast clouts and rotten

rags? Is not the beauty of your sweet children left in wretchedness of disgrace, while, with better honor, nature clothes the brood of the bird in its nest, and the suckling of the wolf in her den? And does not every winter's snow robe what you have not robed, and shroud what you have not shrouded; and every winter's wind bear up to heaven its wasted souls, to witness against you hereafter, by the voice of their Christ—" I was naked, and ye clothed me not?"

131. Lastly—take the Art of Building—the strongest—proudest—most orderly—most enduring of the arts of man; that, of which the produce is in the surest manner accumulative, and need not perish, or be replaced; but if once well done, will stand more strongly than the unbalanced rocks— more prevalently than the crumbling hills. The art which is associated with all civic pride and sacred principle; with which men record their power—satisfy their enthusiasm—make sure their defense—define and make dear their habitation. And, in six thousand years of building, what have we done? Of the greater part of all that skill and strength, *no* vestige is left, but fallen stones, that incumber the fields and impede the streams. But, from this waste of disorder, and of time, and of rage, what *is* left to us? Constructive and progressive creatures, that we are, with ruling brains, and forming hands,

capable of fellowship, and thirsting for fame, can we
not contend, in comfort, with the insects of the forest, or, in achievement, with the worm of the sea.
The white surf rages in vain against the ramparts
built by poor atoms of scarcely nascent life; but
only ridges of formless ruin mark the places where
once dwelt our noblest multitudes. The ant and the
moth have cells for each of their young, but our little
ones lie in festering heaps, in homes that consume
them like graves; and night by night, from the corners of our streets, rises up the cry of the homeless—
"I was a stranger, and ye took me not in."

132. Must it be always thus? Is our life forever to be without profit—without possession?
Shall the strength of its generations be as barren
as death; or cast away their labor, as the wild
fig-tree casts her untimely figs? Is it all a dream
then—the desire of the eyes and the pride ·of life
—or, if it be, might we not live in nobler dream
than this? The poets and prophets, the wise men,
and the scribes, though they have told us nothing about a life to come, have told us much
about the life that is now. They have had—they
also—their dreams, and we have laughed at them.
They have dreamed of mercy, and of justice; they
have dreamed of peace and good-will; they have
dreamed of labor undisappointed, and of rest undisturbed; they have dreamed of fullness in harvest,

and overflowing in store; they have dreamed of wisdom in council, and of providence in law; of gladness of parents, and strength of children, and glory of gray hairs. And at these visions of theirs we have mocked, and held them for idle and vain, unreal and unaccomplishable. What have we accomplished with our realities? Is this what has come of our worldly wisdom, tried against their folly? this, our mightiest possible, against their impotent ideal? or, have we only wandered among the spectra of a baser felicity, and chased phantoms of the tombs, instead of visions of the Almighty; and walked after the imaginations of our evil hearts, instead of after the counsels of Eternity, until our lives—not in the likeness of the cloud of heaven, but of the smoke of hell—have become "as a vapor, that appeareth for a little time, and then vanisheth away?"

133. *Does* it vanish then? Are you sure of that? —sure, that the nothingness of the grave will be a rest from this troubled nothingness; and that the coiling shadow, which disquiets itself in vain, cannot change into the smoke of the torment that ascends forever? Will any answer that they *are* sure of it, and that there is no fear, nor hope, nor desire, nor labor, whither they go? Be it so; will you not, then, make as sure of the life that now is, as you are of the Death that is to come?

Your hearts are wholly in this world—will you
not give them to it wisely, as well as perfectly?
And see, first of all, that you *have* hearts, and
sound hearts, too, to give. Because you have no
heaven to look for, is that any reason that you
should remain ignorant of this wonderful and infinite earth, which is firmly and instantly given
you in possession? Although your days are numbered, and the following darkness sure, is it necessary that you should share the degradation of the
brute, because you are condemned to its mortality;
or live the life of the moth, and of the worm, because you are to companion them in the dust?
Not so; we may have but a few thousands of days
to spend, perhaps hundreds only—perhaps, tens; nay,
the longest of our time and best, looked back on,
will be but as a moment, as the twinkling of an
eye; still, we are men, not insects; we are living
spirits, not passing clouds. "He maketh the winds
His messengers; the momentary fire, His minister;"
and shall we do less than *these?* Let us do the
work of men while we bear the form of them:
and, as we snatch our narrow portion of time out
of Eternity, snatch also our narrow inheritance of
passion out of Immortality—even though our lives
be as a vapor, that appeareth for a little time, and
then vanisheth away.

134. But there are some of you who believe not

this—who think this cloud of life has no such close —that it is to float, revealed and illumined, upon the floor of heaven, in the day when He cometh with clouds, and every eye shall see Him. Some day, you believe, within these five, or ten or twenty years, for every one of us the judgment will be set, and the books opened. If that be true, far more than that must be true. Is there but one day of judgment? Why, for us every day is a day of judgment—every day is a Dies Iræ, and writes its irrevocable verdict in the flame of its West. Think you that judgment waits till the doors of the grave are opened? It waits at the doors of your houses— it waits at the corners of your streets; we are in the midst of judgment—the insects that we crush are our judges—the moments we fret away are our judges—the elements that feed us, judge, as they minister—and the pleasures that deceive us, judge, as they indulge. Let us, for our lives, do the work of Men while we bear the Form of them, if indeed those lives are *Not* as a vapor, and do *Not* vanish away.

135. " The work of men "—and what is that? Well, we may any of us know very quickly, on the condition of being wholly ready to do it. But many of us are for the most part thinking, not of what we are to do, but of what we are to get; and the best of us are sunk into the sin of

Ananias, and it is a mortal one—we want to keep back part of the price; and we continually talk of taking up our cross, as if the only harm in a cross was the *weight* of it—as if it was only a thing to be carried, instead of to be—crucified upon. "They that are His have crucified the flesh, with the affections and lusts." Does that mean, think you, that in time of national distress, of religious trial, of crisis for every interest and hope of humanity—none of us will cease jesting, none cease idling, none put themselves to any wholesome work, none take so much as a tag of lace off their footmen's coats, to save the world? Or does it rather mean, that they are ready to leave houses, lands, and kindreds—yes, and life, if need be? Life? —some of us are ready enough to throw that away, joyless as we have made it. But "*station* in Life" how many of us are ready to quit *that?* Is it not always the great objection, where there is question of finding something useful to do—"We cannot leave our stations in Life?"

Those of us who really cannot—that is to say, who can only maintain themselves by continuing in some business or salaried office, have already something to do; and all that they have to see to, is that they do it honestly and with all their might. But with most people who use that apology, "remaining in the station of life to which Providence has called them," means keeping all the carriages, and all the footmen and large houses they can possibly pay for; and, once for all, I say that if ever Providence *did* put them into stations of that sort—which is not at all a matter of certainty—Providence is just now very distinctly calling them out again. Levi's station in life was the receipt of custom; and Peter's, the shore of Galilee; and Paul's, the antechambers of the High Priest—which "station in life" each had to leave, with brief notice.

And, whatever our station in life may be, at this crisis, those of us who mean to fulfill our duty ought, first, to live on as little as we can; and, secondly, to do all the wholesome work for it we can, and to spend all we can spare in doing all the sure good we can.

And sure good is first in feeding people, then in dressing people, then in lodging people, and lastly in rightly pleasing people, with arts, or sciences, or any other subject of thought.

136. I say first in feeding; and, once for all, do not let yourselves be deceived by any of the common talk of "indiscriminate charity." The order to us is not to feed the deserving hungry, nor the industrious hungry, nor the amiable and well-intentioned hungry, but simply to feed the hungry. It is quite true, infallibly true, that if any man will not work, neither should he eat—think of that, and every time

you sit down to your dinner, ladies and gentlemen, say solemnly, before you ask a blessing, " How much work have I done to-day for my dinner?" But the proper way to enforce that order on those below you, as well as on yourselves, is not to leave vagabonds and honest people to starve together, but very distinctly to discern and seize your vagabond ; and shut your vagabond up out of honest people's way, and very sternly then see that, until he has worked, he does *not* eat. But the first thing is to be sure you have the food to give; and, therefore, to enforce the organization of vast activities in agriculture and in commerce, for the production of the wholesomest food, and proper storing and distribution of it, so that no famine shall any more be possible among civilized beings. There is plenty of work in this business alone, and at once, for any number of people who like to engage in it.

137. Secondly, dressing people—that is to say, urging every one within reach of your influence to be always neat and clean, and giving them means of being so. In so far as they absolutely refuse, you must give up the effort with respect to them, only taking care that no children within your sphere of influence shall any more be brought up with such habits ; and that every person who is willing to dress with propriety shall have encouragement to do so. And the first absolutely necessary

step toward this is the gradual adoption of a consistent dress for different ranks of persons, so that
their rank shall be known by their dress; and the
restriction of the changes of fashion within certain
limits. All which appears for the present quite
impossible; but it is only so far as even difficult
as it is difficult to conquer our vanity, frivolity,
and desire to appear what we are not. And it is
not, nor ever shall be, creed of mine, that these
mean and shallow vices are unconquerable by Christian women.

138. And then, thirdly, lodging people, which you
may think should have been put first, but I put
it third, because we must feed and clothe people
where we find them, and lodge them afterward.
And providing lodgment for them means a great
deal of vigorous legislation, and cutting down of
vested interests that stand in the way, and after
that, or before that, so far as we can get it,
thorough sanitary and remedial action in the houses
that we have; and then the building of more,
strongly, beautifully, and in groups of limited extent, kept in proportion to their streams, and walled
round, so that there may be no festering and
wretched suburb anywhere, but clean and busy
streets within, and the open country without, with
a belt of beautiful garden and orchard round the
walls, so that from any part of the city perfectly

fresh air and grass, and sight of far horizon might be reachable in a few minutes' walk. This is the final aim; but in immediate action every minor and possible good to be instantly done, when, and as, we can; roofs mended that have holes in them—fences patched that have gaps in them—walls buttressed that totter—and floors propped that shake; cleanliness and order enforced with our own hands and eyes, till we are breathless, every day. And all the fine arts will healthily follow. I myself have washed a flight of stone stairs all down, with bucket and broom, in a Savoy inn, where they hadn't washed their stairs since they first went up them? and I never made a better sketch than that afternoon.

139. These, then, are the three first needs of civilized life; and the law for every Christian man and woman is, that they shall be in direct service toward one of these three needs, as far as is consistent with their own special occupation, and if they have no special business, then wholly in one of these services. And out of such exertion in plain duty all other good will come; for in this direct contention with material evil, you will find out the real nature of all evil; you will discern by the various kinds of resistance, what is really the fault and main antagonism to good; also you will find the most unexpected helps and profound lessons given, and truths will come thus down to us

which the speculation of all our lives would never have raised us up to. You will find nearly every educational problem solved, as soon as you truly want to do something; everybody will become of use in their own fittest way, and will learn what is best for them to know in that use. Competitive examination will then, and not till then, be wholesome, because it will be daily, and calm, and in practice; and on these familiar arts, and minute, but certain and serviceable knowledges, will be surely edified and sustained the greater arts and splendid theoretical sciences.

140. But much more than this. On such holy and simple practice will be founded, indeed, at last, an infallible religion. The greatest of all the mysteries of life, and the most terrible, is the corruption of even the sincerest religion, which is not daily founded on rational, effective, humble, and helpful action. Helpful action, observe! for there is just one law, which obeyed, keeps all religions pure—forgotten, makes them all false. Whenever in any religious faith, dark or bright, we allow our minds to dwell upon the points in which we differ from other people, we are wrong, and in the devil's power. That is the essence of the Pharisee's thanksgiving—"Lord, I thank thee that I am not as other men are." At every moment of our lives we should be trying to find out, not in what we differ with other people, but in what we agree with them; and the moment we find we can

agree as to anything that should be done, kind or good (and who but fools couldn't?), then do it; push at it together; you can't quarrel in a side-by-side push; but the moment that even the best men stop pushing, and begin talking, they mistake their pugnacity for piety, and it's all over. I will not speak of the crimes which in past times have been committed in the name of Christ, nor of the follies which are at this hour held to be consistent with obedience to Him; but I *will* speak of the morbid corruption and waste of vital power in religious sentiment, by which the pure strength of that which should be the guiding soul of every nation, the splendor of its youthful manhood, and spotless light of its maidenhood, is averted or cast away. You may see continually girls who have never been taught to do a single useful thing thoroughly; who cannot sew, who cannot cook, who cannot cast an account, nor prepare a medicine, whose whole life has been passed either in play or in pride; you will find girls like these, when they are earnest-hearted, cast all their innate passion of religious spirit, which was meant by God to support them through the irksomeness of daily toil, into grievous and vain meditation over the meaning of the great Book, of which no syllable was ever yet to be understood but through a deed; all the instinctive wisdom and mercy of their womanhood made vain, and the glory of their pure consciences warped into fruitless agony concerning questions which the laws of common serviceable life would have either solved for them in an instant, or kept out of their way. Give such a girl any true work that will make her active in the dawn, and weary at night, with the consciousness that her fellow-creatures have indeed been the better for her day, and the powerless sorrow of her enthusiasm will transform itself into a majesty of radiant and beneficent peace.

So with our youths. We once taught them to make Latin verses, and called them educated; now we teach them to leap and to row, to hit a ball with a bat, and call them educated. Can they plow, can they sow, can they plant at the right time, or build with a steady hand? Is it the effort of their lives to be chaste, knightly, faithful, holy in thought, lovely in word and deed? Indeed it is with some, nay with many, and the strength of England is in them, and the hope; but we have to turn their courage from the toil of war to the toil of mercy; and their intellect from dispute of words to discernment of things; and their knighthood from the errantry of adventure to the state and fidelity of a kingly power. And then, indeed, shall abide, for them, and for us an incorruptible felicity, and an infallible religion; shall abide for us Faith, no more to be assailed by temptation, no more to be de-

fended by wrath and by fear—shall abide with us
Hope, no more to be quenched by the years that
overwhelm, or made ashamed by the shadows that
betray—shall abide for us, and with us, the greatest
of these; the abiding will, the abiding name, of our
Father. For the greatest of these, is Charity.

THE QUEEN OF THE AIR.

FOUR LECTURES.

1. ATHENA IN THE HEAVENS.

2. ATHENA IN THE EARTH.

3. ATHENA IN THE HEART.

4. THE HERCULES OF CAMARINA.

PREFACE.

My days and strength have lately been much broken; and I never more felt the insufficiency of both than in preparing for the press the following desultory memoranda on a most noble subject. But I leave them now as they stand, for no time nor labor would be enough to complete them to my contentment; and I believe that they contain suggestions which may be followed with safety, by persons who are beginning to take interest in the aspects of mythology, which only recent investigation has removed from the region of conjecture into that of rational inquiry. I have some advantage, also, from my field work, in the interpretation of myths relating to natural phenomena; and I have had always near me, since we were at college together, a sure, and unweariedly kind guide, in my friend Charles Newton, to whom we owe the finding of more treasures in mines of marble, than were it rightly estimated, all California could buy. I must not, however, permit the chance of his name being in any wise associated with my errors. Much of my work has been done obstinately in my own way; and he is never responsible for me, though he has often kept me right, or at least enabled me to advance in a right direction. Absolutely right no one can be in such matters; nor does a day pass without convincing every honest student of antiquity of some partial error, and showing him better how to think, and where to look. But I knew that there was no hope of my being able to enter with advantage on the fields of history opened by the splendid investigation of recent philologists; though I could qualify myself, by attention and sympathy, to understand here and there, a verse of Homer's or Hesiod's, as the simple people did for whom they sang.

Even while I correct these sheets for press, a lecture by Professor Tyndall has been put into my hands, which I ought to have heard last 16th of January, but was hindered by mischance; and which I now find, completes, in two important particulars, the evidence of an instinctive truth in ancient symbolism; showing, first, that the Greek conception of an ætherial element pervading space is justified by the closest reasoning of modern physicists; and, secondly, that the blue of the sky, hitherto thought to be caused by watery vapor, is, indeed, reflected from the divided air itself; so that the bright blue of the eyes of Athena, and the deep blue of her ægis, prove to be accurate mythic expressions of natural phenomena which it is an uttermost triumph of recent science to have revealed.

Indeed, it would be difficult to imagine triumph more complete. To form, "within an experimental tube, a bit of more perfect sky than the sky itself!" here is magic of the finest sort! singularly reversed from that of old time, which only asserted its competency to enclose in bottles elementary forces that were —not of the sky.

Let me, in thanking Professor Tyndall for the true wonder of this piece of work, ask his pardon, and that of all masters in physical science, for any words of mine, either in the following pages or elsewhere, that may ever seem to fail in the respect due to their great powers of thought, or in the admiration due to the far scope of their discovery. But I will be judged by themselves, if I have not bitter reason to ask them to teach us more than yet they have taught.

This first day of May, 1869, I am writing where my work was begun thirty-five years ago, within sight of the snows of the higher Alps. In that half of the permitted life of man, I have seen strange evil brought upon every scene that I best loved, or tried to make beloved by others. The light which once flushed those pale summits with its rose at dawn, and purple at sunset, is now umbered and faint; the air which once inlaid the clefts of their golden crags with azure, is now defiled with languid coils of smoke, belched from worse than volcanic fires; their very glacier waves are ebbing, and their snows fading, as if Hell had breathed on them; the waters that once sank at their feet into crystalline rest, are now dimmed and fouled, from deep to deep, and shore to shore. These are no careless words—they are accurately—horribly—true. I know what the Swiss lakes were; no pool of Alpine fountain at its source was clearer. This morning, on the Lake of Geneva, at half a mile from the beach, I could scarcely see my oar-blade a fathom deep.

The light, the air, the waters, all defiled! How of the earth itself? Take this one fact for type of honor done by the modern Swiss to the earth of his native land. There used to be a little rock at the end of the avenue by the port of Neuchâtel; there the last marble of the foot of Jura, sloping to the blue water, and (at this time of year) covered with bright pink tufts of Saponaria. I went, three days since, to gather a blossom at the place. The goodly native rock and its flowers were covered with the dust and refuse of the town; but, in the middle of the avenue, was a newly-constructed artificial rockery, with a fountain twisted through a spinning spout, and an inscription on one of its loose tumbled stones:

" Aux Botanistes,
Le club Jurassique."

Ah, masters of modern science, give me back my Athena out of your vials, and seal, if it may be, once more, Asmodeus therein. You have divided the elements, and united them ; enslaved them upon the earth, and discerned them in the stars. Teach us, now, but this of them, which is all that man need know—that the air is given to him for his life ; and the rain to his thirst, and for his baptism ; and the fire for warmth ; and the sun for sight ; and the earth for his meat— and his rest.

Vevay, May 1, 1869.

THE QUEEN OF THE AIR.

I.

ATHENA CHALINITIS.[*]

(Athena in the Heavens.)

Lecture on the Greek Myths of Storm, given (partly) in University College, London, March 9th, 1869.

1. I WILL not ask your pardon for endeavoring to interest you in the subject of Greek Mythology; but I must ask your permission to approach it in a temper differing from that in which it is frequently treated. We cannot justly interpret the religion of any people, unless we are prepared to admit that we ourselves, as well as they, are liable to error in matters of faith; and that the convictions of others, however singular, may in some points have been well founded, while our own, however reasonable, may in some particulars be mistaken. You must forgive me, therefore, for not always distinctively calling the creeds of the past "superstition," and the creeds of the present day "religion;" as well as for assuming that a faith now confessed may

---

[*] "Athena the Restrainer." The name is given to her as having helped Bellerophon to bridle Pegasus, the flying cloud.

sometimes be superficial, and that a faith long forgotten
may once have been sincere. It is the task of the
Divine to condemn the errors of antiquity, and of the
philologists to account for them : I will only pray you
to read, with patience, and human sympathy, the
thoughts of men who lived without blame in a darkness they could not dispel; and to remember that,
whatever charge of folly may justly attach to the say
ing—"There is no God," the folly is prouder, deeper,
and less pardonable, in saying, "There is no God but
for me."

2. A myth, in its simplest definition, is a story with
a meaning attached to it, other than it seems to have
at first; and the fact that it has such a meaning is
generally marked by some of its circumstances being
extraordinary, or, in the common use of the word, unnatural. Thus, if I tell you that Hercules killed a
water-serpent in the lake of Lerna, and if I mean, and
you understand, nothing more than that fact, the story,
whether true or false, is not a myth. But if by telling
you this, I mean that Hercules purified the stagnation
of many streams from deadly miasmata, my story,
however simple, is a true myth ; only, as, if I left it in
that simplicity, you would probably look for nothing
beyond, it will be wise in me to surprise your attention
by adding some singular circumstance ; for instance,
that the water-snake had several heads, which revived
as fast as they were killed, and which poisoned even

the foot that trod upon them as they slept. And in proportion to the fullness of intended meaning I shall probably multiply and refine upon these improbabilities; as, suppose, if, instead of desiring only to tell you that Hercules purified a marsh, I wished you to understand that he contended with the venom and vapor of envy and evil ambition, whether in other men's souls or in his own, and choked *that* malaria only by supreme toil—I might tell you that this serpent was formed by the Goddess whose pride was in the trial of Hercules; and that its place of abode was by a palm-tree; and that for every head of it that was cut off, two rose up with renewed life; and that the hero found at last he could not kill the creature at all by cutting its heads off or crushing them; but only by burning them down; and that the midmost of them could not be killed even that way, but had to be buried alive. Only in proportion as I mean more, I shall certainly appear more absurd in my statement; and at last, when I get unendurably significant, all practical persons will agree that I was talking mere nonsense from the beginning, and never meant anything at all.

3. It is just possible, however, also, that the story-teller may all along have meant nothing but what he said; and that, incredible as the events may appear, he himself literally believed—and expected you also to believe—all this about Hercules, without any latent moral or history whatever. And it is very necessary,

in reading traditions of this kind, to determine, first of all, whether you are listening to a simple person, who is relating what, at all events, he believes to be true (and may, therefore, possibly have been so to some extent), or to a reserved philosopher, who is veiling a theory of the universe under the grotesque of a fairy tale. It is, in general, more likely that the first supposition should be the right one : simple and credulous persons are, perhaps fortunately, more common than philosophers : and it is of the highest importance that you should take their innocent testimony as it was meant, and not efface, under the graceful explanation which your cultivated ingenuity may suggest, either the evidence their story may contain (such as it is worth) of an extraordinary event having really taken place, or the unquestionable light which it will cast upon the character of the person by whom it was frankly believed. And to deal with Greek religion honestly, you must at once understand that this literal belief was, in the mind of the general people as deeply rooted as ours in the legends of our own sacred book ; and that a basis of unmiraculous event was as little suspected, and an explanatory symbolism as rarely traced by them, as by us.

You must, therefore, observe that I deeply degrade the position which such a myth as that just referred to occupied in the Greek mind, by comparing it (for fear of offending you) to our story of St. George and the Dragon. Still, the analogy is perfect in minor respects; and though it fails to give you any notion of the vitally religious earnestness of the Greek faith, it will exactly illustrate the manner in which faith laid hold of its objects.

4. This story of Hercules and the Hydra, then was to the general Greek mind, in its best days, a tale about a real hero and a real monster. Not one in a thousand knew anything of the way in which the story had arisen, any more than the English peasant generally is aware of the plebeian origin of St. George; or supposes that there were once alive in the world, with sharp teeth and claws, real, and very ugly, flying dragons. On the other hand, few persons traced any moral or symbolical meaning in the story, and the average Greek was as far from imagining any interpretation like that I have just given you, as an average Englishman is from seeing in St. George the Red Cross Knight of Spenser, or in the Dragon the Spirit of Infidelity. But, for all that, there was a certain undercurrent of consciousness in all minds, that the figures meant more than they at first showed; and, according to each man's own faculties of sentiment, he judged and read them; just as a Knight of the Garter reads more in the jewel on his collar than the George and Dragon of a public-house expresses to the host or to his customers. Thus, to the mean person the myth always meant little; to the noble person, much: and the

greater their familiarity with it, the more contemptible it became to the one, and the more sacred to the other: until vulgar commentators explained it entirely away, while Virgil made it the crowning glory of his choral hymn to Hercules.

> " Around thee, powerless to infect thy soul,
> Rose, in his crested crowd, the Lerna worm."

> " Non te rationis egentem
> Lernæus turbâ capitum circumstetit anguis."

And atlhough, in any special toil of the hero's life, the moral interpretation was rarely with definiteness attached to its event, yet in the whole course of the life, not only a symbolical meaning, but the warrant for the existence of a real spiritual power, was apprehended of all men. Hercules was no dead hero, to be remembered only as a victor over monsters of the past—harmless now, as slain. He was the perpetual type and mirror of heroism, and its present and living aid against every ravenous form of human trial and pain.

5. But, if we seek to know more than this, and to ascertain the manner in which the story first crystallized into its shape, we shall find ourselves led back generally to one or other of two sources—either to actual historical events, represented by the fancy under figures personifying them; or else to natural phenomena similarly endowed with life by the imaginative

power, usually more or less under the influence of terror. The historical myths we must leave the masters of history to follow; they, and the events they record, being yet involved in great, though attractive and penetrable mystery. But the stars, and hills, and storms, are with us now, as they were with others of old; and it only needs that we look at them with the earnestness of those childish eyes to understand the first words spoken of them by the children of men. And then, in all the most beautiful and enduring myths, we shall find, not only a literal story of a real person—not only a parallel imagery of moral principle—but an underlying worship of natural phenomena, out of which both have sprung, and in which both forever remain rooted. Thus from the real sun, rising and setting—from the real atmosphere, calm in its dominion of unfading blue, and fierce in its descent of tempest—the Greek forms first the idea of two entirely personal and corporeal gods, whose limbs are clothed in divine flesh, and whose brows are crowned with divine beauty; yet so real that the quiver rattles at their shoulder, and the chariot bends beneath their weight. And, on the other hand, collaterally with these corporeal images, and never for one instant separated from them, he conceives also two omnipresent spiritual influences, of which one illuminates, as the sun, with a constant fire, whatever in humanity is skillful and wise; and the other, like the living air,

breathes the calm of heavenly fortitude, and strength
of righteous anger, into every human breast that is
pure and brave.

6. Now, therefore, in nearly every myth of importance, and certainly in every one of those of which I
shall speak to-night, you have to discern these three
structural parts—the root and the two branches—the
root, in physical existence, sun, or sky, or cloud, or
sea; then the personal incarnation of that; becoming
a trusted and companionable deity, with whom you
may walk hand in hand, as a child with its brother or
its sister; and, lastly, the moral significance of the
image, which is in all the great myths eternally and
beneficently true.

7. The great myths; that is to say, myths made by
great people. For the first plain fact about myth-
making is one which has been most strangely lost
sight of—that you cannot make a myth unless you
have something to make it of. You cannot tell a
secret which you don't know. If the myth is about
the sky, it must have been made by somebody who
had looked at the sky. If the myth is about justice
and fortitude, it must have been made by some one
who knew what it was to be just or patient. According to the quantity of understanding in the person will
be the quantity of significance in his fable; and the
myth of a simple and ignorant race must necessarily
mean little, because a simple and ignorant race have

little to mean. So the great question in reading a story is always, not what wild hunter dreamed, or what childish race first dreaded it; but what wise man first perfectly told, and what strong people first perfectly lived by it. And the real meaning of any myth is that which it has at the noblest age of the nation among whom it is current. The farther back you pierce, the less significance you will find, until you come to the first narrow thought, which indeed contains the germ of the accomplished tradition; but only as the seed contains the flower. As the intelligence and passion of the race develop, they cling to and nourish their beloved and sacred legend : leaf by leaf it expands under the touch of more pure affections, and more delicate imagination, until at last the perfect fable burgeons out into symmetry of milky stem, and honied bell.

8. But through whatever changes it may pass, remember that our right reading of it is wholly dependent on the materials we have in our own minds for an intelligent answering sympathy. If it first arose among a people who dwelt under stainless skies, and measured their journeys by ascending and declining stars, we certainly cannot read their story, if we have never seen anything above us in the day, but smoke; or anything round us in the night but candles. If the tale goes on to change clouds or planets into living creatures—to invest them with fair forms—and inflame

them with mighty passions, we can only understand the story of the human-hearted things, in so far as we ourselves take pleasure in the perfectness of visible form, or can sympathize, by an effort of imagination, with the strange people who had other loves than that of wealth, and other interests than those of commerce. And, lastly, if the myth complete itself to the fulfilled thoughts of the nation, by attributing to the gods, whom they have carved out of their fantasy, continual presence with their own souls; and their every effort for good is finally guided by the sense of the companionship, the praise, and the pure will of immortals, we shall be able to follow them into this last circle of their faith only in the degree in which the better parts of our own being have been also stirred by the aspects of nature, or strengthened by her laws. It may be easy to prove that the ascent of Apollo in his chariot signifies nothing but the rising of the sun. But what does the sunrise itself signify to us? If only languid return to frivolous amusement, or fruitless labor, it will, indeed, not be easy for us to conceive the power, over a Greek, of the name of Apollo. But if, for us also, as for the Greek, the sunrise means daily restoration to the sense of passionate gladness and of perfect life—if it means the thrilling of new strength through every nerve—the shedding over us of a better peace than the peace of night, in the power of the dawn—and the purging of evil vision and fear by the baptism of its dew—if the sun itself is an influence, to us also, of spiritual good—and becomes thus in reality, not in imagination, to us also, a spiritual power—we may then soon over-pass the narrow limit of conception which kept that power impersonal, and rise with the Greek to the thought of an angel who rejoiced as a strong man to run his course, whose voice, calling to life and to labor, rang round the earth, and whose going forth was to the ends of heaven.

9. The time, then, at which I shall take up for you, as well as I can decipher it, the tradition of the gods of Greece, shall be near the beginning of its central and formed faith—about 500 B.C., a faith of which the character is perfectly represented by Pindar and Æschylus, who are both of them outspokenly religious, and entirely sincere men; while we may always look back to find the less developed thought of the preceding epoch given by Homer, in a more occult, subtle, half-instinctive and involuntary way.

10. Now, at that culminating period of the Greek religion we find, under one governing Lord of all things, four subordinate elemental forces, and four spiritual powers living in them, and commanding them. The elements are of course the well-known four of the ancient world—the earth, the water, the fire, and the air; and the living powers of them are Demeter, the Latin Ceres; Poseidon, the Latin Neptune;

Apollo, who has retained always his Greek name; and Athena, the Latin Minerva. Each of these are descended from, or changed from, more ancient, and therefore more mystic deities of the earth and heaven, and of a finer element of æther supposed to be beyond the heavens; * but at this time we find the four quite definite, both in their kingdoms and in their personalities. They are the rulers of the earth that we tread upon, and the air that we breathe; and are with us as closely, in their vivid humanity, as the dust that they animate, and the winds that they bridle. I shall briefly define for you the range of their separate dominions, and then follow, as far as we have time, the most interesting of the legends which relate to the queen of the air.

11. The rule of the first spirit, Demeter, the earth mother, is over the earth, first, as the origin of all life —the dust from whence we were taken: secondly, as the receiver of all things back at last into silence— "Dust thou art and unto dust shalt thou return." And, therefore, as the most tender image of this appearing and fading life, in the birth and fall of flowers, her daughter, Proserpine, plays in the fields of Sicily, and thence is torn away into darkness, and becomes the queen of Fate—not merely of death, but of the gloom which closes over and ends, not beauty only,

---

* And by modern science now also asserted, and with probability argued, to exist.

but sin; and chiefly of sins the sin against the life she gave: so that she is, in her highest power, Persephone, the avenger and purifier of blood—"The voice of thy brother's blood cries to me *out of the ground*." Then, side by side with this queen of the earth, we find a demigod of agriculture by the plow—the lord of grain, or of the thing ground by the mill. And it is a singular proof of the simplicity of Greek character at this noble time, that of all representations left to us of their deities by their art, few are so frequent, and none perhaps so beautiful, as the symbol of this spirit of agriculture.

12. Then the dominant spirit of the element water is Neptune, but subordinate to him are myriads of other water spirits, of whom Nereus is the chief, with Palæmon, and Leucothea, the "white lady" of the sea; and Thetis, and nymphs innumerable who, like her, could "suffer a sea change," while the river deities had each independent power, according to the preciousness of their streams to the cities fed by them—the "fountain Arethuse, and thou, honored flood, smooth-sliding Mincius, crowned with vocal reeds." And, spiritually, this king of the waters is lord of the strength and daily flow of human life—he gives it material force and victory; which is the meaning of the dedication of hair, as the sign of the strength of life, to the river or the native land.

13. Demeter, then, over the earth, and its giving

and receiving of life. Neptune over the waters, and the flow and force of life—always among the Greeks typified by the horse, which was to them as a crested sea-wave, animated and bridled. Then the third element, fire, has set over it two powers; over earthly fire, the assistant of human labor, is set Hephæstus, lord of all labor in which is the flush and the sweat of the brow; and over heavenly fire, the source of day, is set Apollo, the spirit of all kindling, purifying, and illuminating intellectual wisdom, each of these gods having also their subordinate or associated powers — servant or sister or companion muse.

14. Then, lastly we come to the myth which is to be our subject of closer inquiry—the story of Athena and of the deities subordinate to her. This great goddess, the Neith of the Egyptians, the Athena or Athenaia of the Greeks, and, with broken power, half usurped by Mars, the Minerva of the Latins, is, physically, the queen of the air; having supreme power both over its blessing of calm, and wrath of storm; and spiritually, she is the queen of the breath of man, first of the bodily breathing which is life to his blood, and strength to his arm in battle; and then of the mental breathing, or inspiration, which is his moral health and habitual wisdom; wisdom of conduct and of the heart, as opposed to the wisdom of imagination and the brain; moral, as distinct from intellectual; inspired as distinct from illuminated.

15. By a singular, and fortunate, though I believe wholly accidental coincidence, the heart-virtue, of which she is the spirit, was separated by the ancients into four divisions, which have since obtained acceptance from all men as rightly discerned, and have received, as if from the quarters of the four winds of which Athena is the natural queen, the name of "cardinal" virtues: namely, Prudence (the right seeing, and foreseeing, of events through darkness); Justice (the righteous bestowal of favor and of indignation); Fortitude (patience under trial by pain); and Temperance (patience under trial by pleasure). With respect to these four virtues, the attributes of Athena are all distinct. In her prudence, or sight in darkness, she is "Glaukopis," "owl-eyed." * In her justice, which is the dominant virtue, she wears two robes, one of light and one of darkness; the robe of light, saffron color or the color of the daybreak, falls to her feet, covering her wholly with favor and love—the calm of the sky in blessing; it is embroidered along its edge with her victory over the giants (the troublous powers of the earth), and the likeness of it was woven yearly by the Athenian maidens and carried to the temple of their own Athena, not to the Parthenon, that was the temple of all the world's Athena—but this they carried to the temple of their own only one

* There are many other meanings in the epithet; see, farther on § 91.

who loved them, and stayed with them always. Then her robe of indignation is worn on her breast and left arm only, fringed with fatal serpents, and fastened with Gorgonian cold, turning men to stone; physically the lightning and the hail of chastisement by storm. Then in her fortitude she wears the crested and un-stooping helmet; * and lastly, in her temperance, she is the queen of maidenhood—stainless as the air of heaven.

16. But all these virtues mass themselves in the Greek mind into the two main ones—of justice, or noble passion, and fortitude, or noble patience; and of these, the chief powers of Athena, the Greeks had divinely written for them, and for all men after them, two mighty songs—one, of the Menis,† *mens*, passion, or zeal, of Athena, breathed into a mortal whose name is "ache of heart," and whose short life is only the incarnate brooding and burst of storm; and the other is of the foresight and fortitude of Athena, maintained by her in the heart of a mortal whose name is given to him from a longer grief, Odysseus, the full of sorrow, the much-enduring, and the long-suffering.

---

*I am compelled, for clearness' sake, to mark only one meaning at a time. Athena's helmet is sometimes a mask—sometimes a sign of anger—sometimes of the highest light of æther: but I cannot speak of all this at once.

† This first word of the Iliad, Menis, afterward passes into the Latin Mens; is the root of the Latin name for Athena, "Minerva," and so of the English "mind."

17. The minor expressions by the Greeks in word, in symbol and in religious service, of this faith, are so many and so beautiful, that I hope some day to gather at least a few of them into a separate body of evidence respecting the power of Athena and its relations to the ethical conception of the Homeric poems, or, rather, to their ethical nature; for they are not conceived didactically, but are didactic in their essence, as all good art is. There is an increasing insensibility to this character, and even an open denial of it, among us now, which is one of the most curious errors of modernism— the peculiar and judicial blindness of an age which, having long practiced art and poetry for the sake of pleasure only, has become incapable of reading their language when they were both didactic: and also, having been itself accustomed to a professedly didactic teaching, which yet, for private interests, studiously avoids collision with every prevalent vice of its day (and especially with avarice), has become equally dead to the intensely ethical conceptions of a race which habitually divided all men into two broad classes of worthy or worthless; good, and good for nothing. And even the celebrated passage of Horace about the Iliad is now misread or disbelieved, as if it was impossible that the Iliad could be instructive because it is not like a sermon. Horace does not say that it is like a sermon, and would have been still less likely to say so, if he ever had had the advantage of hearing a sermon. "I

have been reading that story of Troy again " (thus he writes to a noble youth of Rome whom he cared for), " quietly at Præneste, while you have been busy at Rome; and truly I think that what is base and what is noble, and what useful and useless, may be better learned from that, than from all Chrysippus' and Crantor's talk put together." * Which is profoundly true, not of the Iliad only, but of all other great art whatsoever; for all pieces of such art are didactic in the purest way, indirectly and occultly, so that, first, you shall only be bettered by them if you are already hard at work in bettering yourself; and when you *are* bettered by them, it shall be partly with a general acceptance of their influence, so constant and subtle that you shall be no more conscious of it than of the healthy digestion of food; and partly by a gift of un-expected truth, which you shall only find by slow mining for it; which is withheld on purpose, and close-locked, that you may not get it till you have forged the key of it in a furnace of your own heating. And this withholding of their meaning is continual and confessed, in the great poets. Thus Pindar says of himself: " There is many an arrow in my quiver, full of speech to the wise, but, for the many, they need interpreters." And neither Pindar, nor Æschylus, nor

---

* Note, once for all, that unless when there is question about some particular expression, I never translate literally, but give the real force of what is said, as I best can, freely.

Hesiod nor Homer nor any of the greater poets or teachers of any nation or time, ever spoke but with intentional reservation : nay, beyond this, there is often a meaning which they themselves cannot interpret—which it may be for ages long after them to interpret—in what they said, so far as it recorded true imaginative vision. For all the greatest myths have been seen, by the men who tell them, involuntarily and passively—seen by them with as great distinctness (and in some respects, though not in all, under conditions as far beyond the control of their will) as a dream sent to any of us by night when we dream clearest ; and it is this veracity of vision that could not be refused, and of moral that could not be foreseen, which in modern historical inquiry has been left wholly out of account : being indeed the thing which no merely historical investigator can understand, or even believe ; for it belongs exclusively to the creative or artistic group of men, and can only be interpreted by those of their race, who themselves in some measure also see visions and dream dreams.

So that you may obtain a more truthful idea of the nature of Greek religion and legend from the poems of Keats, and the nearly as beautiful, and, in general grasp of subject, far more powerful, recent work of Morris, than from frigid scholarship, however extensive. Not that the poet's impressions or renderings of things are wholly true, but their truth is vital, not formal. They are like sketches from the life by Reynolds or Gainsborough, which may be demonstrably inaccurate or imaginary in many traits, and indistinct in others, yet will be in the deepest sense like, and true; while the work of historical analysis is too often weak with loss, through the very labor of its miniature touches, or useless in clumsy and vapid veracity of externals, and complacent security of having done all that is required for the portrait, when it has measured the breadth of the forehead, and the length of the nose.

18.   The first of requirements, then, for the right reading of myths, is the understanding of the nature of all true vision by noble persons; namely, that it is founded on constant laws common to all human nature; that it perceives, however darkly, things which are for all ages true—that we can only understand it so far as we have some perception of the same truth—and that its fullness is developed and manifested more and more by the reverberation of it from minds of the same mirror-temper, in succeeding ages. You will understand Homer better by seeing his reflection in Dante, as you may trace new forms and softer colors in a hill-side, redoubled by a lake.

I shall be able partly to show you, even to-night, how much in the Homeric vision of Athena, has been made clearer by the advance of time, being thus essentially and eternally true; but I must in the outset indicate the relation to that central thought of the imagery of the inferior deities of storm.

19. And first I will take the myth of Æolus (the "sage Hippotades" of Milton), as it is delivered pure by Homer from the early times.

Why do you suppose Milton calls him "sage?" One does not usually think of the winds as very thoughtful or deliberate powers. But hear Homer: "Then we came to the Æolian island, and there dwelt Æolus Hippotades, dear to the deathless gods: there he dwelt in a floating island, and round it was a wall of brass that could not be broken; and the smooth rock of it ran up sheer. To whom twelve children were born in the sacred chambers—six daughters and six strong sons; and they dwell forever with their beloved father, and their mother strict in duty ; and with them are laid up a thousand benefits; and the misty house around them rings with fluting all the day long." Now, you are to note first, in this description, the wall of brass and the sheer rock. You will find, throughout the fables of the tempest-group, that the brazen wall and precipice (occurring in another myth as the brazen tower of Danæ) are always connected with the idea of the towering cloud lighted by the sun, here truly described as a floating island. Secondly, you hear that all treasures were laid up in them ; therefore, you know this Æolus is lord of the beneficent winds ("he bringeth the wind out of his treasuries"); and presently afterward Homer calls him the "steward" of the winds, the master of the storehouse of them.

And this idea of gifts and preciousness in the winds of
heaven is carried out in the well-known sequel of the
fable.   Æolus gives them to Ulysses, all but one, bound
in leathern bags, with a glittering cord of silver; and
so like bags of treasure that the sailors think they are
so, and open them to see.   And when Ulysses is thus
driven back to Æolus, and prays him again to help
him, note the deliberate words of the king's refusal—
"Did I not," he says, "send thee on thy way heartily,
that thou mightest reach thy country, thy home, and
whatever is dear to thee?   It is not lawful for me
again to send forth favorably on his journey a man
hated by the happy gods."   This idea of the beneficence of Æolus remains to the latest times, though
Virgil, by adopting the vulgar change of the cloud
island into Lipari, has lost it a little; but even when it
is finally explained away by Diodorus, Æolus is still a
kind-hearted monarch, who lived on the coast of Sor-
rento, invented the use of sails, and established a system of storm signals.

20.   Another beneficent storm-power, Boreas, occu-
pies an important place in early legend, and a singularly principal one in art; and I wish I could read to
you a passage of Plato about the legend of Boreas and
Oreithyia,* and the breeze and shade of the Ilissus—
notwithstanding its severe reflection upon persons who

---

* Translated by Max Müller in the opening of his essay on "Com-
parative Mythology."   (*Chips from a German workshop,* vol. ii.)

waste their time on mythological studies : but I must go on at once to the fable with which you are all generally familiar, that of the harpies.

This is always connected with that of Boreas or the north wind, because the two sons of Boreas are enemies of the harpies, and drive them away into frantic flight. The myth in its first literal form means only the battle between the fair north wind and the foul south one : the two harpies, "Stormswift" and "Swiftfoot," are the sisters of the rainbow—that is to say, they are the broken drifts of the showery south wind, and the clear north wind drives them back ; but they quickly take a deeper and more malignant significance. You know the short, violent, spiral gusts that lift the dust before coming rain : the harpies get identified first with these, and then with more violent whirlwinds, and so they are called "harpies," "the snatchers," and are thought of as entirely destructive; their manner of destroying being twofold—by snatching away, and by defiling and polluting. This is a month in which you may really see a small harpy at her work almost whenever you choose. The first time that there is threatening of rain after two or three days of fine weather, leave your window well open to the street, and some books or papers on the table ; and if you do not, in a little while, know what the harpies mean and how they snatch, and how they defile, I'll give up my Greek myths.

21. That is the physical meaning. It is now easy to find the mental one. You must all have felt the expression of ignoble anger in those fitful gusts of sudden storm. There is a sense of provocation and apparent bitterness of purpose in their thin and senseless fury, wholly different from the noble anger of the greater tempests. Also, they seem useless and unnatural, and the Greek thinks of them always as vile in malice, and opposed, therefore, to the sons of Boreas, who are kindly winds, that fill sails, and wave harvests—full of bracing health and happy impulses. From this lower and merely malicious temper, the harpies rise into a greater terror, always associated with their whirling motion, which is indeed indicative of the most destructive winds: and they are thus related to the nobler tempests, as Charybdis to the sea ; they are devouring and desolating, merciless, making all things disappear that come in their grasp: and so, spiritually, they are the gusts of vexatious, fretful, lawless passion, vain and over-shadowing, discontented and lamenting, meagre and insane—spirits of wasted energy, and wandering disease, and unappeased famine, and unsatisfied hope. So you have, on the one side, the winds of prosperity and health, on the other, of ruin and sickness. Understand that, once deeply—any who have ever known the weariness of vain desires ; the pitiful, unconquerable, coiling and recoiling and self-involved returns of some sickening famine

and thirst of heart : and you will know what was in the sound of the harpy Celæno's shriek from her rock ; and why, in the seventh circle of the " Inferno," the harpies make their nests in the warped branches of the trees that are the souls of suicides.

22. Now you must always be prepared to read Greek legends as you trace threads through figures on a silken damask : the same thread runs through the web, but it makes part of different figures. Joined with other colors you hardly recognize it, and in different lights, it is dark or light. Thus the Greek fables blend and cross curiously in different directions, till they knit themselves into an arabesque where sometimes you cannot tell black from purple, nor blue from emerald—they being all the truer for this, because the truths of emotion they represent are interwoven in the same way, but all the more difficult to read, and to explain in any order. Thus the harpies, as they represent vain desire, are connected with the sirens, who are the spirits of constant desire : so that it is difficult sometimes in early art to know which are meant, both being represented alike as birds with women's heads; only the sirens are the great constant desires—the infinite sicknesses of heart— which, rightly placed, give life, and wrongly placed, waste it away ; so that there are two groups of sirens, one noble and saving, as the other is fatal. But there are no animating or saving harpies ; their nature is always vexing and full of

weariness, and thus they are curiously connected with
the whole group of legends about Tantalus.

23. We all know what it is to be tantalized; but
we do not often think of asking what Tantalus was
tantalized for—what he had done, to be forever kept
hungry in sight of food? Well, he had not been condemned to this merely for being a glutton. By Dante
the same punishment is assigned to simple gluttony, to
purge it away—but the sins of Tantalus were of a
much wider and more mysterious kind. There are four
great sins attributed to him—one, stealing the food of
the gods to give it to men; another, sacrificing his son
to feed the gods themselves (it may remind you for a
moment of what I was telling you of the earthly
character of Demeter, that, while the other gods all
refuse, she, dreaming about her lost daughter, eats
part of the shoulder of Pelops before she knows what
she is doing); another sin, is telling the secrets of the
gods; and only the fourth—stealing the golden dog
of Pandareos—is connected with gluttony. The
special sense of this myth is marked by Pandareos receiving the happy privilege of never being troubled
with indigestion; the dog, in general, however,
mythically represents all utterly senseless and carnal
desires; mainly that of gluttony; and in the mythic
sense of hades—that is to say, so far as it represents
spiritual ruin in this life, and not a literal hell—the
dog Cerberus as its gate-keeper—with this special

marking of his character of sensual passion, that he fawns on all those who descend, but rages against all who would return (the Virgilian "*facilis descensus*" being a later recognition of this mythic character of Hades): the last labor of Hercules is the dragging him up to the light; and in some sort, he represents the voracity or devouring of Hades itself; and the mediæval representation of the mouth of hell perpetuates the same thought. Then, also, the power of evil passion is partly associated with the red and scorching light of Sirius, as opposed to the pure light, of the sun: he is the dog-star of ruin; and hence the continual Homeric dwelling upon him, and comparison of the flame of anger to his swarthy light; only, in his scorching, it is thirst, not hunger, over which he rules physically; so that the fable of Icarius, his first master, corresponds, among the Greeks, to the legend of the drunkenness of Noah.

The story of Actæon, the raging death of Hecuba, and the tradition of the white dog which ate part of Hercules' first sacrifice, and so gave name to the Cynosarges, and all various phases of the same thought—the Greek notion of the dog being throughout confused between its serviceable fidelity, its watchfulness, its foul voracity, shamelessness, and deadly madness, while, with the curious reversal or recoil of the meaning which attaches itself to nearly every great myth—and which we shall presently see notably exemplified in the relations of the serpent to Athena—the dog becomes in philosophy a type of severity and abstinence.

24. It would carry us too far aside were I to tell you the story of Pandareos' dog—or rather, of Jupiter's dog, for Pandareos was its guardian only; all that bears on our present purpose is that the guardian of this golden dog had three daughters, one of whom was subject to the power of the sirens; and is turned into the nightingale; and the other two were subject to the power of the harpies, and this was what happened to them. They were very beautiful, and they were beloved by the gods in their youth, and all the great goddesses were anxious to bring them up rightly. Of all types of young ladies' education, there is nothing so splendid as that of the younger daughters of Pandareos. They have literally the four greatest goddesses for their governesses. Athena teaches them domestic accomplishments, how to weave, and sew, and the like; Artemis teaches them to hold themselves up straight; Hera, how to behave proudly and oppressively to company; and Aphrodite—delightful governess—feeds them with cakes and honey all day long. All goes well, until just the time when they are going to be brought out; then there is a great dispute whom they are to marry, and in the midst of it they are carried off by the harpies, given by them to be slaves to the furies, and

never seen more. But of course there is nothing in Greek myths; and one never heard of such things as vain desires, and empty hopes, and clouded passions, defiling and snatching away the souls of maidens, in a London season.

I have no time to trace for you any more harpy legends, though they are full of the most curious interest; but I may confirm for you my interpretation of this one, and prove its importance in the Greek mind, by noting that Polygnotus painted these maidens, in his great religious series of paintings at Delphi, crowned with flowers and playing at dice; and that Penelope remembers them in her last fit of despair, just before the return of Ulysses, and prays bitterly that she may be snatched away at once into nothingness by the harpies, like Pandareos' daughters, rather than be tormented longer by her deferred hope, and anguish of disappointed love.

25. I have hitherto spoken only of deities of the winds. We pass now to a far more important group, the Deities of Cloud. Both of these are subordinate to the ruling power of the air, as the demigods of the fountains and minor seas are to the great deep: but, as the cloud-firmament detaches itself more from the air, and has a wider range of ministry than the minor streams and seas, the highest cloud deity, Hesmes, has a rank more equal with Athena than Nereus or Proteus with Neptune; and there is greater difficulty in

tracing his character, because his physical dominion over the clouds can, of course, be asserted only where clouds are; and, therefore, scarcely at all in Egypt; * so that the changes which Hermes undergoes in becoming a Greek from an Egyptian and Phœnician god, are greater than in any other case of adopted tradition. In Egypt Hermes is a deity of historical record and a conductor of the dead to judgment; the Greeks take away much of this historical function, assigning it to the Muses; but, in investing him with the physical power over clouds, they give him that which the Muses disdain, the power of concealment and of theft. The snatching away by the harpies is with brute force; but the snatching away by the clouds is connected with the thought of hiding and of making things seem to be what they are not; so that Hermes is the god of lying, as he is of mist; and yet with this ignoble function of making things vanish and disappear, is connected the remnant of his grand Egyptian authority of leading away souls in the cloud of death (the actual dimness of sight caused by mortal

---

* I believe that the conclusions of recent scholarship are generally opposed to the Herodotean ideas of any direct acceptance by the Greeks of Egyptian myths: and very certainly, Greek art is developed by giving the veracity and simplicity of real life to eastern savage grotesque; and not by softening the severity of pure Egyptian design. But it is of no consequence whether one conception was, or was not, in this case, derived from the other; my object is only to mark the essential differences between them.

wounds physically suggesting the darkness and descent of clouds, and continually being so described in the Iliad); while the sense of the need of guidance on the untrodden road follows necessarily. You cannot but remember how this thought of cloud guidance and cloud receiving of souls at death, has been elsewhere ratified.

26. Without following that higher clue, I will pass to the lovely group of myths connected with the birth of Hermes on the Greek mountains. You know that the valley of Sparta is one of the noblest mountain ravines in the world, and that the western flank of it is formed by an unbroken chain of crags, forty miles long, rising opposite Sparta, to a height of 8,000 feet and known as the chain of Taygetus. Now, the nymph from whom that mountain ridge is named, was the mother of Lacedæmon; therefore, the mythic ancestress of the Spartan race. She is the nymph Taygeta and one of the seven stars of spring; one of those Pleiades of whom is the question of Job— "Canst thou bind the sweet influences of Pleiades, or loose the bands of Orion?" "The sweet influences of Pleiades," of the stars of spring—nowhere sweeter than among the pine-clad slopes of the hills of Sparta and Arcadia, when the snows of their higher summits, beneath the sunshine of April, fell into fountains and rose into clouds; and in every ravine was a newly-awakened voice of waters—soft increase of whisper

among its sacred stones: and on every crag its form
ing and fading veil of radiant cloud; temple above
temple, of the divine marble that no tool can pollute,
nor ruin undermine. And, therefore, beyond this central valley, this great Greek vase of Arcadia, on the
"*hollow*" mountain, Cyllene, or " pregnant " mountain,
called also " cold," because there the vapors rest,* and
born of the eldest of those stars of spring, that Maia,
from whom your own month of May has its name,
bringing to you, in the green of her garlands and the
white of her hawthorn, the unrecognized symbols of
the pastures and the wreathed snows of Arcadia,
where long ago she was queen of stars: there, first
cradled and wrapped in swaddling-clothes; then raised,
in a moment of surprise, into his wandering power—
is born the shepherd of the clouds, winged-footed and
deceiving—blinding the eyes of Argus—escaping from
the grasp of Apollo—restless messenger between the
highest sky and topmost earth—" the herald Mercury,
new lighted on a heaven-kissing hill."

27. Now, it will be wholly impossible, at present, to
trace for you any of the minor Greek expressions of this
thought, except only that Mercury, as the cloud shepherd, is especially called Eriophoros, the wool-bearer.
You will recollect the name from the common woolly

---

* On the altar of Hermes on its summit, as on that of the Lacinian
Hera, no wind ever stirred the ashes. By those altars, the Gods of
Heaven were appeased; and all their storms at rest.

rush "eriophorum" which has a cloud of silky seed; and note also that he wears distinctively the flat cap, *petasos*, named from a word meaning to expand : which shaded from the sun, and is worn on journeys. You have the epithet of mountains "cloud-capped" as an established form with every poet, and the Mont Pilate of Lucerne is named from a Latin word signifying specially a *woolen* cap ; but Mercury has besides, a general Homeric epithet, curiously and intensely concentrated in meaning, "the profitable or serviceable by wool," [*] that is to say, by shepherd wealth ; hence, "pecuniarily," rich or serviceable, and so he passes at last into a general mercantile deity ; while yet the cloud sense of the wool is retained by Homer always, so that he gives him this epithet when it would otherwise have been quite meaningless (in Iliad, xxiv. 440), when he drives Priam's chariot, and breaths force into his horses, precisely as we shall find Athena drive Diomed : and yet the serviceable and profitable sense —and something also of gentle and soothing character in the mere wool-softness, as used for dress, and religious rites—is retained also in the epithet, and thus the gentle and serviceable Hermes is opposed to the deceitful one.

---

[*] I am convinced that the ἐρι in ἐριούνιος is not intensive ; but retained from ἔριον : but even if I am wrong in thinking this, the mistake is of no consequence with respect to the general force of the term as meaning the *profitableness* of Hermes. Athena's epithet of αγελεις has a parallel significance.

28. In connection with this driving of Priam's chariot, remember, that as Autolycus is the son of Hermes the deceiver, Myrtilus (the Auriga of the stars) is the son of Hermes the guide. The name Hermes itself means impulse; and he is especially the shepherd of the flocks of the sky, in driving, or guiding, or stealing them; and yet his great name, Argeiphontes, not only—as in different passages of the olden poets—means "shining white," which is said of him as being himself the silver cloud lighted by the sun; but "Argus-Killer," the killer of brightness, which is said of him as he veils the sky, and especially the stars, which are the eyes of Argus; or literally, eyes of brightness, which Juno, who is, with Jupiter, part of the type of highest heaven, keeps in her peacock's train. We know that this interpretation is right, from a passage in which Euripides describes the shield of Hippomedon, which bore for its sign, "Argus the all-seeing, covered with eyes; open toward the rising of the stars, and closed toward their setting."

And thus Hermes becomes the spirit of the movement of the sky or firmament; not merely the fast-flying of the transitory cloud, but the great motion of the heavens and stars themselves. Thus, in his highest power, he corresponds to the *"primo mobile"* of the later Italian philosophy, and, in his simplest, is the guide of all mysterious and cloudy movement, and of all successful subtleties. Perhaps the prettiest minor recognition of his character is when, on the night foray of Ulysses and Diomed, Ulysses wears the helmet stolen by Autolycus, the son of Hermes.

29. The position in the Greek mind of Hermes as the lord of cloud, is, however, more mystic and ideal than that of any other deity, just on account of the constant and real presence of the cloud itself under different forms, giving rise to all kinds of minor fables. The play of the Greek imagination in this direction is so wide and complex, that I cannot even give you an outline of its range in my present limits. There is first a great series of storm-legends connected with the family of the historic Æolus, centralized by the story of Athamas, with his two wives, "the Cloud," and the "White Goddess," ending in that of Phrixus and Helle, and of the golden fleece (which is only the cloud-burden of Hermes Eriophoros). With this, there is the fate of Salmoneus, and the destruction of Glaucus by his own horses; all these minor myths of storm concentrating themselves darkly into the legend of Bellerophon and the Chimæra, in which there is an under story about the vain subduing of passion and treachery, and the end of life in fading melancholy—which, I hope, not many of you could understand even were I to show it you: (the merely physical meaning of the Chimæra is the cloud of volcanic lightning, connected wholly with earth-fire, but resembling the heavenly cloud in its height and its thunder).

Finally, in the Æolic group, there is the legend of Sisyphus, which I mean to work out thoroughly by itself: its root is in the position of Corinth as ruling the isthmus and the two seas—the Corinthian Acropolis, two thousand feet high, being the center of the crossing currents of the winds, and of the commerce of Greece. Therefore, Athena, and the fountain cloud Pegasus, are more closely connected with Corinth than even with Athens in their material, though not in their moral power; and Sisyphus founds the Isthmian games in connection with a melancholy story about the sea gods; but he himself is κερδιστος ἀνδρῶν, the most " gaining " and subtle of men ; who, having the key of the isthmus, becomes the type of transit, transfer, or trade, as such; and of the apparent gain from it, which is not gain : and this is the real meaning of his punishment in hell—eternal toil and recoil (the modern idol of capital being, indeed, the stone of Sisyphus with a vengeance, *crushing* in its recoil). But, throughout, the old ideas of the cloud power and cloud feebleness—the deceit of its hiding—and the emptiness of its vanishing—the Autolycus enchantment of making black seem white—and the disappointed fury of Ixion (taking shadow for power), mingle in the moral meaning of this and its collateral legends : and give an aspect, at last, not only of foolish cunning, but of impiety or literal " idolatry," " imagination worship," to the dreams of avarice and injus tice, until this notion of atheism and insolent blindness becomes principal; and the "Clouds" of Aristophanes, with the personified "just" and "unjust" sayings in the latter part of the play, foreshadow, almost feature by feature, in all that they were written to mock and to chastise, the worse elements of the impious "δῖνος" and tumult in men's thoughts, which have followed on their avarice in the present day, making them alike forsake the laws of their ancient gods, and misapprehended or reject the true words of their existing teachers.

30. All this we have from the legends of the historic Æolus only; but, besides these, there is the beautiful story of Semele, the mother of Bacchus. She is the cloud with the strength of the vine in its bosom, consumed by the light which matures the fruit; the melting away of the cloud into the clear air at the fringe of its edges being exquisitely rendered by Pinard's epithet for her, Semele, "with the stretched-out hair" (ταννέθειρα). Then there is the entire tradition of the Danaides, and of the tower of Danae and golden shower; the birth of Perseus connecting this legend with that of the Gorgons and Graiæ, who are the true clouds of thunderous and ruinous tempest. I must, in passing, mark for you that the form of the sword or sickle of Perseus, with which he kills Medusa is another image of the whirling harpy vortex, and belongs especially to the sword of destruction or anni-

hilation; whence it is given to the two angels who gather for destruction the evil harvest and evil vintage of the earth (Rev. xiv. 15). I will collect afterward and complete what I have already written respecting the Pegasean and Gorgonian legends, noting here only what is necessary to explain the central myth of Athena herself, who represents the ambient air, which included all cloud, and rain, and dew, and darkness, and peace, and wrath of heaven. Let me now try to give you, however briefly, some distinct idea of the several agencies of this great goddess.

31. I. She is the air giving life and health to all animals.

II. She is in the air giving vegetative power to the earth.

III. She is the air giving motion to the sea, and rendering navigation posssible.

IV. She is the air nourishing artificial light, torch, or lamplight; as opposed to that of the sun, on one hand, and of *consuming** fire on the other.

V. She is the air conveying vibration of sound.

I will give you instances of her agency in all these functions.

32. First, and chiefly, she is air as the spirit of life, giving vitality to the blood. Her psychic relation to the vital force in matter lies deeper, and we will

---

* Not a scientific, but a very practical and expressive distinction.

examine it afterward; but a great number of the most interesting passages in Homer regard her as flying over the earth in local and transitory strength, simply and merely the goddess of fresh air.

It is curious that the British city which has some what saucily styled itself the modern Athens, is indeed more under her especial tutelage and favor in this respect than perhaps any other town in the island. Athena is first simply what in the modern Athens you so practically find her, the breeze of the mountain and the sea; and wherever she comes, there is purification, and health and power. The sea-beach round this isle of ours is the frieze of our Parthenon; every wave that breaks on it thunders with Athena's voice; nay, whenever you throw your window wide open in the morning, you let in Athena, as wisdom and fresh air at the same instant; and whenever you draw a pure, long, full breath of right heaven, you take Athena into your heart, through your blood; and, with the blood, into the thoughts of your brain.

Now this giving of strength by the air, observe, is mechanical as well as chemical. You cannot strike a good blow but with your chest full; and in hand to hand fighting, it is not the muscle that fails first, it is the breath; the longest-breathed will, on the average, be the victor—not the strongest. Note how Shakespeare always leans on this. Of Mortimer, in " changing hardiment with great Glendower:"

> "Three times they breathed, and three times did they drink,
> Upon agreement, of swift Severn's flood."

And again, Hotspur sending challenge to Prince Harry:

> "That none might draw short breath to-day
> But I and Harry Monmouth."

Again of Hamlet, before he receives his wound:

> "He's fat and scant of breath."

Again, Orlando in the wrestling:

> "Yes; I beseech your grace
> I am not yet well breathed."

Now of all people that ever lived, the Greeks knew best what breath meant, both in exercise and in battle, and therefore the queen of the air becomes to them at once the queen of bodily strength in war; not mere brutal muscular strength—that belongs to Ares—but the strength of young lives passed in pure air and swift exercise—Camilla's virginal force, that "flies o'er the unbending corn, and skims along the main."

33. Now I will rapidly give you two or three instances of her direct agency in this function. First, when she wants to make Penelope bright and beautiful; and to do away with the signs of her waiting and her grief. "Then Athena thought of another thing;

she laid her into deep sleep, and loosed all her limbs, and made her taller, and made her smoother, and fatter, and whiter than sawn ivory; and breathed ambrosial brightness over her face; and so she left her and went up to heaven." Fresh air and sound sleep at night, young ladies! You see you may have Athena for lady's maid whenever you choose. Next, hark how she gives strength to Achilles when he is broken with fasting and grief. Jupiter pities him and says to her: "'Daughter mine are you forsaking your own soldier, and don't you care for Achilles any more? see how hungry and weak he is—go and feed him with ambrosia.' So he urged the eager Athena; and she leaped down out of heaven like a happy falcon, shrill-voiced; and she poured nectar and ambrosia, full of delight, into the breast of Achilles, that his limbs might not fail with famine; then she returned to the solid dome of her strong father." And then comes the great passage about Achilles arming—for which we have no time. But here is again Athena giving strength to the whole Greek army. She came as a falcon to Achilles, straight at him—a sudden drift of breeze; but to the army she must come widely—she sweeps round them all. "As when Jupiter spreads the purple rainbow over heaven, portending battle or cold storm, so Athena, wrapping herself round with a purple cloud, stooped to the Greek soldiers, and raised up each of them." Note that purple, in Homer's use of it, nearly always means "fiery," "full of light." It is the light of the rainbow, not the color of it, which Homer means you to think of.

34.   But the most curious passage of all, and fullest of meaning, is when she gives strength to Menelaus, that he may stand unwearied against Hector.   He prays to her: "And blue-eyed Athena was glad that he prayed to her, first; and she gave him strength in his shoulders, and in his limbs, and she gave him the courage"—of what animal, do you suppose? Had it been Neptune or Mars, they would have given him the courage of a bull, or a lion; but Athena gives him the courage of the most fearless in attack of all creatures —small or great, and very small it is, but wholly incapable of terror—she gives him the courage of a fly.

35.   Now this simile of Homer's is one of the best instances I can give you of the way in which great writers seize truths unconsciously which are for all time.   It is only recent science which has completely shown the perfectness of this minute symbol of the power of Athena; proving that the insect's life and breath are co-ordinated; that its wings are actually forcing-pumps, of which the stroke compels the thoracic respiration; and that it thus breathes and flies simultaneously by the action of the same muscles, so that respiration is carried on most vigorously during flight, " while the air-vessels, supplied by many pairs of lungs instead of one, traverse the organs of flight in far

greater numbers than the capillary blood-vessels of our own system, and give enormous and untiring muscular power, a rapidity of action measured by thousands of strokes in the minute, and an endurance, by miles and hours of flight." *

Homer could not have known this; neither that the buzzing of the fly was produced as in a wind instrument, by a constant current of air through the trachea. But he had seen, and, doubtless, meant us to remember, the marvelous strength and swiftness of the insect's flight (the glance of the swallow itself is clumsy and slow compared to the darting of common house-flies at play); he probably attributed its murmur to the wings, but in this also there was a type of what we shall presently find recognized in the name of Pallas—the vibratory power of the air to convey sound—while, as a purifying creature, the fly holds its place beside the old symbol of Athena in Egypt, the vulture; and as a venemous and tormenting creature, has more than the strength of the serpent in proportion to its size, being thus entirely representative of the influence of the air both in purification and pestilence; and its courage is so notable that, strangely enough, forgetting Homer's simile, I happened to take the fly for an expression of the audacity of freedom in speaking of quite another subject.† Whether it

---

* Ormerod. *Natural History of Wasps.*

† See farther on, § 148.

should be called courage or mere mechanical instinct, may be questioned, but assuredly no other animal, exposed to continual danger, is so absolutely without sign of fear.

36. You will, perhaps, have still patience to hear two instances, not of the communication as strength, but of the personal agency of Athena as the air. When she comes down to help Diomed against Ares, she does not come to fight instead of him, but she takes his charioteer's place.

> "She snatched the reins, she lashed with all her force,
>   And full on Mars impelled the foaming horse."

Ares is the first to cast his spear; then, note this, Pope says:

> "Pallas opposed her hand, and caused to glance,
>   Far from the car, the strong, immortal lance."

She does not oppose her hand in the Greek—the wind could not meet the lance straight—she catches it in her hand, and throws it off. There is no instance in which a lance is so parried by a mortal hand in all the Iliad, and it is exactly the way the wind would parry it, catching it, and turning it aside. If there are any good rifle-shots here—they know something about Athena's parrying—and in old times the English masters of feathered artillery knew more yet. Compare also the turning of Hector's lance from Achilles: Iliad xx. 439.

37. The last instance I will give you is as lovely as it is subtle. Throughout the Iliad, Athena is herself the will or menis of Achilles. If he is to be calmed, it is she who calms him; if angered, it is she who inflames him. In the first quarrel with Atrides, when he stands at pause, with the great sword half drawn, " Athena came from heaven, and stood behind him, and caught him by the yellow hair." Another god would have stayed his hand upon the hilt, but Athena only lifts his hair. " And he turned and knew her, and her dreadful eyes shone upon him." There is an exquisite tenderness in this laying her hand upon his hair, for it is the talisman of his life, vowed to his own Thessalian river if he ever returned to its shore, and cast upon Patroclus' pile, so ordaining that there should be no return.

38. Secondly—Athena is the air giving vegetative impulse to the earth. She is the wind and the rain— and yet more the pure air itself, getting at the earth fresh turned by spade or plough—and, above all, feeding the fresh leaves; for though the Greeks knew nothing about carbonic acid, they did know that trees fed on the air.

Now, note first in this, the myth of the air getting at plowed ground. You know I told you the lord of all labor by which man lived was Hephæstus; therefore Athena adopts a child of his, and of the earth— Erichthonius—literally, " the tearer up of the ground "

—who is the head (though not in direct line) of the kings of Attica; and having adopted him, she gives him to be brought up by the three nymphs of the dew. Of these, Aglauros, the dweller in the fields, is the envy or malice of the earth; she answers nearly to the envy of Cain, the tiller of the ground against his shepherd brother, in her own envy against her two sisters, Herse the cloud dew, who is the beloved of the shepherd Mercury; and Pandrosos, the diffused dew, or words of heaven. Literally, you have in this myth the dew of the blessing of Esau—"Thy dwelling shall be of the fatness of the earth, and of the dew of heaven from above." Aglauros is for her envy turned into a black stone; and hers is one of the voices—the other being that of Cain—which haunts the circle of envy in the Purgatory:

" Io sono Aglauro, chi divenne sasso."

But to her two sisters, with Erichthonius (or the hero Erectheus), is built the most sacred temple of Athena in Athens; the temple to their own dearest Athena— to her, and to the dew together; so that it was divided into two parts: one, the temple of Athena of the city, and the other that of the dew. And this expression of her power, as the air bringing the dew to the hill pastures, in the central temple of the central city of the heathen, dominant over the future intellectual world, is, of all the facts connected with her worship as the spirit of life, perhaps the most important. I have no time now to trace for you the hundredth part of the different ways in which it bears both upon natural beauty, and on the best order and happiness of men's lives. I hope to follow out some of these trains of thought in gathering together what I have to say about field herbage; but I must say briefly here that the great sign, to the Greeks, of the coming of spring in the pastures, was not, as with us, in the primrose, but in the various flowers of the asphodel tribe (of which I will give you some separate account presently); therefore it is that the earth answers with crocus flame to the cloud on Ida; and the power of Athena in eternal life is written by the light of the asphodel on the Elysian fields.

But farther, Athena is the air, not only to the lilies of the field, but to the leaves of the forest. We saw before the reason why Hermes is said to be the son of Maia, the eldest of the sister stars of spring. Those stars are called not only Pleiades, but Vergiliæ, from a word mingling the ideas of the turning or returning of spring-time with the outpouring of rain. The mother of Virgil bearing the name of Maia, Virgil himself received his name from the seven stars; and he, in forming, first, the mind of Dante, and through him that of Chaucer (besides whatever special minor influence came from the Pastorals and Georgics), became the fountain-head of all the best literary power connected with the love of vegetative nature among civilized races of men. Take the fact for what it is worth; still it is a strange seal of coincidence, in word and in reality, upon the Greek dream of the power over human life, and its purest thoughts, in the stars of spring. But the first syllable of the name of Virgil has relation also to another group of words, of which the English ones, virtue, and virgin, bring down the force to modern days. It is a group containing mainly the idea of "spring" or increase of life in vegetation —the rising of the new branch of the tree out of the bud, and of the new leaf out of the ground. It involves, secondarily, the idea of greenness and of strength but primarily, that of living increase of a new rod from a stock, stem, or root (" There shall come forth a rod out of the stem of Jesse "); and chiefly the stem of certain plants—either of the rose tribe, as in the budding of the almond rod of Aaron ; or of the olive tribe, which has triple significance in this symbolism, from the use of its oil for sacred anointing, for strength in the gymnasium, and for light. Hence, in numberless divided and reflected ways, it is connected with the power of Hercules and Athena : Hercules plants the wild olive, for its shade, on the course of Olympia, and it thenceforward gives the Olympic crown of consummate honor and rest ; while the prize at the Panathenaic games is a vase of its oil (meaning encouragement to continuance of effort) ; and from the paintings on these Panathenaic vases we get the most precious clue to the entire character of Athena. Then to express its propagation by slips, the trees from which the oil was to be taken were called "Moriai," trees of division (being all descendants of the sacred one in the Erechtheum). And thus, in one direction, we get to the "children like olive plants round about thy table" and the olive grafting of St. Paul; while the use of the oil for anointing gives chief name to the rod itself by the stem of Jesse, and to all those who were by that name signed for his disciples first in Antioch. Remember, farther, since that name was first given, the influence of the symbol, both in extreme unction, and in consecration of priests and kings to their "divine right;" and think, if you can reach with any grasp of thought, what the influence on the earth has been, of those twisted branches whose leaves give gray bloom to the hill-sides under every breeze that blows from the midland sea. But, above and beyond all, think how strange it is that the chief Agonia of humanity, and the chief giving of strength from heaven for its fulfillment, should have been under its night shadow in Palestine.

39. Thirdly—Athena is the air in its power over the sea.

On the earliest Panathenaic vase known—the "Burgon" vase in the British museum—Athena has a dolphin on her shield. The dolphin has two principal meanings in Greek symbolism. It means, first, the sea; secondarily, the ascending and descending course of any of the heavenly bodies from one sea horizon to another—the dolphins' arching rise and replunge (in a summer evening, out of calm sea, their black backs roll round with exactly the slow motion of a water-wheel; but I do not know how far Aristotle's exaggerated account of their leaping or their swiftness has any foundation) being taken as a type of the emergence of the sun or stars from the sea in the east, and plunging beneath in the west. Hence, Apollo, when in his personal power he crosses the sea, leading his Cretan colonists to Pytho, takes the form of a dolphin, becomes Apollo Delphinius, and names the founded colony "Delphi." The lovely drawing of the Delphic Apollo on the hydria of the Vatican (Le Normand and De Witte, vol. ii. p. 6), gives the entire conception of this myth. Again, the beautiful coins of Tarentum represent Taras coming to found the city, riding on a dolphin, whose leaps and plunges have partly the rage of the sea in them, and partly the spring of the horse, because the splendid riding of the Tarentines had made their name proverbial in Magna Græcia. The story of Arion is a collateral fragment of the same thought; and, again, the plunge before their transformation, of the ships of Æneas. Then, this idea of career upon, or conquest of the sea, either by the creatures themselves, or by dolphin-like ships (compare the Merlin prophecy :

> " They shall ride
> Over ocean wide
> With hempen bridle, and horse of tree,")

connects itself with the thought of undulation, and of the wave-power in the sea itself, which is always expressed by the serpentine bodies either of the sea-gods or of the sea-horse; and when Athena carries, as she does often in later work, a serpent for her shield-sign, it is not so much the repetition of her own ægis-snakes as the farther expression of her power over the sea-wave ; which, finally, Virgil gives in its perfect unity with her own anger, in the approach of the serpents against Laocoon from the sea ; and then, finally, when her own storm-power is fully put forth on the ocean also, and the madness of the ægis-snake is given to the wave-snake, the sea-wave becomes the devouring hound at the waist of Scylla, and Athena takes Scylla for her helmet-crest; while yet her beneficent and essential power on the ocean, in making navigation possible, is commemorated in the Panathenaic festival by her peplus being carried to the Erechtheum suspended from the mast of a ship.

In plate cxv. of vol. ii., Le Normand, are given two sides of a vase, which, in rude and childish way, assembles most of the principal thoughts regarding Athena in this relation. In the first, the sunrise is represented by the ascending chariot of Apollo, foreshortened; the light is supposed to blind the eyes, and no face of the god is seen (Turner, in the Ulysses and Polyphemus sunrise, loses the form of the god in light, giving the chariot-horses only; rendering in his own manner, after two thousand two hundred years of various fall and revival of the arts, precisely the same thought as the old Greek potter). He ascends out of the sea; but the sea itself has not yet caught the light. In the second design, Athena as the morning breeze, and Hermes as the morning cloud, fly over the sea before the sun. Hermes turns back his head; his face is unseen in the cloud, as Apollo's in the light; the grotesque appearance of an animal's face is only the cloud-phantasm modifying a frequent form of the hair of Hermes beneath the back of his cap. Under the morning breeze, the dolphins leap from the rippled sea, and their sides catch the light.

The coins of the Lucanian Heracleia give a fair representation of the helmed Athena, as imagined in later Greek art, with the embossed Scylla.

40. Fourthly: Athena is the air nourishing artificial light — unconsuming fire. Therefore, a lamp was always kept burning in the Erechtheum; and the torch-race belongs chiefly to her festival, of which the meaning is to show the danger of the perishing of the light even by excess of the air that nourishes it: and so that the race is not to the swift, but to the wise.

The household use of her constant light is symbolized in the lovely passage in the Odyssey, where Ulysses and his son move the armor while the servants are shut in their chambers and there is no one to hold torches for them; but Athena herself, "having a golden lamp," fills all the rooms with light. Her presence in war-strength with her favorite heroes is always shown by the "unwearied" fire hovering on their helmets and shields; and the image gradually becomes constant and accepted, both for the maintenance of household watchfulness, as in the parable of the ten virgins, or as the symbol of direct inspiration, in the rushing wind and divided flames of Pentecost: but together with this thought of unconsuming and constant fire, there is always mingled in the Greek mind the sense of the consuming by excess, as of the flame by the air, so also of the inspired creature by its own fire (thus, again, "the zeal of thine house hath eaten me up"—"my zeal hath consumed me, because of thine enemies," and the like); and especially Athena has this aspect toward the truly sensual and bodily strength; so that to Ares, who is himself insane and consuming, the opposite wisdom seems to be insane and consuming: "All we the other gods have thee against us, O Jove! when we would give grace to men; for thou hast begotten the maid without a mind —the mischievous creature, the doer of unseemly evil. All we obey thee and are ruled by thee. Her only thou wilt not resist in anything she says or does, because thou didst bear her—consuming child as she is."

41. Lastly: Athena is the air, conveying vibration of sound.

In all the loveliest representations in central Greek art of the birth of Athena, Apollo stands close to the sitting Jupiter, singing with a deep, quiet joyfulness, to his lyre. The sun is always thought of as the master of time and rhythm, and as the origin of the composing and inventive discovery of melody; but the air, as the actual element and substance of the voice, the prolonging and sustaining power of it, and the symbol of its moral passion. Whatever in music is measured and designed, belongs therefore to Apollo and the Muses; whatever is impulsive and passionate to Athena: hence her constant strength of voice or cry (as when she aids the shout of Achilles) curiously opposed to the dumbness of Demeter. The Apolline lyre, therefore, is not so much the instrument producing sound, as its measurer and divider by length or tension of string into given notes, and I believe it is in a double connection with its office as a measurer of time or motion, and its relation to the transit of the sun in the sky, that Hermes forms it from the tortoise-shell, which is the image of the dappled concave of the cloudy sky. Thenceforward all the limiting or restraining modes of music belong to the Muses; but the passionate music is wind music, as in the Doric flute. Then, when this inspired music becomes degraded in its passion, it sinks into the pipe of Pan, and the double pipe of Marsyas, and is then rejected by Athena. The myth which represents her doing so is that she invented the double pipe from hearing the hiss of the Gorgonian serpents; but when she played upon it, chancing to see her face reflected in water, she saw that it was distorted, whereupon she threw down the flute, which Marsyas found. Then, the strife of Apollo and Marsyas represents the enduring contest between music in which the words and thought lead, and the lyre measures or melodizes them (which Pindar means when he calls his hymns "kings over the lyre"), and music in which the words are lost and the wind or impulse leads—generally, therefore, between intellectual, and brutal, or meaningless, music. Therefore, when Apollo prevails, he flays Marsyas, taking the limit and external bond of his shape from him, which is death, without touching the mere muscular strength; yet shameful and dreadful in dissolution.

42. And the opposition of these two kinds of sound is continually dwelt upon by the Greek philosophers, the real fact at the root of all their teaching being this—that true music is the natural expression of a lofty passion for a right cause; that in proportion to the kingliness and force of any personality,

the expression either of its joy or suffering becomes measured, chastened, calm, and capable of interpretation only by the majesty of ordered, beautiful, and worded sound. Exactly in proportion to the degree in which we become narrow in the cause and conception of our passions, incontinent in the utterance of them, feeble of perseverance in them, sullied or shameful in the indulgence of them, their expression by musical sound becomes broken, mean, fatuitous, and at last impossible; the measured waves of the air of heaven will not lend themselves to expression of ultimate vice, it must be forever sunk into discordance or silence. And since, as before stated, every work of right art has a tendency to reproduce the ethical state which first developed it, this, which of all the arts is most directly ethical in origin, is also the most direct in power of discipline; the first, the simplest, the most effective of all instruments of moral instruction; while in the failure and betrayal of its functions, it becomes the subtlest aid of moral degradation. Music is thus, in her health, the teacher of perfect order, and is the voice of the obedience of angels, and the companion of the course of the spheres of heaven; and in her depravity she is also the teacher of perfect disorder and disobedience, and the Gloria in Excelsis becomes the Marseillaise. In the third section of this volume, I reprint two chapters from another essay of mine ("The Cestus of Aglaia"), on modesty or measure, and on liberty, containing farther reference to music in her two powers; and I do this now, because, among the many monstrous and misbegotten fantasies which are the spawn of modern license, perhaps the most impishly opposite to the truth is the conception of music which has rendered possible the writing, by educated persons, and, more strangely yet, the tolerant criticism, of such words as these: "*This so persuasive art is the only one that has no didactic efficacy, that engenders no emotions save such as are without issue on the side of moral truth, that expresses nothing of God, nothing of reason, nothing of human liberty.*" I will not give the author's name; the passage is quoted in the *Westminster Review* for last January [1869].

43. I must also anticipate something of what I have to say respecting the relation of the power of Athena to organic life, so far as to note that her name, Pallas, probably refers to the quivering or vibration of the air; and to its power, whether as vital force, or communicated wave, over every kind of matter, in giving it vibratory movement; first, and most intense, in the voice and throat of the bird; which is the air incarnate; and so descending through the various orders of animal life to the vibrating and semi-voluntary murmur of the insect; and, lower still, to the hiss, or quiver of the tail, of the half-lunged snake and deaf adder; all these, nevertheless, being wholly under the rule of Athena as representing either breath, or vital

nervous power; and, therefore, also in their simplicity, the "oaten pipe and pastoral song," which belong to her dominion over the asphodel meadows, and breathe on their banks of violets.

Finally, is it not strange to think of the influence of this one power of Pallas in vibration (we shall see a singular mechanical energy of it presently in the serpent's motion); in the voices of war and peace? How much of the repose—how much of the wrath, folly and misery of men, has literally depended on this one power of the air—on the sound of the trumpet and of the bell—on the lark's song and the bee's murmur.

44. Such is the general conception in the Greek mind of the physical power of Athena. The spiritual power associated with it is of two kinds; first, she is the spirit of life in material organism; not strength in the blood only, but formative energy in the clay: and, secondly, she is inspired and impulsive wisdom in human conduct and human art, giving the instinct of infallible decision and of faultless invention.

It is quite beyond the scope of my present purpose—and, indeed, will only be possible for me at all after marking the relative intention of the Apolline myths —to trace for you the Greek conception of Athena as the guide of moral passion. But I will at least endeavor, on some near occasion,* to define some of the

---

* I have tried to do this in mere outline in the two following sections of this volume.

actual truths respecting the vital force in created organism and inventive fancy in the works of man, which are more or less expressed by the Greeks, under the personality of Athena. You would, perhaps, hardly bear with me if I endeavored farther to show you—what is nevertheless perfectly true—the analogy between the spiritual power of Athena in her gentle ministry, yet irresistible anger, with the ministry of another spirit whom we also, holding for the universal power of life, are forbidden, at our worst peril, to quench or to grieve.

45. But, I think to-night, you should not let me close without requiring of me an answer on one vital point, namely, how far these imaginations of gods—which are vain to us—were vain to those who had no better trust? and what real belief the Greek had in these creations of his own spirit, practical and helpful to him in the sorrow of earth? I am able to answer you explicitly in this. The origin of his thoughts is often obscure and we may err in endeavoring to account for their form of realization; but the effect of that realization on his life is not obscure at all. The Greek creed was, of course, different in its character, as our own creed is, according to the class of persons who held it. The common people's was quite literal, simple and happy: their idea of Athena was as clear as a good Roman Catholic peasant's idea of the Madonna. In Athens itself, the center of thought

and refinement, Pisistratus obtained the reins of government through the ready belief of the populace that a beautiful woman, armed like Athena, was the goddess herself. Even at the close of the last century some of this simplicity remained among the inhabitants of the Greek islands ; and when a pretty English lady first made her way into the grotto of Antiparos, she was surrounded on her return, by all the women of the neighboring village, believing her to be divine, and praying her to heal them of their sicknesses.

46. Then, secondly, the creed of the upper classes was more refined and spiritual, but quite as honest, and even more forcible in its effect on the life. You might imagine that the employment of the artifice just referred to implied utter unbelief in the persons contriving it ; but it really meant only that the more worldly of them would play with a popular faith for their own purposes, as doubly-minded persons have often done since, all the while sincerely holding the same ideas themselves in a more abstract form ; while the good and unworldly men, the true Greek heroes, lived by their faith as firmly as St. Louis, or the Cid, or the Chevalier Bayard.

47. Then, thirdly, the faith of the poets and artists was, necessarily, less definite, being continually modified by the involuntary action of their own fancies ; and by the necessity of presenting, in clear ver-

bal or material form, things of which they had no authoritative knowledge. Their faith was, in some respects, like Dante's or Milton's: firm in general conception, but not able to vouch for every detail in the forms they gave it: but they went considerably farther, even in that minor sincerity, than subsequent poets; and strove with all their might to be as near the truth as they could. Pindar says, quite simply: "I cannot think so-and-so of the gods. It must have been this way—it cannot have been that way—that the thing was done." And as late among the Latins as the days of Horace, this sincerity remains. Horace is just as true and simple in his religion as Wordsworth; but all power of understanding any of the honest classic poets has been taken away from most English gentleman by the mechanical drill in verse-writing at school. Throughout the whole of their lives afterward, they never can get themselves quit of the notion that all verses were written as an exercise, and that Minerva was only a convenient word for the last of an hexameter, and Jupiter for the last but one.

48. It is impossible that any notion can be more fallacious or more misleading in its consequences. All great song, from the first day when human lips contrived syllables, has been sincere song. With deliberate didactic purpose the tragedians—with pure and native passion the lyrists—fitted their perfect words to their dearest faiths. "*Operosa parvus carmina*

fingo." "I, little thing that I am, weave my laborious songs" as earnestly as the bee among the bells of thyme on the Matin mountains. Yes, and he dedicates his favorite pine to Diana, and he chants his autumnal hymn to the Faun that guards his fields, and he guides the noble youths and maids of Rome in their choir to Apollo, and he tells the farmer's little girl that the gods will love her, though she has only a handful of salt and meal to give them—just as earnestly as ever English gentleman taught Christian faith to English youth in England's truest days.

49. Then, lastly, the creed of the philosophers of sages varied according to the character and knowledge of each; their relative acquaintance with the secrets of natural science—their intellectual and sectarian egotism—and their mystic or monastic tendencies, for there is a classic as well as a mediæval monasticism. They ended in losing the life of Greece in play upon words; but we owe to their early thought some of the soundest ethics and the foundation of the best practical laws, yet known to mankind.

50. Such was the general vitality of the heathen creed in its strength. Of its direct influence on conduct, it is, as I said, impossible for me to speak now; only, remember always, in endeavoring to form a judgment of it, that what of good or right the heathens did, they did looking for no reward. The purest forms of our own religion have always consisted in

sacrificing less things to win greater; time, to win eternity—the world, to win the skies. The order, "sell that thou hast," is not given without the promise, "thou shalt have treasure in heaven;" and well for the modern Christian if he accepts the alternative as his Master left it—and does not practically read the command and promise thus: "Sell that thou hast in the best market and thou shalt have treasure in eternity also." But the poor Greeks of the great ages expected no reward from heaven but honor, and no reward from earth but rest; though, when on those conditions, they patiently and proudly fulfilled their task of the granted day, an unreasoning instinct of an immortal benediction broke from their lips in song: and they, even they, had sometimes a prophet to tell them of a land "where there is sun alike by day and alike by night—where they shall need no more to trouble the earth by strength of hands for daily bread—but the ocean breezes blow around the blessed islands and golden flowers burn on their bright trees for evermore."

II.

ATHENA KERAMITIS.*

(*Athena in the Earth.*)

Study, supplementary to the preceeding lecture, of the supposed, and actual, relations of Athena to the vital force in material organism.

51. It has been easy to decipher approximately the Greek conception of the physical power of Athena in cloud and sky, because we know ourselves what clouds and skies are, and what the force of the wind is in forming them. But it is not at all easy to trace the Greek thoughts about the power of Athena in giving life, because we do not ourselves know clearly what life is, or in what way the air is necessary to it, or what there is, besides the air, shaping the forms that it is put into. And it is comparatively of small consequence to find out what the Greeks thought or meant, until we have determined what we ourselves think, or mean, when we translate the Greek word for "breathing" into the Latin-English word "spirit."

52. But it is of great consequence that you should

---

* "Athena, fit for being made into pottery." I coin the expression as a counterpart of λῆ παρθένια, "Clay intact."

fix in your minds—and hold, against the baseness of mere materialism on the one hand, and against the fallacies of controversial speculation on the other—the certain and practical sense of this word " spirit "—the sense in which you all know that its reality exists, as the power which shaped you into your shape, and by which you love, and hate, when you have received that shape. You need not fear, on the one hand, that either the sculpturing or the loving power can ever be beaten down by the philosophers into a metal, or evolved by them into a gas; but on the other hand, take care that you yourselves, in trying to elevate your conception of it, do not lose its truth in a dream, or even in a word. Beware always of contending for words : you will find them not easy to grasp, if you know them in several languages. This very word, which is so solemn in your mouths, is one of the most doubtful. In Latin, it means little more than breathing, and may mean merely accent; in French it is not breath, but wit, and our neighbors are therefore obliged, even in their most solemn expressions, to say " wit " when we say " ghost." In Greek, " pneuma," the word we translate " ghost," means either wind or breath, and the relative word " psyche," has, perhaps, a more subtle power ; yet St. Paul's words " pneumatic body " and " psychic body," involve a difference in his mind which no words will explain. But in Greek and in English, and in Saxon and in Hebrew, and in every articulate tongue of humanity the "spirit of man" truly means his passion and virtue, and is stately according to the height of his conception, and stable according to the measure of his endurance.

53. Endurance, or patience, that is the central sign of spirit; a constancy against the cold and agony of death; and as, physically, it is by the burning power of the air that the heat of the flesh is sustained, so this Athena, spiritually, is the queen of all glowing virtue, the unconsuming fire and inner lamp of life. And thus, as Hephæstus is lord of the fire of the hand and Apollo of the fire of the brain, so Athena of the fire of the heart; and as Hercules wears for his chief armor the skin of the Nemean lion, his chief enemy, whom he slew: and Apollo has for his highest name "the Pythian," from his chief enemy, the python, slain; so Athena bears always on her breast the deadly face of her chief enemy slain, the Gorgonian cold, and venomous agony, that turns living men to stone.

54. And so long as you have that fire of the heart within you, and know the reality of it, you need be under no alarm as to the possibility of its chemical or mechanical analysis. The philosophers are very humorous in their ecstasy of hope about it; but the real interest of their discoveries in this direction is very small to human-kind. It is quite true that the tympanum of the ear vibrates under sound, and that

the surface of the water in a ditch vibrates too: but the ditch hears nothing for all that: and my hearing is still to me as blessed a mystery as ever, and the interval between the ditch and me, quite as great. If the trembling sound in my ears was once of the marriage-bell which began my happiness, and is now of the passing-bell which ends it, the difference between those two sounds to me cannot be counted by the number of concussions. There have been some curious speculations lately as to the conveyance of mental consciousness by "brain-waves." What does it matter how it is conveyed? The consciousness itself is not a wave. It may be accompanied here or there by any quantity of quivers and shakes, up or down, of anything you can find in the universe that is shakeable—what is that to me? My friend is dead, and my—according to modern views—vibratory sorrow is not one whit less, or less mysterious, to me, than my old quiet one.

55. Beyond, and entirely unaffected by, any questionings of this kind, there are, therefore, two plain facts which we should all know: first, that there is a power which gives their several shapes to things, or capacities of shape; and, secondly, a power which gives them their several feelings, or capacities of feeling; and that we can increase or destroy both of these at our will. By care and tenderness, we can extend the range of lovely life in plants and animals; by our

neglect and cruelty, we can arrest it, and bring pestilence in its stead. Again, by right discipline we can increase our strength of noble will and passion, or destroy both. And whether these two forces are local conditions of the elements in which they appear, or are part of a great force in the universe, out of which they are taken, and to which they must be restored, is not of the slightest importance to us in dealing with them; neither is the manner of their connection with light and air. What precise meaning we ought to attach to expressions such as that of the prophecy to the four winds that the dry bones might be breathed upon and might live, or why the presence of the vital-power should be dependent on the chemical action of the air and its awful passing away materially signified by the rendering up of that breath or ghost, we cannot at present know, and need not at any time dispute. What we assuredly know is that the states of life and death are different, and the first more desirable than the other, and by effort attainable, whether we understand being "born of the spirit" to signify having the breath of heaven in our flesh, or its power in our hearts.

56. As to its power on the body, I will endeavor to tell you, having been myself much led into studies involving necessary reference both to natural science and mental phenomena, what, at least, remains to us after science has done its worst; what the myth of

Athena, as a formative and decisive power—a spirit of creation and volition, must eternally mean for all of us.

57. It is now (I believe I may use the strong word) "ascertained" that heat and motion are fixed in quantity, and measurable in the portions that we deal with. We can measure out portions of power, as we can measure portions of space; while yet, as far as we know, space may be infinite, and force infinite. There may be heat as much greater than the sun's, as the sun's heat is greater than a candle's; and force as much greater than the force by which the world swings, as that is greater than the force by which a cobweb trembles. Now, on heat and force, life is inseparably dependent; and I believe, also, on a form of substance, which the philosophers call "protoplasm." I wish they would use English instead of Greek words. When I want to know why a leaf is green, they tell me it is colored by "chlorophyll," which at first sounds very instructive; but if they would only say plainly that a leaf is colored green by a thing which is called "green leaf," we should see more precisely how far we had got. However, it is a curious fact that life is connected with a cellular structure called protoplasm, or, in English, "first stuck together:" whence, conceivably through deuteroplasms, or second stickings, and tritoplasms, or third stickings,* we reach the

---

* Or, perhaps, we may be indulged with one consummating gleam

highest plastic phase in the human pottery, which differs from common chinaware, primarily, by a measureable degree of heat, developed in breathing, which it borrows from the rest of the universe while it lives, and which it as certainly returns to the rest of the universe, when it dies.

58. Again, with this heat certain assimilative powers are connected, which the tendency of recent discovery is to simplify more and more into modes of one force; or finally into mere motion, communicable in various states, but not destructible. We will assume that science has done its utmost; and that every chemical or animal force is demonstrably resolvable into heat or motion, reciprocally changing into each other. I would myself like better, in order of thought, to consider motion as a mode of heat than heat as a mode of motion : still, granting that we have got thus far, we have yet to ask, what is heat? or what motion? What is this "*primo mobile*," this transitional power, in which all things live, and move, and have their be-

---

of "glycasm"—visible "Sweetness"—according to the good old monk "Full moon," or "All moonshine." I cannot get at his original Greek, but am content with M. Durand's clear French (Manual d'Iconographie Chrétienne. Paris 1845): "Lorsque vous aurez fait le proplasme, et esquissé un visage, vous ferez les chairs avec le glycasme dont nous avons donné la recette. Chez lef vieillards, vous indiquerez les rides, et chez les jeunes gens, les angles dez yeux. C'est ainsi qui l'on fait les chairs, suivant Panselinos."

ing? It is by definition something different from matter, and we may call it as we choose—"first cause," or "first light," or "first heat;" but we can show no scientific proof of its not being personal, and coinciding with the ordinary conception of a supporting spirit in all things.

59. Still, it is not advisable to apply the word "spirit" or "breathing" to it, while it is only enforcing chemical affinities; but, when the chemical affinities are brought under the influence of the air, and of the sun's heat, the formative force enters an entirely different phase. It does not now merely crystallize indefinite masses, but it gives to limited portions of matter the power of gathering, selectively, other elements proper to them, and binding these elements into their own peculiar and adopted form.

This force, now properly called life, or breathing, or spirit, is continually creating its own shells of definite shape out of the wreck round it: and this is what I meant by saying, in the "Ethics of the Dust"—"you may always stand by form against force." For the mere force of junction is not spirit; but the power that catches out of chaos charcoal, water, lime, or what not and fastens them down into a given form, is properly called "spirit;" and we shall not diminish, but strengthen our conception of this creative energy by recognizing its presence in lower states of matter than our own—such recognition being enforced upon us by delight we instinctively receive from all the forms of matter which manifest it; and yet more, by the glorifying of those forms, in the parts of them that are most animated, with the colors that are pleasantest to our senses. The most familiar instance of this is the best, and also the most wonderful: the blossoming of plants.

60. The spirit in the plant—that is to say, its power of gathering dead matter out of the wreck round it, and shaping it into its own chosen shape—is of course strongest at the moment of its flowering, for it then not only gathers, but forms, with the greatest energy.

And where this life is in it at full power, its form becomes invested with aspects that are chiefly delightful to our own human passions; namely, first, with the loveliest outlines of shape; and secondly, with the most brilliant phases of the primary colors, blue, yellow, and red or white, the unison of all; and, to make it all more strange, this time of peculiar and perfect glory is associated with relations of the plants or blossoms to each other, correspondent to the joy of love in human creatures, and having the same object in the continuance of the race. Only, with respect to plants, as animals, we are wrong in speaking as if the object of this strong life were only the bequeathing of itself. The flower is the end or proper object of the seed, not the seed of the flower. The reason for seeds is that flowers may be; not the reason of flowers that seeds may be. The flower itself is the creature which the spirit makes; only, in connection with its perfectness, is placed the giving birth to its successor.

61. The main fact, then, about a flower is that it is the part of the plant's form developed at the moment of its intensest life: and this inner rapture is usually marked externally for us by the flush of one or more of the primary colors. What the character of the flower shall be, depends entirely upon the portion of the plant into which this rapture of spirit has been put. Sometimes the life is put into its outer sheath, and then the outer sheath becomes white and pure, and full of strength and grace; sometimes the life is put into the common leaves, just under the blossom, and they become scarlet or purple; sometimes the life is put into the stalks of the flower and they flush blue; sometimes into its outer inclosure or calyx; mostly into its inner cup; but, in all cases the presence of the strongest life is asserted by characters in which the human sight takes pleasure, and which seem prepared with distinct reference to us, or rather, bear, in being delightful, evidence of having been produced by the power of the same spirit as our own.

62. And we are led to feel this still more strongly because all the distinctions of species,* both in plants

---

* The facts on which I am about to dwell are in no wise antagonistic to the theories which Mr. Darwin's unwearied and unerring in-

and animals, appear to have similar connection with human character. Whatever the origin of species may be, or however those species, once formed, may be influenced by external accident, the groups into which birth or accident have reduced them have distinct relation to the spirit of man. It is perfectly possible, and ultimately conceivable, that the crocodile and the lamb may have descended from the same ancestral atom of protoplasm; and that the physical laws of the operation of calcareous slime and of meadow grass, on that protoplasm, may in time have developed opposite natures and aspects of the living frames; but the practically important fact for us is the existence of a power which creates that calcareous earth itself—which creates, that separately—and quartz, separately; and gold, separately; and charcoal, separately; and then so directs the relation of these elements as that the gold shall destroy the souls of men by being yellow; and the charcoal destroy their souls by being hard and bright; and the quartz represent to them an ideal purity; and the calcareous earth, soft, shall beget crocodiles, and dry and hard, sheep; and that the as-

vestigations are every day rendering more probable. The æsthetic relations of species are independent of their origin. Nevertheless, it has always seemed to me, in what little work I have done upon organic forms, as if the species mocked us by their deliberate imitation of each other when they met: yet did not pass one into another.

pects and qualities of these two products, crocodiles and lambs, shall be, the one repellent to the spirit of man, the other attractive to it, in a quite inevitable way; representing to him states of moral evil and good; and becoming myths to him of destruction or redemption, and, in the most literal sense, "words" of God.

63. And the force of these facts cannot be escaped from by the thought that there are species innumerable, passing into each other by regular gradations, out of which we choose what we most love or dread, and say they were indeed prepared for us. Species are not innumerable; neither are they now connected by consistent gradation. They touch at certain points only; and even then are connected, when we examine them deeply, in a kind of reticulated way, not in chains, but in checkers; also, however connected, it is but by a touch of the extremities, as it were, and the characteristic form of the species is entirely individual. The rose nearly sinks into a grass in the sanguisorba; but the formative spirit does not the less clearly separate the ear of wheat from the dog-rose, and oscillate with tremulous constancy round the central forms of both, having each their due relation to the mind of man. The great animal kingdoms are connected in the same way. The bird through the penguin drops toward the fish, and the fish in the cetacean reascends to the mammal,

yet there is no confusion of thought possible between the perfect forms of an eagle, a trout, and a war-horse, in their relations to the elements, and to man.

64. Now we have two orders of animals to take some note of in connection with Athena, and one vast order of plants, which will illustrate this matter very sufficiently for us.

The orders of animals are the serpent and the bird; the serpent, in which the breath or spirit is less than in any other creature, and the earth-power greatest—the bird, in which the breath or spirit is more full than in any other creature, and the earth power least.

65. We will take the bird first. It is little more than a drift of the air brought into form by plumes; the air is in all its quills, it breathes through its whole frame and flesh, and glows with air in its flying, like blown flame: it rests upon the air, subdues it, surpasses it, outraces it; *is* the air, conscious of itself, conquering itself, ruling itself.

Also, in the throat of the bird is given the voice of the air. All that in the wind itself is weak, wild, useless in sweetness, is knit together in its song. As we may imagine the wild form of the cloud closed into the perfect form of the bird's wings, so the wild voice of the cloud into its ordered and commanded voice; unwearied, rippling through the clear heaven in its gladness, interpreting all intense passion through the soft spring nights, bursting into acclaim and rapture of choir at daybreak, or lisping and twittering among the boughs and hedges through heat of day, like little winds that only make the cow-slip bells shake, and ruffle the petals of the wild rose.

66. Also, upon the plumes of the bird are put the colors of the air: on these the gold of the cloud, that cannot be gathered by any covetousness; the rubies of the clouds that are not the price of Athena, but *are* Athena; the vermilion of the cloud-bar and the flame of the cloud-crest and the snow of the cloud, and its shadow, and the melted blue of the deep wells of the sky—all these, seized by the creating spirit and woven by Athena herself into films and threads of plume; with wave on wave following and fading along breast and throat and opened wings, infinite as the dividing of the foam and the sifting of the sea-sand; even the white down of the cloud seeming to flutter up between the stronger plumes, seen, but too soft for touch.

And so the spirit of the air is put into and upon this created form; and it becomes, through twenty centuries, the symbol of divine help, descending, as the fire, to speak, but as the dove, to bless.

67. Next, in the serpent, we approach the source of a group of myths, world-wide, founded on great and common human instincts, respecting which I must note one or two points which bear intimately on all

our subject. For it seems to me that the scholars who are at present occupied in interpretation of human myths have most of them forgotten that there are any such things as natural myths; and that the dark sayings of men may be both difficult to read and not always worth reading; but the dark sayings of nature will probably become clearer for the looking into and will very certainly be worth reading. And, indeed, all guidance to the right sense of the human and variable myths will probably depend on our first getting at the sense of the natural and invariable ones. The dead hieroglyph may have meant this or that— the living hieroglyph means always the same; but remember, it is just as much a hieroglyph as the other; nay, more, a " sacred or reserved sculpture," a thing with an inner language. The serpent crest of the king's crown, or of the god's, on the pillars of Egypt, is a mystery; but the serpent itself, gliding past the pillar's foot, is it less a mystery? Is there indeed, no tongue, except the mute forked flash from its lips, in that running brook of horror on the ground?

68. Why that horror? We all feel it, yet how imaginative it is, how disproportioned to the real strength of the creature! There is more poison in an ill-kept drain, in a pool of dish-washings at a cottage door, than in the deadliest asp of Nile. Every back-yard which you look down into from the railway, as

it carries you out by Vauxhall or Deptford, holds its coiled serpent: all the walls of those ghastly suburbs are enclosures of tank temples for serpent-worship; yet you feel no horror in looking down into them, as you would if you saw the livid scales and lifted head. There is more venom, mortal, inevitable, in a single word, sometimes, or in the gliding entrance of a wordless thought, than ever *"vanti Libia con sua rena."* But that horror is of the myth, not of the creature. There are myriads lower than this and more loathsome, in the scale of being; the links between dead matter and animation drift everywhere unseen. But it is the strength of the base element that is so dreadful in the serpent; it is the very omnipotence of the earth. That rivulet of smooth silver—how does it flow, think you? It literally rows on the earth with every scale for an oar; it bites the dust with the ridges of its body. Watch it, when it moves slowly: A wave, but without wind! a current, but with no fall! all the body moving at the same instant, yet some of it to one side, some to another, or some forward and the rest of the coil backward; but all with the same calm will and equal way—no contraction, no extension; one soundless, causeless march of sequent rings and spectral procession of spotted dust, with dissolution in its fangs, dislocation in its coils. Startle it; the winding stream will become a twisted arrow; the wave of poisoned life will lash through the grass

like a cast lance.* It scarcely breathes with its one
lung (the other shriveled and abortive); it is passive
to the sun and shade and is cold or hot like a stone;
yet " it can outclimb the monkey, outswim the fish,
outleap the zebra, outwrestle the athlete and crush
the tiger." † It is a divine hieroglyph of the de-
moniac power of the earth, of the entire earthly
nature. As the bird is the clothed power of the air,
so this is the clothed power of the dust; as the bird
the symbol of the spirit of life, so this of the grasp
and sting of death.

69. Hence the continual change in the interpretation put upon it in various religions. As the worm of
corruption, it is the mightiest of all adversaries of the

---

*I cannot understand this swift forward motion of serpents. The
seizure of prey by the constrictor, though invisibly swift, is quite
simple in mechanism; it is simply the return to its coil of an opened
watch-spring and is just as instantaneous. But the steady and continuous motion, without a visible fulcrum (for the whole body moves
at the same instant, and I have often seen even small snakes glide as
fast as I could walk), seems to involve a vibration of the scales quite
too rapid to be conceived. The motion of the crest and dorsal fin of
the hippocampus, which is one of the intermediate types between
serpent and fish, perhaps gives some resemblance of it, dimly visible
for the quivering turns the fin into a mere mist. The entrance of
the two barbs of a bee's sting by alternate motion, " the teeth of one
barb acting as a fulcrum for the other," must be something like the
serpent motion on a small scale.

† Richard Owen.

gods—the special adversary of their light and creative power—Python against Apollo. As the power of the earth against the air, the giants are serpent-bodied in the Gigantomachia; but as the power of the earth upon the seed—consuming it into new life ("that which thou sowest is not quickened except it die")—serpents sustain the chariot of the spirit of agriculture.

70. Yet, on the other hand, there is a power in the earth to take away corruption, and to purify (hence the very fact of burial, and many uses of earth, only lately known); and in this sense, the serpent is a healing spirit—the representative of Æsculapius, and of Hygieia; and is a sacred earth-type in the temple of the dew; being there especially a symbol of the native earth of Athens; so that its departure from the temple was a sign to the Athenians that they were to leave their homes. And then, lastly, as there is a strength and healing in the earth, no less than the strength of air, so there is conceived to be a wisdom of earth no less than a wisdom of the spirit; and when its deadly power is killed, its guiding power becomes true; so that the Python serpent is killed at Delphi, where yet the oracle is from the breath of the earth.

71. You must remember, however, that in this, as in every other instance, I take the myth at its central time. This is only the meaning of the serpent to the

Greek mind which could conceive an Athena. Its
first meaning to the nascent eyes of men, and its continued influence over degraded races, are subjects of
the most fearful mystery. Mr. Fergusson has just
collected the principal evidence bearing on the matter
in a work of very great value, and if you read his
opening chapters, they will put you in possession of
the circumstances needing chiefly to be considered.
I cannot touch upon any of them here, except only to
point out that though the doctrine of the so-called
" corruption of human nature," asserting that there is
nothing but evil in humanity, is just as blasphemous
and false as a doctrine of the corruption of physical
nature would be, asserting there was nothing but evil
in the earth—there is yet the clearest evidence of a
disease, plague, or cretinous imperfection of develop-
ment, hitherto allowed to prevail against the greater
part of the races of men ; and this in monstrous ways,
more full of mystery than the serpent-being itself. I
have gathered for you to-night only instances of what
is beautiful in Greek religion ; but even in its best
time there were deep corruptions in other phases of it,
and degraded forms of many of its deities, all originating in a misunderstood worship of the principle
of life; while in the religions of lower races, little
else than these corrupted forms of devotion can be
found ; all having a strange and dreadful consistency
with each other, and infecting Christianity, even at

its strongest periods, with fatal terror of doctrine, and ghastliness of symbolic conception, passing through fear into frenzied grotesque, and thence into sensuality.

In the Psalter of St. Louis itself, half of its letters are twisted snakes; there is scarcely a wreathed ornament, employed in Christian dress, or architecture, which cannot be traced back to the serpent's coil; and there is rarely a piece of monkish decorated writing in the world, that is not tainted with some ill-meant vileness of grotesque—nay, the very leaves of the twisted ivy-pattern of the fourteenth century can be followed back to wreaths for the foreheads of bacchanalian gods. And truly, it seems to me, as I gather in my mind the evidences of insane religion, degraded art, merciless war, sullen toil, detestable pleasure, and vain or vile hope, in which the nations of the world have lived since first they could bear record of themselves—it seems to me, I say, as if the race itself were still half-serpent, not extricated yet from its clay; a lacertine breed of bitterness—the glory of it emaciate with cruel hunger, and blotted with venomous stain; and the track of it, on the leaf a glittering slime, and in the sand a useless furrow.

72. There are no myths, therefore, by which the moral state and fineness of intelligence of different races can be so deeply tried or measured, as by those of the serpent and the bird; both of them having an

especial relation to the kind of remorse for sin, or grief in fate, of which the national minds that spoke by them had been capable. The serpent and vulture are alike emblems of immortality and purification among races which desired to be immortal and pure : and as they recognize their own misery, the serpent becomes to them the scourge of the Furies, and the vulture finds its eternal prey in their breast. The bird long contests among the Egyptians with the still received serpent symbol of power. But the Draconian image of evil is established in the serpent Apap ; while the bird's wings, with the globe, become part of the better symbol of deity, and the entire form of the vulture, as an emblem of purification, is associated with the earliest conception of Athena. In the type of the dove with the olive branch, the conception of the spirit of Athena in renewed life prevailing over ruin, is embodied for the whole of futurity : while the Greeks, to whom, in a happier climate and higher life than that of Egypt, the vulture symbol of cleansing became unintelligible, took the eagle, instead, for their hieroglyph of supreme spiritual energy, and it thenceforward retains its hold on the human imagination, till it is established among Christian myths as the expression of the most exalted form of evangelistic teaching. The special relation of Athena to her favorite bird we will trace presently : the peacock of Hera, and dove of Aphrodite, are comparatively unimportant myths : but the bird power is soon made entirely human by the Greeks in their flying angel of victory (partially human, with modified meaning of evil, in the harpy and siren); and thenceforward it associates itself with the Hebrew cherubim, and has had the most singular influence on the Christian religion by giving its wings to render the conception of angels mysterious and un-tenable, and check rational endeavor to determine the nature of subordinate spiritual agency ; while yet it has given to that agency a vague poetical influence of the highest value in its own imaginative way.

73. But with the early serpent-worship there was associated another—that of the groves—of which you will also find the evidence exhaustively collected in Mr. Fergusson's work. This tree-worship may have taken a dark form when associated with the Draconian one ; or opposed, as in Judea, to a purer faith ; but in itself, I believe, it was always healthy, and though it retains little definite hieroglyphic power in subsequent religion, it becomes, instead of symbolic, real ; the flowers and trees are themselves beheld and beloved with a half-worshiping delight, which is always noble and healthful.

And it is among the most notable indications of the volition of the animating power, that we find the ethical signs of good and evil set on these also, as well as upon animals ; the venom of the serpent, and in some respects its image also, being associated even with the passionless growth of the leaf out of the ground while the distinctions of species seem appointed; with more definite ethical address to the intelligence of man as their material products become more useful to him.

74. I can easily show this, and, at the same time, make clear the relation to other plants of the flowers which especially belong to Athena, by examining the natural myths in the groups of the plants which would be used at any country dinner, over which Athena would, in her simplest household authority, cheerfully rule, here, in England. Suppose Horace's favorite dish of beans, with the bacon; potatoes; some savory stuffing of onions and herbs with the meat; celery, and a radish or two, with the cheese; nuts and apples for dessert, and brown bread.

75. The beans are, from earliest time, the most important and interesting of the seeds of the great tribe of plants from which came the Latin and French name for all kitchen vegetables, things that are gathered with the hand—podded seeds that cannot be reaped or beaten or shaken down, but must be gathered green. "Leguminous" plants, all of them having flowers like butterflies, seeds in (frequently pendent) pods—"*lætum siliqua quassante legumen*"— smooth and tender leaves, divided into many minor ones; strange adjuncts of tendril, for climbing (and

sometimes of thorn); exquisitely sweet, yet pure scents of blossom and almost always harmless, if not serviceable seeds. It is, of all tribes of plants, the most definite; its blossoms being entirely limited in their parts, and not passing into other forms. It is also the most usefully extended in range and scale; familiar in the height of the forest—acacia, laburnum, Judas-tree; familiar in the sown field—bean and vetch and pea; familiar in the pasture—in every form of clustered clover and sweet trefoil tracery; the most entirely serviceable and human of all orders of plants.

76. Next, in the potato, we have the scarcely innocent underground stem of one of a tribe set aside for evil; having the deadly nightshade for its queen, and including the henbane, the witch's mandrake and the worst natural curse of modern civilization— tobacco.* And the strange thing about this tribe is, that though thus set aside for evil, they are not a group distinctly separate from those that are happier in function. There is nothing in other tribes of plants like the form of the bean blossom; but there is another family with forms and structure closely connected with this venomous one. Examine the purple and yellow bloom of the common hedge nightshade;

---

* It is not easy to estimate the demoralizing effect on the youth of Europe of the cigar, in enabling them to pass their time happily in idleness.

you will find it constructed exactly like some of the forms of the cyclamen; and, getting this clue, you will find at last the whole poisonous and terrible group to be—sisters of the primulas!

The nightshades are, in fact, primroses with a curse upon them; and a sign set in their petals, by which the deadly and condemned flowers may always be known from the innocent ones—that the stamens of the nightshades are between the lobes, and of the primulas, opposite the lobes, of the corolla.

77. Next, side by side in the celery and radish, you have the two great groups of the umbelled and cruciferous plants; alike in conditions of rank among herbs; both flowering in clusters; but the umbelled group, flat, the crucifers, in spires—both of them mean and poor in the blossom, and losing what beauty they have by too close crowding—both of them having the most curious influence on human character in the temperate zones of the earth, from the days of the parsley crown, and hemlock drink, and mocked Euripidean chervil, until now : but chiefly among the northern nations, being especially plants that are of some humble beauty, and (the crucifers) of endless use, when they are chosen and cultivated; but that run to wild waste, and are the signs of neglected ground, in their rank or ragged leaves, and meager stalks, and pursed or podded seed clusters. Capable, even under cultivation, of no perfect beauty, though reaching some sub-

dued delightfulness in the lady's smock and the wall-
flower; for the most part, they have every floral
quality meanly, and in vain—they are white, without
purity; golden, without preciousness; redundant,
without richness; divided, without fineness; massive,
without strength; and slender without grace. Yet
think over that useful vulgarity of theirs; and of the
relations of German and English peasant character to
its food of kraut and cabbage (as of Arab character to
its food of palm-fruit), and you will begin to feel what
purposes of the forming spirit are in these distinctions
of species.

78. Next we take the nuts and apples—the nuts
representing one of the groups of catkined trees,
whose blossoms are only tufts and dust; and the other,
the rose tribe, in which fruit and flower alike have
been the types, to the highest races of men, of all passionate temptation, or pure delight, from the coveting
of Eve to the crowning of the Madonna, above the

> " Rosa sempiterna,
> Che si dilata, rigrada, e ridole
> Odor di lode al Sol."

We have no time now for these, we must go on to the
humblest group of all, yet the most wonderful, that of
the grass, which has given us our bread; and from
that we will go back to the herbs.

79. The vast family of plants which, under rain,

make the earth green for man, and, under sunshine, give him bread, and, in their springing in the early year, mixed with their native flowers, have given us (far more than the new leaves of trees) the thought and word of "spring" divide themselves broadly into three great groups—the grasses, sedges, and rushes. The grasses are essentially a clothing for healthy and pure ground, watered by occasional rain, but in itself dry, and fit for all cultivated pasture and corn. They are distinctively plants with round and jointed stems, which have long green flexible leaves, and heads of seed, independently emerging from them. The sedges are essentially the clothing of waste and more or less poor or uncultivated soils, coarse in their structure, frequently triangular in stem—hence called "acute" by Virgil—and with their heads of seed not extricated from their leaves. Now, in both the sedges and grasses the blossom has a common structure, though undeveloped in the sedges, but composed always of groups of double husks, which have mostly a spinous process in the center, sometimes projecting into a long awn or beard ; this central process being characteristic also of the ordinary leaves of mosses, as if a moss were a kind of ear of corn made permanently green on the ground, and with a new and distinct fructification. But the rushes differ wholly from the sedge and grass in their blossom structure. It is not a dual cluster, but a twice threefold one, so far separate from the grasses, and so closely connected with a higher order of plants, that I think you will find it convenient to group the rushes at once with that higher order to which, if you will for the present let me give the general name of Drosidæ, or dew plants, it will enable me to say what I have to say of them much more shortly and clearly.

80. These Drosidæ, then, are plants delighting in interrupted moisture—moisture which comes either partially or at certain seasons—into dry ground. They are not water-plants; but the signs of water resting among dry places. Many of the true water-plants have triple blossoms, with a small triple calyx holding them; in the Drosidæ, the floral spirit passes into the calyx also, and the entire flower becomes a six-rayed star, bursting out of the stem laterally, as if it were the first of flowers, and had made its way to the light by force through the unwilling green. They are often required to retain moisture or nourishment for the future blossom through long times of drought; and this they do in bulbs under ground, of which some become a rude and simple, but most wholesome, food for man.

81. So now, observe, you are to divide the whole family of the herbs of the field into three great groups —Drosidæ, Carices,* Gramineæ—dew-plants, sedges,

---

* I think Carex will be found ultimately better than Cyperus for the generic name, being the Virgilian word, and representing a larger sub-species.

and grasses. Then, the Drosidæ are divided into five great orders—lilies, asphodels, amaryllids, irids and rushes. No tribes of flowers have had so great, so varied, or so healthy an influence on man as this great group of Drosidæ, depending, not so much on the whiteness of some of their blossoms, or the radiance of others, as on the strength and delicacy of the substance of their petals; enabling them to take forms of faultless elastic curvature, either in cups, as the crocus, or expanding bells, as the true lily, or heath-like bells, as the hyacinth, or bright and perfect stars, like the star of Bethlehem, or, when they are affected by the strange reflex of the serpent nature which forms the labiate group of all flowers, closing into forms of exquisitely fantastic symmetry in the gladiolus. Put by their side their nereid sisters, the water-lilies, and you have in them the origin of the loveliest forms of ornamental design, and the most powerful floral myths yet recognized among human spirits, born by the streams of Ganges, Nile, Arno, and Avon.

82. For consider a little what each of those five tribes* has been to the spirit of man. First, in their nobleness: the lilies gave the lily of the annunciation; the asphodels, the flower of the Elysian fields; the irids,

---

* Take this rough distinction of the four tribes—lilies, superior ovary, white seeds; asphodels, superior ovary, black seeds; irids, inferior ovary, style (typically) rising into central crest; amaryllids, inferior ovary, stamens (typically) joined in central cup. Then the rushes are a dark group, through which they stoop to the grasses.

the fleur-de-lys of chivalry; and the amaryllids, Christ's lily of the field: while the rush, trodden always under foot, became the emblem of humility. Then take each of the tribes, and consider the extent of their lower influence. Perdita's "The crown imperial, lilies of all kinds," are the first tribe; which, giving the type of perfect purity in the Madonna's lily, have, by their lovely form, influenced the entire decorative design of Italian sacred art; while ornament of war was continually enriched by the curves of the triple petals of the Florentine "giglio," and French fleur-de-lys; so that it is impossible to count their influence for good in the middle ages, partly as a symbol of womanly character, and partly of the utmost brightness and refinement and chivalry in the city which was the flower of cities.

Afterward, the group of the turban-lilies, or tulips, did some mischief (their splendid stains having made them the favorite caprice of florists); but they may be pardoned all such guilt for the pleasure they have given in cottage gardens, and are yet to give, when lowly life may again be possible among us; and the crimson bars of the tulips in their trim beds, with their likeness in crimson bars of morning above them, and its dew glittering heavy, globed in their glossy cups, may be loved better than the gray nettles of the ash heap, under gray sky, unveined by vermilion or by gold.

83. The next great group of the asphodels divides itself also into two principal families; one, in which the flowers are like stars, and clustered characteristically in balls, though opening sometimes into looser heads; and the other, in which the flowers are in long bells, opening suddenly at the lips, and clustered in spires on a long stem, or drooping from it when bent by their weight.

The star-group, of the squills, garlics, and onions, has always caused me great wonder. I cannot understand why its beauty, and serviceableness, should have been associated with the rank scent which has been really among the most powerful means of degrading peasant life, and separating it from that of the higher classes.

The belled group, of the hyacinth and convallaria, is as delicate as the other is coarse: the unspeakable azure light along the ground of the wood hyacinth in English spring; the grape hyacinth, which is in south France, as if a cluster of grapes and a hive of honey had been distilled and compressed together into one small boss of celled and beaded blue; the lilies of the valley everywhere, in each sweet and wild recess of rocky lands; count the influences of these on childish and innocent life; then measure the mythic power of the hyacinth and asphodel as connected with Greek thoughts of immortality; finally, take their useful and nourishing power in ancient and modern peasant life, and it will be strange if you do not feel what fixed relation exists between the agency of the creating spirit in these, and in us who live by them.

84. It is impossible to bring into any tenable compass for our present purpose, even hints of the human influence of the two remaining orders of amaryllids and irids; only note this generally, that while these in northern countries share with the primulas the field of spring, it seems that in Greece, the primulaceæ are not an extended tribe, while the crocus, narcissus, and amaryllis lutea, the " lily of the field " (I suspect also that the flower whose name we translate " violet " was in truth an iris), represented to the Greek the first coming of the breath of life on the renewed herbage; and became in his thoughts the true embroidery of the saffron robe of Athena. Later in the year, the dianthus (which though belonging to an entirely different race of plants, has yet a strange look of having been made out of the grasses by turning the sheath-membrane at the root of their leaves into a flower) seems to scatter, in multitudinous families, its crimson stars far and wide. But the golden lily and crocus, together with the asphodel, retain always the old Greek's fondest thoughts—they are only " golden " flowers that are to burn on the trees, and float on the streams of paradise.

85. I have but one tribe of plants more to note at our country feast—the savory herbs; but must go a

little out of my way to come at them rightly. All flowers whose petals are fastened together, and most of those whose petals are loose, are best thought of first as a kind of cup or tube opening at the mouth. Sometimes the opening is gradual, as in the convolvulus or campanula; oftener there is a distinct change of direction between the tube and expanding lip, as in the primrose; or even a contraction under the lip, making the tube into a narrow-necked phial or vase, as in the heaths, but the general idea of a tube expanding into a quatrefoil, cinquefoil, or sixfoil, will embrace most of the forms.

86. Now it is easy to conceive that flowers of this kind, growing in close clusters, may, in process of time, have extended their outside petals rather than the interior ones (as the outer flowers of the clusters of many umbellifers actually do), and thus, elongated and variously distorted forms have established themselves; then if the stalk is attached to the side instead of the base of the tube, its base becomes a spur, and thus all the grotesque forms of the mints, violets and larkspurs gradually might be composed. But, however this may be, there is one great tribe of plants separate from the rest, and of which the influence seems shed upon the rest in different degrees; and these would give the impression, not so much of having been developed by change, as of being stamped with a character of their own, more or less serpentine

or dragon-like. And I think you will find it convenient to call these generally *Draconidæ;* disregarding their present ugly botanical name, which I do not care even to write once—you may take for their principal types the foxglove, snapdragon and calceolaria; and you will find they all agree in a tendency to decorate themselves by spots and with bosses or swollen places in their leaves, as if they had been touched by poison. The spot of the foxglove is especially strange, because it draws the color out of the tissue all around it, as if it had been stung, and as if the central color was really an inflamed spot, with paleness round. Then also they carry to its extreme the decoration by bulging or pouting the petal; often beautifully used by other flowers in a minor degree, like the beating out of bosses in hollow silver, as in the kalmia, beaten out apparently in each petal by the stamens instead of a hammer; or the borage, pouting inward; but the snapdragons and calceolarias carry it to its extreme.

87. Then the spirit of these Draconidæ seems to pass more or less into other flowers, whose forms are properly pure vases; but it affects some of them slightly—others not at all. It never strongly affects the heaths; never once the roses; but it enters like an evil spirit into the buttercup, and turns it into a larkspur, with a black, spotted, grotesque center, and a strange, broken, blue, gorgeous and intense, yet impure, glittering on

the surface as if it were strewn with broken glass, and stained or darkening irregularly into red. And then at last the serpent charm changes the ranunculus into monkshood, and makes it poisonous. It enters into the forget-me-not, and the star of heavenly turquoise is corrupted into the viper's bugloss, darkened with the same strange red as the larkspur, and fretted into a fringe of thorn; it enters, together with a strange insect-spirit, into the asphodels, and (though with a greater interval between the groups) they change into spotted orchideæ; it touches the poppy, it becomes a fumaria; the iris, and it pouts into a gladiolus; the lily, and it checkers itself into a snake's-head, and secretes in the deep of its bell, drops, not of venom indeed, but honey-dew, as if it were a healing serpent. For there is an Æsculapian as well as an evil serpentry among the Draconidæ, and the fairest of them, the *erba della Madonna* of Venice (*Linaria Cymbalaria*), descends from the ruins it delights in to the herbage at their feet, and touches it; and behold, instantly, a vast group of herbs for healing—all draconid in form— spotted and crested, and from their lip-like corrolas named "labiatæ;" full of various balm and warm strength for healing, yet all of them without splendid honor or perfect beauty, "ground ivies," richest when crushed under the foot; the best sweetness and gentle brightness of the robes of the field—thyme, and marjoram, and euphrasy.

88. And observe, again and again, with respect to all these divisions and powers of plants; it does not matter in the least by what concurrences of circumstance or necessity they may gradually have been developed: the concurrence of circumstance is itself the supreme and inexplicable fact. We always come at last to a formative cause, which directs the circumstance, and mode of meeting it. If you ask an ordinary botanist the reason of the form of a leaf, he will tell you it is a "developed tubercle," and that its ultimate form "is owing to the directions of its vascular threads." But what directs its vascular threads? "They are seeking for something they want," he will probably answer. What made them want that? What made them seek for it thus? Seek for it, in five fibres, or in three? Seek for it, in serration, or in sweeping curves? Seek for it, in servile tendrils, or impetuous spray? Seek for it, in woolen wrinkles rough with stings, or in glossy surfaces, green with pure strength, and winterless delight?

89. There is no answer. But the sum of all is, that over the entire surface of the earth and its waters, as influenced by the power of the air under solar light, there is developed a series of changing forms, in clouds, plants and animals, all of which have reference in their action, or nature, to the human intelligence that perceives them; and on which, in their aspects of horror and beauty, and their qualities of good

and evil, there is engraved a series of myths, or words of the forming power, which, according to the true passion and energy of the human race, they have been enabled to read into religion. And this forming power has been by all nations partly confused with the breath or air through which it acts, and partly understood as a creative wisdom, proceeding from the Supreme Deity; but entering into and inspiring all intelligences that work in harmony with Him. And whatever intellectual results may be in modern days obtained by regarding this effluence only as a motion of vibration, every formative human art hitherto, and the best states of human happiness and order, have depended on the apprehension of its mystery (which is certain), and of its personality, which is probable.

90. Of its influence on the formative arts, I have a few words to say separately: my present business is only to interpret, as we are now sufficiently enabled to do, the external symbols of the myth under which it was represented by the Greeks as a goddess of counsel taken first into the breast of their supreme deity, then created out of his thoughts, and abiding closely beside him; always sharing and consummating his power.

91. And in doing this we have first to note the meaning of the principal epithet applied to Athena, "Glaukopis," "with eyes full of light," the first syllable being connected, by its root, with words signify-

ing sight, not with words signifying color. As far as I can trace the color perception of the Greeks, I find it all founded primarily on the degree of connection between color and light; the most important fact to them in the color of red being its connection with fire and sunshine; so that "purple" is, in its original sense, "fire-color," and the scarlet, or orange, of dawn, more than any other fire-color. I was long puzzled by Homer's calling the sea purple; and misled into thinking he meant the color of cloud shadows on green sea; whereas he really means the gleaming blaze of the waves under wide light. Aristotle's idea (partly true) is that light, subdued by blackness, becomes red; and blackness, heated or lighted, also becomes red. Thus, a color may be called purple because it is light subdued (and so death is called "purple" or "shadowy" death); or else it may be called purple as being shade kindled with fire, and thus said of the lighted sea; or even of the sun itself, when it is thought of as a red luminary opposed to the whiteness of the moon: "*purpureos inter soles, et candida lunæ sidera;*" or of golden hair: "*pro purpureo pœnam solvens scelerata capillo;*" while both ideas are modified by the influence of an earlier form of the word, which has nothing to do with fire at all, but only with mixing or staining; and then, to make the whole group of thoughts inextricably complex, yet rich and subtle in proportion to their intricacy, the various rose and crimson colors of the murex-dye—the crimson and purple of the poppy, and fruit of the palm—and the association of all these with the hue of blood : partly direct, partly through a confusion between the word signifying " slaughter " and " palm-fruit color," mingle themselves in, and renew the whole nature of the old word ; so that, in later literature, it means a different color, or emotion of color, in almost every place where it occurs ; and casts forever around the reflection of all that has been dipped in its dyes.

92. So that the word is really a liquid prism, and stream of opal. And then, last of all, to keep the whole history of it in the fantastic course of a dream, warped here and there into wild grotesque, we moderns, who have preferred to rule over coal-mines instead of the sea (and so have turned the everlasting lamp of Athena into a Davy's safety-lamp in the hand of Britannia, and Athenian heavenly lightning into British subterranean " damp"), have actually got our purple out of coal instead of the sea ! And thus, grotesquely, we have had enforced on us the doubt that held the old word between blackness and fire, and have completed the shadow, and the fear of it, by giving it a name from battle, " Magenta."

93. There is precisely a similar confusion between light and color in the word used for the blue of the eyes of Athena—a noble confusion, however, brought

about by the intensity of the Greek sense that the heaven is light, more than that it is blue. I was not thinking of this when I wrote, in speaking of pictorial chiaroscuro, " The sky is not blue color merely : it is blue fire and cannot be painted " (Mod. P. iv. p. 36) ; but it was this that the Greeks chiefly felt of it, and so " Glaukopis " chiefly means gray-eyed : gray standing for a pale or luminous blue ; but it only means " owl-eyed " in thought of the roundness and expansion, not from the color ; this breadth and brightness being, again, in their moral sense typical of the breadth, intensity and singleness of the sight in prudence (" if thine eye be single, thy whole body shall be full of light "). Then the actual power of the bird to see in twilight enters into the type, and perhaps its general fineness of sense. " Before the human form was adopted, her (Athena's) proper symbol was the owl, a bird which seems to surpass all other creatures in acuteness of organic perception, its eye being calculated to observe objects which to all others are enveloped in darkness, its ear to hear sounds distinctly, and its nostrils to discriminate effluvia with such nicety that it has been deemed prophetic, from discovering the putridity of death even in the first stages of disease." *

---

* Payne Knight in his " Inquiry into the Symbolical Language of Ancient Art," not trustworthy, being little more than a mass of conjectural memoranda, but the heap is suggestive, if well sifted.

I cannot find anywhere an account of the first known occurrence of the type; but, in the early ones on Attic coins, the wide round eyes are clearly the principal things to be made manifest.

94. There is yet, however, another color of great importance in the conception of Athena—the dark blue of her ægis. Just as the blue or gray of her eyes was conceived as more light than color, so her ægis was dark blue, because the Greeks thought of this tint more as shade than color, and, while they used various materials in ornamentation, lapislazuli, carbonate of copper, or perhaps, smalt, with real enjoyment of the blue tint, it was yet in their minds as distinctly representative of darkness as scarlet was of light, and, therefore, anything dark,* but especially the color of

---

*In the breastplate and shield of Atrides the serpents and bosses are all of this dark color, yet the serpents are said to be like rainbows; but through all this splendor and opposition of hue, I feel distinctly that the literal "splendor," with its relative shade, are prevalent in the conception; and that there is always a tendency to look through the hue to its cause. And in this feeling about color the Greeks are separated from the eastern nations, and from the best designers of Christian times. I cannot find that they take pleasure in color for its own sake; it may be in something more than color, or better: but it is not in the hue itself. When Homer describes cloud breaking from a mountain summit, the crags became visible in light, not in color; he feels only their flashing out in bright edges and trenchant shadows: above, the "infinite," "unspeakable" æther is torn open—but not the *blue* of it. He has scarcely any abstract pleasure in blue, or green, or gold; but only in their shade or flame.

heavy thunder-cloud, was described by the same term. The physical power of this darkness of the ægis, fringed with lightning, is given quite simply when Jupiter himself uses it to overshadow Ida and the Plain of Troy, and withdraws it at the prayer of Ajax for light; and again when he grants it to be worn for a time by Apollo, who is hidden by its cloud when he strikes down Patroclus; but its spiritual power is chiefly expressed by a word signifying deeper

I have yet to trace the causes of this (which will be a long task, belonging to art questions, not to mythological ones); but it is, I believe, much connected with the brooding of the shadow of death over the Greeks without any clear hope of immortality. The restriction of the color on their vases to dim red (or yellow) with black and white, is greatly connected with their sepulchral use, and with all the melancholy of Greek tragic thought; and in this gloom the failure of color-perception is partly noble, partly base: noble, in its earnestness, which raises the design of Greek vases as far above the designing of mere colorist nations like the Chinese, as men's thoughts are above children's; and yet it is partly base and earthly; and inherently defective in one human faculty: and I believe it was one cause of the perishing of their art so swiftly, for indeed there is no decline so sudden, or down to such utter loss and ludicrous depravity as the fall of Greek design on its vases from the fifth to the third century, B. C. On the other hand, the pure colored-gift, when employed for pleasure only, degrades in another direction; so that among the Indians, Chinese, and Japanese, all intellectual progress in art has been for ages rendered impossible by the prevalence of that faculty: and yet it is as I have said again and again, the spiritual power of art; and its true brightness is the essential characteristic of all healthy schools.

shadow—the gloom of Erebus, or of our evening, which, when spoken of the ægis, signifies, not merely the indignation of Athena, but the entire hiding or withdrawal of her help, and beyond even this, her deadliest of all hostility—the darkness by which she herself deceives and beguiles to final ruin those to whom she is wholly adverse; this contradiction of her own glory being the uttermost judgment upon human falsehood. Thus it is she who provokes Pandarus to the treachery which purposed to fulfill the rape of Helen by the murder of her husband in time of truce; and *then* the Greek king, holding his wounded brother's hand, prophesies against Troy the darkness of the ægis which shall be over all, and forever.*

95. This, then, finally, was the perfect color-conception of Athena—the flesh snow-white (the hands, feet, and face of marble, even when the statue was hewn roughly in wood); the eyes of keen pale blue, often in statues represented by jewels; the long robe to the feet, crocus-colored; and the ægis thrown over it of thunderous purple; the helmet golden (Il. v. 744) and I suppose its crest also, as that of Achilles.

If you think carefully of the meaning and character which is now enough illustrated for you in each of these colors, and remember that the crocus-color and the purple were both of them developments, in opposite directions, of the great central idea of fire-color

---

* ἐρεμνὴν Αἰγίδα πᾶσι.—Il. iv. 166.

or scarlet, you will see that this form of the creative spirit of the earth is conceived as robed in the blue, and purple, and scarlet, the white, and the gold, which have been recognized for the sacred chord of colors, from the day when the cloud descended on a rock more mighty than Ida.

96. I have spoken throughout, hitherto, of the conception of Athena, as it is traceable in the Greek mind; not as it was rendered by Greek art. It is matter of extreme difficulty, requiring a sympathy at once affectionate and cautious, and a knowledge reaching the earliest springs of the religion of many lands, to discern through the imperfection, and, alas! more dimly yet, through the triumphs of formative art, what kind of thoughts they were that appointed for it the tasks of its childhood, and watched by the awakening of its strength.

The religious passion is nearly always vividest when the art is weakest; and the technical skill only reaches its deliberate splendor when the ecstacy which gave it birth has passed away forever. It is as vain an attempt to reason out the visionary power or guiding influence of Athena in the Greek heart, from anything we now read, or possess, of the work of Phidias, as it would be for the disciples of some new religion to infer the spirit of Christianity from Titian's "Assumption." The effective vitality of the religious conception can be traced only through the efforts of trembling hands and strange pleasures of untaught eyes; and the beauty of the dream can no more be found in the first symbols by which it is expressed, than a child's idea of fairyland can be gathered from its pencil scrawl, or a girl's love for her broken doll explained by the defaced features. On the other hand, the Athena of Phidias was, in very fact, not so much the deity, as the darling of the Athenian people. Her magnificence represented their pride and fondness, more than their piety; and the great artist, in lavishing upon her dignities which might be ended abruptly by the pillage they provoked, resigned, apparently without regret, the awe of her ancient memory; and (with only the careless remonstrance of a workman too strong to be proud) even the perfectness of his own art. Rejoicing in the protection of their goddess, and in their own hour of glory the people of Athena robed her, at their will, with the preciousness of ivory and gems; forgot or denied the darkness of the breastplate of judgment and vainly bade its unappeasable serpents relax their coils in gold.

97. It will take me many a day yet—if days, many or few, are given to me—to disentangle in any wise the proud and practiced disguises of religious creeds from the instinctive arts which, grotesquely and indecorously, yet with sincerity, strove to embody them, or to relate. But I think the reader, by help even of the imperfect

indications already given to him, will be able to follow, with a continually increasing security, the vestiges of the myth of Athena; and to reanimate its almost evanescant shade, by connecting it with the now recognized facts of existent nature, which it, more or less dimly, reflected and foretold. I gather these facts together in brief sum.

98. The deep of air that surrounds the earth enters into union with the earth at its surface, and with its waters; so as to be the apparent cause of their ascending into life. First, it warms them, and shades, at once, staying the heat of the sun's rays in its own body, but warding their force with its clouds. It warms and cools at once, with traffic of balm and frost; so that the white wreaths are withdrawn from the field of the Swiss peasant by the glow of Libyan rock. It gives its own strength to the sea; forms and fills every cell of its foam; sustains the precipices, and designs the valleys of its waves; gives the gleam to their moving under the night, and the white fire to their plains under sunrise; lifts their voices along the rocks, bears above them the spray of birds, pencils through them the dimpling of unfooted sands. It gathers out of them a portion in the hollow of its hand; dyes, with that, the hills into dark blue, and their glaciers with dying rose; inlays with that, for sapphire, the dome in which it has to set the cloud; shapes out of that the heavenly flocks; divides them, numbers, cherishes,

bears them on its bosom, calls them to their journeys, waits by their rest; feeds from them the brooks that cease not, and strews with them the dews that cease. It spins and weaves their fleece into wild tapestry, rends it, and renews; and flits and flames, and whispers, among the golden threads, thrilling them with a plectrum of strange fire that traverses them to and fro, and is inclosed in them like life.

It enters into the surface of the earth, subdues it, and falls together with it into fruitful dust, from which can be molded flesh; it joins itself, in dew, to the substance of adamant; and becomes the green leaf out of the dry ground; it enters into the separated shapes of the earth it has tempered, commands the ebb and flow of the current of their life, fills their limbs with its own lightness, measures their existence by its indwelling pulse, molds upon their lips the words by which one soul can be known to another; is to them the hearing of the ear, and the beating of the heart; and, passing away, leaves them to the peace that hears and moves no more.

99. This was the Athena of the greatest people of the days of old. And opposite to the temple of this spirit of the breath, and life-blood, of man and of beast, stood, on the Mount of Justice, and near the chasm which was haunted by the goddess-avengers, an altar to a god unknown—proclaimed at last to them, as one who, indeed, gave to all men, life, and breath, and all

things; and rain from heaven, filling their hearts with food and gladness—a God who had made of one blood all nations of men who dwell on the face of all the earth, and had determined the times of their fate, and the bounds of their habitation.

100. We ourselves, fretted here in our narrow days, know less, perhaps, in very deed, than they, what manner of spirit we are of, or what manner of spirit we ignorantly worship. Have we, indeed, desired the desire of all nations? and will the Master whom we meant to seek, and the Messenger in whom we thought we delighted, confirm, when He comes to His temple —or not find in its midst—the tables heavy with gold for bread, and the seats that are bought with the price of the dove? Or is our own land also to be left by its angered spirit—left among those, where sunshine vainly sweet, and passionate folly of storm, waste themselves in the silent places of knowledge that has passed away, and of tongues that have ceased?

This only we may discern assuredly: this, every true light of science, every mercifully-granted power, every wisely-restricted thought, teach us more clearly day by day, that in the heavens above, and the earth beneath, there is one continual and omnipotent presence of help, and of peace, for all men who know that they live, and remember that they die.

III.

ATHENA ERGANE.*

(Athena in the Heart.)

Various Notes relating to the Conception of Athena as the Directress of the Imagination and Will.

101. I HAVE now only a few words to say, bearing on what seems to me present need, respecting the third function of Athena, conceived as the directress of human passion, resolution and labor.

Few words, for I am not yet prepared to give accurate distinction between the intellectual rule of Athena and that of the Muses; but, broadly, the Muses, with their king, preside over meditative, historical and poetic arts, whose end is the discovery of light or truth and the creation of beauty: but Athena rules over moral passion and practically useful art. She does not make men learned, but prudent and subtle: she does not teach them to make their work beautiful, but to make it right.

In different places of my writings and through

---

* "Athena the worker, or having rule over work." The name was first given to her by the Athenians.

many years of endeavor to define the laws of art, I have insisted on this rightness in work, and on its connection with virtue of character, in so many partial ways, that the impression left on the reader's mind—if, indeed, it was ever impressed at all—has been confused and uncertain. In beginning the series of my corrected works, I wish this principle (in my own mind the foundation of every other) to be made plain, if nothing else is; and will try, therefore, to make it so, as far as, by any effort, I can put it into unmistakable words. And, first, here is a very simple statement of it, given lately in a lecture on the architecture of the valley of the Somme, which will be better read in this place than in its incidental connection with my account of the porches of Abbeville.

102. I had used, in a preceding part of the lecture, the expression, " by what faults " this Gothic architecture fell. We continually speak thus of works of art. We talk of their faults and merits as of virtues and vices. What do we mean by talking of the faults of a picture, or the merits of a piece of stone?

The faults of a work of art are the faults of its workman, and its virtues his virtues.

Great art is the expression of the mind of a great man, and mean art, that of the want of mind of a weak man. A foolish person builds foolishly, and a wise one, sensibly; a virtuous one, beautifully; and a vicious one, basely. If stone work is well put together, it means that a thoughtful man planned it, and a careful man cut it, and an honest man cemented it. If it has too much ornament, it means that its carver was too greedy of pleasure; if too little, that he was rude, or insensitive, or stupid, and the like. So that when once you have learned how to spell these most precious of all legends—pictures and buildings—you may read the characters of men and of nations in their art, as in a mirror; nay, as in a microscope and magnified a hundredfold; for the character becomes passionate in the art, and intensifies itself in all its noblest or meanest delights. Nay, not only as in a microscope, but as under a scalpel and in dissection; for a man may hide himself from you, or misrepresent himself to you, every other way; but he cannot in his work: there, be sure, you have him to the inmost. All that he likes, all that he sees, all that he can do—his imagination, his affections, his perseverance, his impatience, his clumsiness, cleverness, everything is there. If the work is a cobweb, you know it was made by a spider; if a honey-comb, by a bee; a worm-cast is thrown up by a worm and a nest wreathed by a bird; and a house built by a man, worthily, if he is worthy, and ignobly, if he is ignoble.

And always from the least to the greatest, as the made thing is good or bad, so is the maker of it.

103. You all use this faculty of judgment more or less, whether you theoretically admit the principle or

not. Take that floral gable; * you don't suppose the man who built Stonehenge could have built that, or that the man who built that, *would* have built Stonehenge? Do you think an old Roman would have liked such a piece of filigree work? or that Michael Angelo would have spent his time in twisting these stems of roses in and out? Or, of modern handicraftsmen, do you think a burglar, or a brute, or a pickpocket could have carved it? Could Bill Sykes have done it? or the Dodger, dexterous with finger and tool? You will find in the end, that *no man could have done it but exactly the man who did it;* and by looking close at it, you may, if you know your letters, read precisely the manner of man he was.

104. Now I must insist on this matter, for a grave reason. Of all facts concerning art, this is the one most necessary to be known, that, while manufacture is the work of hands only, art is the work of the whole spirit of man; and as that spirit is, so is the deed of it : and by whatever power of vice or virtue any art is produced, the same vice or virtue it reproduces and teaches. That which is born of evil begets evil; and that which is born of valor and honor, teaches valor and honor. All art is either infection or education. It *must* be one or other of these.

---

* The elaborate pediment above the central porch at the west end of Rouen Cathedral, pierced into a transparent web of tracery, and enriched with a border of " twisted eglantine."

105. This, I repeat, of all truths respecting art is the one of which understanding is the most precious, and denial the most deadly. And I assert it the more because it has of late been repeatedly, expressly, and with contumely, denied; and that by high authority; and I hold it one of the most sorrowful facts connected with the decline of the arts among us, that English gentlemen, of high standing as scholars and artists, should have been blinded into the acceptance, and betrayed into the assertion, of a fallacy which only authority such as theirs could have rendered for an instant credible. For the contrary of it is written in the history of all great nations; it is the one sentence always inscribed on the steps of their thrones; the one concordant voice in which they speak to us out of their dust.

All such nations first manifest themselves as a pure and beautiful animal race, with intense energy and imagination. They live lives of hardship by choice, and by grand instinct of manly discipline: they become fierce and irresistible soldiers; the nation is always its own army, and their king, or chief head of government, is always their first soldier. Pharaoh, or David, or Leonidas, or Valerius, or Barbarossa, or Cœur de Lion, or St. Louis, or Dandolo, or Frederick the Great: Egyptian, Jew, Greek, Roman, German, English, French, Venetian—that is inviolable law for them all; their king must be their first soldier, or they cannot be in progressive power. Then after their great military period comes the domestic period; in which, without betraying the discipline of war, they add to their great soldiership the delights and possessions of a delicate and tender home-life: and then, for all nations, is the time of their perfect art, which is the fruit, the evidence, the reward of their national ideal of character, developed by the finished care of the occupations of peace. That is the history of all true art that ever was, or can be: palpably the history of it—unmistakably—written on the forehead of it in letters of light—in tongues of fire, by which the seal of virtue is branded as deep as ever iron burned into a convict's flesh the seal of crime. But always, hitherto, after the great period, has followed the day of luxury, and pursuit of the arts for pleasure only. And all has so ended.

106. Thus far of Abbeville building. Now I have here asserted two things—first, the foundation of art in moral character; next, the foundation of moral character in war. I must make both these assertions clearer, and prove them.

First, of the foundation of art in moral character. Of course art-gift and amiability of disposition are two different things, for a good man is not necessarily a painter, nor does an eye for color necessarily imply an honest mind. But great art implies the union of both powers: it is the expression, by an art-gift, of a pure soul. If the gift is not there, we can have no art at all; and if the soul—and a right soul, too—is not there, the art is bad, however dexterous.

107. But also, remember, that the art-gift itself is only the result of the moral character of generations. A bad woman may have a sweet voice; but that sweetness of voice comes of the past morality of her race. That she can sing with it at all, she owes to the determination of laws of music by the morality of the past. Every act, every impulse, of virtue and vice, affects in any creature, face, voice, nervous power, and vigor and harmony of invention, at once. Perseverance in rightness of human conduct, renders, after a certain number of generations, human art possible; every sin clouds it, be it ever so little a one; and persistent vicious living and following of pleasure render, after a certain number of generations, all art impossible. Men are deceived by the long-suffering of the laws of nature; and mistake, in a nation, the reward of the virtue of its sires for the issue of its own sins. The time of their visitation will come, and that inevitably; for it is always true, that if the fathers have eaten sour grapes, the children's teeth are set on edge. And for the individual, as soon as you have learned to read, you may, as I said, know him to the heart's core, through his art. Let his art-gift be never so great, and cultivated to the height by the schools of a great race of men; and it is still but a tapestry

thrown over his own being and inner soul; and the bearing of it will show, infallibly, whether it hangs on a man, or on a skeleton. If you are dimmed-eyed, you may not see the difference in the fall of the folds at first, but learn how to look, and the folds themselves will become transparent, and you shall see through them the death's shape, or the divine one, making the tissue above it as a cloud of light, or as a winding-sheet.

108. Then farther, observe, I have said (and you will find it true, and that to the uttermost) that, as all lovely art is rooted in virtue, so it bears fruit of virtue, and is didactic in its own nature. It is often didactic also in actually expressed thought, as Giotto's, Michael Angelo's, Durer's, and hundreds more; but that is not its special function—it is didactic chiefly by being beautiful; but beautiful with haunting thought, no less than with form, and full of myths that can be read only with the heart.

For instance, at this moment there is open beside me as I write, a page of Persian manuscript, wrought with wreathed azure and gold, and soft green, and violet, and ruby, and scarlet, into one field of pure resplendence. It is wrought to delight the eyes only, and does delight them; and the man who did it assuredly had eyes in his head; but not much more. It is not didactic art, but its author was happy: and it will do the good, and the harm, that mere pleasure

can do.   But opposite me is an early Turner drawing
of the lake of Geneva, taken about two miles from
Geneva, on the Lausanne road, with Mont Blanc in
the distance.   The old city is seen lying beyond the
waveless waters, veiled with a sweet misty veil of
Athena's weaving: a faint light of morning, peaceful
exceedingly, and almost colorless, shed from behind
the Voirons, increases into soft amber along the slope
of the Saleve, and is just seen, and no more, on the
fair warm fields of its summit, between the folds of a
white cloud that rests upon the grass, but rises, high
and tower-like, into the zenith of dawn above.

109.   There is not as much color in that low amber
light upon the hill-side as there is in the palest dead
leaf.   The lake is not blue, but gray in mist, passing
into deep shadow beneath the Voirons' pines ; a few dark
clusters of leaves, a single white flower—scarcely seen
—are all the gladness given to the rocks of the shore.
One of the ruby spots of the eastern manuscript would
give color enough for all the red that is in Turner's
entire drawing.   For the mere pleasure of the eye
there is not so much in all those lines of his, throughout the entire landscape, as in half an inch square of
the Persian's page.   What made him take pleasure in
the low color that is only like the brown of a dead
leaf ? in the cold gray of dawn—in the one white
flower among the rocks—in these—and no more than
these ?

110. He took pleasure in them because he had been bred among English fields and hills; because the gentleness of a great race was in his heart, and its powers of thought in his brain; because he knew the stories of the Alps, and of the cities at their feet; because he had read the Homeric legends of the clouds, and beheld the gods of dawn, and the givers of dew to the fields; because he knew the faces of the crags, and the imagery of the passionate mountains, as a man knows the face of his friend; because he had in him the wonder and sorrow concerning life and death which are the inheritances of the Gothic soul from the days of its first sea kings; and also the compassion and the joy that are woven into the innermost fabric of every great imaginative spirit, born now in countries that have lived by the Christian faith with any courage or truth. And the picture contains also, for us, just this which its maker had in him to give; and can convey it to us, just so far as we are of the temper in which it must be received. It is didactic if we are worthy to be taught, not otherwise. The pure heart, it will make more pure; the thoughtful, more thoughtful. It has in it no words for the reckless or the base.

111. As I myself look at it, there is no fault nor folly of my life—and both have been many and great —that does not rise up against me, and take away my joy, and shorten my power of possession, of sight, of

understanding. And every past effort of my life, every gleam of rightness or good in it, is with me now, to help me in my grasp of this art, and its vision. So far as I can rejoice in, or interpret either, my power is owing to what of right there is in me. I dare to say it, that, because through all my life I have desired good, and not evil; because I have been kind to many; have wished to be kind to all; have willfully injured none; and because I have loved much, and not selfishly—therefore, the morning light is yet visible to me on those hills, and you, who read, may trust my thought and word in such work as I have to do for you; and you will be glad afterward that you have trusted them.

112. Yet remember—I repeat it again and yet again—that I may for once, if possible, make this thing assuredly clear—the inherited art-gift must be there, as well as the life in some poor measure, or rescued fragment, right. This art-gift of mine could not have been won by any work or by any conduct: it belongs to me by birthright, and came by Athena's will from the air of English country villages, and Scottish hills. I will risk whatever charge of folly may come on me, for printing one of my many childish rhymes, written on a frosty day in Glen Farg, just north of Loch Leven. It bears date 1st January, 1828. I was born on the 8th of February, 1819; and all that I ever could be, and all that I cannot be, the weak little rhyme already shows:

" Papa, how pretty those icicles are,
   That are seen so near—that are seen so far ;
   Those dropping waters that come from the rocks
   And many a hole, like the haunt of a fox ;
   That silvery stream that runs babbling along,
   Making a murmuring, dancing song.
   Those trees that stand waving upon the rock's side
   And men, that, like spectres, among them glide;
   And waterfalls that are heard from far,
   And come in sight when very near ;
   And the water-wheel that turns slowly round,
   Grinding the corn that—requires to be ground—

(Political economy of the future !)

   " And mountains at a distance seen,
      And rivers winding through the plain ;
      And quarries with their craggy stones,
      And the wind among them moans."

So foretelling stones of Venice, and this essay on Athena.

Enough now concerning myself.

113. Of Turner's life, and of its good and evil—both great, but the good immeasurably the greater—his work is in all things a perect and transparent evidence. His biography is simple: " He did this, nor will ever another do its like again." Yet read what I have said of him, as compared with the great Italians, in the passages taken from the " Cestus of Aglaia," farther on, § 158.

114. This, then, is the nature of the connection of

morals with art. Now, secondly, I have asserted the foundation of both these, at least hitherto, in war. The reason of this too manifest fact is that, until now, it has been impossible for any nation, except a warrior one, to fix its mind wholly on its men, instead of on their possessions. Every great soldier nation thinks, necessarily, first of multiplying its bodies and souls of men, in good temper and strict discipline. As long as this is its political aim, it does not matter what it temporarily suffers, or loses, either in numbers or in wealth; its morality and its arts (if it have national art-gift) advance together; but so soon as it ceases to be a warrior nation, it thinks of its possessions instead of its men; and then the moral and poetic powers vanish together.

115. It is thus, however, absolutely necessary to the virtue of war that it should be waged by personal strength, not by money or machinery. A nation that fights with a mercenary force, or with torpedos instead of its own arms, is dying. Not but that there is more true courage in modern than even in ancient war; but this is, first, because all the remaining life of European nations is with a morbid intensity thrown into their soldiers; and, secondly, because their present heroism is the culmination of centuries of inbred and traditional valor, which Athena taught them by forcing them to govern the foam of the sea-wave and of the horse —not the steam of kettles.

116.   And farther note this, which is vital to us in
the present crisis : If war is to be made by money and
machinery, the nation which is the largest and most
covetous multitude will win.   You may be as
scientific as you choose ; the mob that can pay more
for sulphuric acid and gunpowder will at last poison its
bullets, throw acid in your faces, and make an end of
you ; of itself, also, in good time, but of you first.
And to the English people the choice of its fate is
very near now.   It may spasmodically defend its
property with iron walls a fathom thick a few years
longer—a very few.   No walls will defend either it
or its havings, against the multitude that is breeding
and spreading, faster than the clouds, over the habita-
ble earth.   We shall be allowed to live by small ped-
ler's business, and ironmongery—since we have chosen
those for our line of life—as long as we are found
useful black servants to the Americans ; and are content to dig coals and sit in the cinders ; and have still
coals to dig—they once exhausted, or got cheaper
elsewhere, we shall be abolished.   But if we think
more wisely, while there is yet time, and set our
minds again on multiplying Englishmen, and not on
cheapening English wares ; if we resolve to submit to
wholesome laws of labor and economy, and, setting
our political squabbles aside, try how many strong
creatures, friendly and faithful to each other, we can
crowd into every spot of English dominion, neither

poison nor iron will prevail against us; nor traffic—nor hatred: the noble nation will yet, by the grace of Heaven, rule over the ignoble, and force of heart hold its own against fire-balls.

117. But there is yet a farther reason for the dependence of the arts on war. The vice and injustice of the world are constantly springing anew, and are only to be subdued by battle; the keepers of order and law must always be soldiers. And now, going back to the myth of Athena, we see that though she is first a warrior maid, she detests war for its own sake; she arms Achilles and Ulysses in just quarrels, but she disarms Ares. She contends, herself, continually against disorder and convulsion, in the earth giant; she stands by Hercules' side in victory over all monstrous evil; in justice only she judges and makes war. But in this war of hers she is wholly implacable. She has little notion of converting criminals. There is no faculty of mercy in her when she has been resisted. Her word is only, "I will mock when your fear cometh." Note the words that follow: "When your fear cometh as desolation, and your destruction as a whirlwind;" for her wrath is of irresistible tempest: once roused, it is blind and deaf—rabies— madness of anger—darkness of the *Dies Iræ*.

And that is, indeed, the sorrowfulest fact we have to know about our own several lives. Wisdom never forgives. Whatever resistance we have offered to her law, she avenges forever—the lost hour can never be redeemed, and the accomplished wrong never atoned for. The best that can be done afterward, but for that, had been better—the falsest of all the cries of peace, where there is no peace, is that of the pardon of sin, as the mob expect it. Wisdom can "put away" sin, but she cannot pardon it; and she is apt, in her haste, to put away the sinner as well, when the black ægis is on her breast.

118. And this is also a fact we have to know about our national life, that it is ended as soon as it has lost the power of noble anger. When it paints over, and apologizes for its pitiful criminalities; and endures its false weights, and its adulterated food—dares not to decide practically between good and evil, and can neither honor the one, nor smite the other, but sneers at the good as if it were hidden evil, and consoles the evil with pious sympathy, and conserves it in the sugar of its leaden heart—the end is come.

119. The first sign, then, of Athena's presence with any people, is that they become warriors, and that the chief thought of every man of them is to stand rightly in his rank, and not fail from his brother's side in battle. Wealth, and pleasure, and even love, are all under Athena's orders, sacrificed to this duty of standing fast in the rank of war.

But farther: Athena presides over industry as well as battle; typically, over women's industry: that

brings comfort with pleasantness.   Her word to us
all is : "Be well exercised, and rightly clothed. Clothed,
and in your right minds : not insane and in rags, nor
in soiled fine clothes clutched from each other's shoulders.   Fight and weave.   Then I myself will answer
for the course of the lance, and the colors of the
loom."

And now I will ask the reader to look with some
care through these following passages respecting modern multitudes and their occupations, written long ago,
but left in fragmentary form, in which they must now
stay, and be of what use they can.

120.   It is not political economy to put a number of
strong men down on an acre of ground, with no lodging, and nothing to eat.   Nor is it political economy
to build a city on good ground, and fill it with store
of corn and treasure, and put a score of lepers to live
in it.   Political economy creates together the means
of life, and the living persons who are to use them ;
and of both, the best and the most that it can, but
imperatively the best, not the most.   A few good and
healthy men, rather than a multitude of diseased
rogues ; and a little real milk and wine rather than
much chalk and petroleum ; but the gist of the whole
business is that the men and their property must both
be produced together—not one to the loss of the other.
Property must not be created in lands desolate by exile
of their people, nor multiplied and depraved humanity
in lands barren of bread.

121. Nevertheless, though the men and their possessions are to be increased at the same time, the first object of thought is always to be the multiplication of a worthy people. The strength of the nation is in its multitude, not in its territory ; but only in its sound multitude. It is one thing, both in a man and a nation to gain flesh, and another to be swollen with putrid, humors. Not that multitude ever ought to be inconsistent with virtue. Two men should be wiser than one, and two thousand than two ; nor do I know another so gross fallacy in the records of human stupidity as that excuse for neglect of crime by greatness of cities. As if the first purpose of congregation were not to devise laws and repress crimes ! as if bees and wasps could live honestly in flocks—men, only in separate dens—as if it were easy to help one another on the opposite sides of a mountain, and impossible on the opposite side of a street ! But when the men are true and good, and stand shoulder to shoulder, the strength of any nation is in its quantity of life, not in its land nor gold. The more good men a state has in proportion to its territory, the stronger the state. And as it has been the madness of economists to seek for gold instead of life, so it has been the madness of kings to seek for land instead of life. They want the town on the other side of the river and seek it at the spear point : it never enters their stupid heads that to double the honest souls in the town on *this* side of the river

would make them stronger kings; and that this doubling might be done by the plowshare instead of the spear, and through happiness instead of misery.

Therefore, in brief, this is the object of all true policy and true economy : "utmost multitude of good men on every given space of ground"—imperatively always good, sound, honest men, not a mob of white-faced thieves. So that, on the one hand, all aristocracy is wrong which is inconsistent with numbers; and, on the other, all numbers are wrong which are inconsistent with breeding.

122. Then, touching the accumulation of wealth for the maintenance of such men, observe, that you must never use the terms "money" and "wealth" as synonymous. Wealth consists of the good, and therefore useful, things in the possession of the nation : money is only the written or coined sign of the relative quantities of wealth in each person's possession. All money is a divisible title-deed, of immense importance as an expression of right to property; but absolutely valueless as property itself. Thus, supposing a nation isolated from all others, the money in its possession is, at its maximum value, worth all the property of the nation, and no more, because no more can be got for it. And the money of all nations is worth, at its maximum, the property of all nations, and no more, for no more can be got for it. Thus, every article of property produced increases, by its value, the value of

all the money in the world, and every article of property destroyed, diminishes the value of all the money in the world. If ten men are cast away on a rock, with a thousand pounds in their pockets, and there is on the rock neither food nor shelter, their money is worth simply nothing; for nothing is to be had for it: if they build ten huts, and recover a cask of biscuit from the wreck, then their thousand pounds, at its maximum value, is worth ten huts and a cask of biscuit. If they make their thousand pounds into two thousand by writing new notes, their two thousand pounds are still only worth ten huts and a cask of biscuit. And the law of relative value is the same for all the world and all the people in it, and all their property, as for ten men on a rock. Therefore, money is truly and finally lost in the degree in which its value is taken from it (ceasing in that degree to be money at all); and it is truly gained in the degree in which value is added to it. Thus, suppose the money coined by the nation to be a fixed sum, divided very minutely (say into francs and cents), and neither to be added to, nor diminished. Then every grain of food and inch of lodging added to its possessions makes every cent in its pockets worth proportionally more, and every grain of food it consumes, and inch of roof it allows to fall to ruin, makes every cent in its pockets worth less; and this with mathematical precision. The immediate value of the money at particular times and places depends, indeed, on the humors of the pos-sessors of property : but the nation is in the one case gradually getting richer; and will feel the pressure of poverty steadily everywhere relaxing, whatever the humors of individuals may be; and, in the other case, is gradually growing poorer, and the pressure of its poverty will every day tell more and more in ways that it cannot explain, but will most bitterly feel.

123. The actual quantity of money which it coins, in relation to its real property, is, therefore, only of consequence for convenience of exchange; but the proportion in which this quantity of money is divided among individuals expresses their various rights to greater or less proportions of the national property, and must not, therefore, be tampered with. The government may at any time, with perfect justice, double its issue of coinage, if it gives every man who had ten pounds in his pocket, another ten pounds, and every man who had ten pence another ten pence; for it thus does not make any of them richer; it merely divides their counters for them into twice the number. But if it gives the newly-issued coins to other people, or keeps them itself, it simply robs the former holders to precisely that extent. This most important func-tion of money, as a title-deed, on the non-violation of which all national soundness of commerce and peace of life depend, has been never rightly distinguished by

economists from the quite unimportant function of money as a means of exchange. You can exchange goods—at some inconvenience, indeed, but still you can contrive to do it—without money at all: but you cannot maintain your claim to the savings of your past life without a document declaring the amount of them, which the nation and its government will respect.

124. And as economists have lost sight of this great function of money in relation to individual rights, so they have equally lost sight of its function as a representative of good things. That, for every good thing produced, so much money is put into everybody's pocket, is the one simple and primal truth for the public to know, and for economists to teach. How many of them have taught it? Some have; but only incidentally; and others will say it is a truism. If it be, do the public know it? Does your ordinary English householder know that every costly dinner he gives has destroyed forever as much money as it is worth? Does every well-educated girl—do even the women in high political position—know that every fine dress they wear themselves, or cause to be worn, destroys precisely so much of the national money as the labor and material of it are worth? If this be a truism, it is one that needs proclaiming somewhat louder.

125. That, then, is the relation of money and goods.

So much goods, so much money; so little goods, so little money. But, as there is this true relation between money and "goods," or good things, so there is a false relation between money and "bads," or bad things. Many bad things will fetch a price in exchange; but they do not increase the wealth of the country. Good wine is wealth—drugged wine is not; good meat is wealth—putrid meat is not; good pictures are wealth—bad pictures are not. A thing is worth precisely what it can do for you; not what you choose to pay for it. You may pay a thousand pounds for a cracked pipkin, if you please; but you do not by that transaction make the cracked pipkin worth one that will hold water, nor that, nor any pipkin whatsoever, worth more than it was before you paid such sum for it. You may, perhaps, induce many potters to manufacture fissured pots and many amateurs of clay to buy them; but the nation is, through the whole business so encouraged, rich by the addition to its wealth of so many potsherds—and there an end. The thing is worth what it can do for you, not what you think it can; and most national luxuries, now-a-days, are a form of potsherd, provided for the solace of a self-complacent Job, voluntary sedent on his ash-heap.

126. And, also, so far as good things already exist, and have become media of exchange, the variations in their prices are absolutely indifferent to the nation.

Whether Mr. A. buys a Titian from Mr. B. for twenty, or for two thousand pounds, matters not sixpence to the national revenue; that is to say, it matters in nowise to the revenue whether Mr. A. has the picture, and Mr. B. the money, or Mr. B. the picture, and Mr. A. the money. Which of them will spend the money most wisely, and which of them will keep the picture most carefully, is, indeed, a matter of some importance; but this cannot be known by the mere fact of exchange.

127. The wealth of a nation then, first, and its peace and well-being besides, depend on the number of persons it can employ in making good and useful things. I say its well-being also, for the character of men depends more on their occupations than on any teaching we can give them, or principles with which we can imbue them. The employment forms the habits of body and mind, and these are the constitution of the man—the greater part of his moral or persistent nature, whatever effort, under special excitement, he may make to change or overcome them. Employment is the half, and the primal half, of education —it is the warp of it; and the fineness or the endurance of all subsequently woven pattern depends wholly on its straightness and strength. And, whatever difficulty there may be in tracing through past history the remoter connections of event and cause, one chain of sequence is always clear: the formation,

namely, of the character of nations by their employ. ments, and the determination of their final fate by their character. The moment, and the first direction of decisive revolutions, often depend on accident; but their persistent course, and their consequences, depend wholly on the nature of the people. The passing of the reform bill by the late English parliament may have been more or less accidental: the results of the measure now rest on the character of the English people, as it has been developed by their recent interests, occupations, and habits of life. Whether, as a body, they employ their new powers for good or evil, will depend, not on their facilities of knowledge, nor even on the general intelligence they may possess; but on the number of persons among them whom wholesome employments have rendered familiar with the duties, and modest in their estimate of the promises, of life.

128. But especially in framing laws respecting the treatment or employment of improvident and more or less vicious persons, it is to be remembered that as men are not made heroes by the performance of an act of heroism, but must be brave before they can perform it, so they are not made villains by the commission of a crime, but were villains before they committed it; and that the right of public interference with their conduct begins when they begin to corrupt themselves; not merely at the moment when they have proved themselves hopelessly corrupt.

All measures of reformation are effected in exact proportion to their timeliness ; partial decay may be cut away and cleansed ; incipient error corrected ; but there is a point at which corruption can no more be stayed, nor wandering recalled. It has been the manner of modern philanthropy to remain passive until that precise period, and to leave the sick to perish, and the foolish to stray, while it spent itself in frantic exertions to raise the dead, and reform the dust.

The recent direction of a great weight of public opinion against capital punishment is, I trust, the sign of an awakening perception that punishment is the last and worst instrument in the hands of the legislator for the prevention of crime. The true instruments of reformation are employment and reward —not punishment. Aid the willing, honor the virtuous, and compel the idle into occupation, and there will be no need for the compelling of any into the great and last indolence of death.

129. The beginning of all true reformation among the criminal classes depends on the establishment of institutions for their active employment, while their criminality is still unripe, and their feelings of relf-respect, capacities of affection, and sense of justice, not altogether quenched. That those who are desirous of employment should always be able to find it, will hardly, at the present day, be disputed : but that

those who are undesirous of employment should of all persons be the most strictly compelled to it, the public are hardly yet convinced; and they must be convinced. If the danger of the principal thoroughfares in their capital city, and the multiplication of crimes more ghastly than ever yet disgraced a nominal civilization, are not enough, they will not have to wait long before they receive sterner lessons. For our neglect of the lower orders has reached a point at which it begins to bear its necessary fruit, and every day makes the fields, not whiter, but more sable, to harvest.

130. The general principles by which employment should be regulated may be briefly stated as follows:

1st. There being three great classes of mechanical powers at our disposal, namely (*a*) vital or muscular power; (*b*) natural mechanical power of wind, water, and electricity; and (*c*) artificially-produced mechanical power; it is the first principle of economy to use all available vital power first, then the inexpensive natural forces, and only at last to have recourse to artificial power. And this because it is always better for a man to work with his own hands to feed and clothe himself, than to stand idle while a machine works for him; and if he cannot by all the labor healthily possible to him, feed and clothe himself, then it is better to use an inexpensive machine—as a windmill or watermill—than a costly one like a steam-engine, so long as we have natural force enough at our disposal. Whereas at present we continually hear economists regret that the water-power of the cascades or streams of a country should be lost, but hardly ever that the muscular power of its idle inhabitants should be lost; and, again, we see vast districts, as the south of Provence, where a strong wind* blows steadily all day long for six days out of seven throughout the year, without a windmill, while men are continually employed a hundred miles to the north, in digging fuel to obtain artificial power. But the principle point of all to be kept in view is, that in every idle arm and shoulder throughout the country there is a certain quantity of force, equivalent to the force of so much fuel; and that it is mere insane waste to dig for coal for our force, while the vital force is unused; and not only unused, but, in being so, corrupting and polluting itself. We waste our coal, and spoil our humanity at one and the same instant. Therefore, wherever there is an idle arm, always save coal with it, and the stores of England will last all the longer. And precisely the same argument answers the common one about "taking employment out of the hands of the industrious laborer." Why, what is "employment" but the putting out of vital force instead of mechanical force? We

---

* In order fully to utilize this natural power, we only require machinery to turn the variable into a constant velocity—no insurmountable difficulty.

are continually in search of means of strength—to pull, to hammer, to fetch, to carry; we waste our future resources to get this strength, while we leave all the living fuel to burn itself out in mere pestiferous breath, and production of its variously noisome forms of ashes! Clearly, if we want fire for force, we want men for force first. The industrious hands must already have so much to do that they can do no more, or else we need not use machines to help them. Then use the idle hands first.· Instead of dragging petroleum with a steam-engine, put it on a canal, and drag it with human arms and shoulders. Petroleum cannot possibly be in a hurry to arrive anywhere. We can always order that, and many other things, time enough before we want it. So, the carriage of everything which does not spoil by keeping may most wholesomely and safely be done by water-traction and sailing vessels; and no healthier work can men be put to, nor better discipline, than such active porterage.

131. 2nd. In employing all the muscular power at our disposal we are to make the employments we choose as educational as possible. For a wholesome human employment is the first and best method of education, mental as well as bodily. A man taught to plow, row, or steer well, and a woman taught to cook properly, and make a dress neatly, are already educated in many essential moral habits. Labor considered as a discipline has hitherto been thought of

only for criminals; but the real and noblest function of labor is to prevent crime, and not to be *re*formatory but formatory.

132. The third great principle of employment is, that whenever there is pressure of poverty to be met, all enforced occupation should be directed to the production of useful articles only, that is to say, of food, of simple clothing, of lodging, or of the means of conveying, distributing, and preserving these. It is yet little understood by economists, and not at all by the public that the employment of persons in a useless business cannot relieve ultimate distress. The money given to employ ribbon-makers at Coventry is merely so much money withdrawn from what would have employed lace-makers at Honiton : or makers of something else, as useless, elsewhere. We *must* spend our money in some way, at some time, and it cannot at any time be spent without employing somebody. If we gamble it away, the person who wins it must spend it; if we lose it in a railroad speculation, it has gone into some one else's pockets, or merely gone to pay navvies for making a useless embankment, instead of to pay ribbon or button makers for making useless ribbons or buttons; we cannot lose it (unless by actually destroying it) without giving employment of some kind ; and therefore, whatever quantity of money exists, the relative quantity of employment must some day come out of it; but the distress of the nation sig-

nifies that the employments given have produced nothing that will support its existence. Men cannot live
on ribbons, or buttons, or velvet, or by going quickly
from place to place; and every coin spent in useless ornament, or useless motion, is so much withdrawn from
the national means of life. One of the most beautiful uses of railroads is to enable A to travel from the
town of X to take away the business of B in the town
of Y; while, in the meantime, B travels from the
town of Y to take away A's business in the town of X.
But the national wealth is not increased by these op-
erations. Whereas every coin spent in cultivating
ground, in repairing lodging, in making necessary and
good roads, in preventing danger by sea or land, and
in carriage of food or fuel where they are required, is
so much absolute and direct gain to the whole nation.
To cultivate land round Coventry makes living easier
at Honiton, and every acre of sand gained from the
sea in Lincolnshire, makes life easier all over England.

4th, and lastly. Since for every idle person, some
one else must be working somewhere to provide him
with clothes and food, and doing, therefore, double the
quantity of work that would be enough for his own
needs, it is only a matter of pure justice to compel the
idle person to work for his maintenance himself. The
conscription has been used in many countries, to take
away laborers who supported their families, from their

useful work, and maintain them for purposes chiefly of military display at the public expense. Since this has been long endured by the most civilized nations, let it not be thought they would not much more gladly endure a conscription which should seize only the vicious and idle, already living by criminal procedures at the public expense; and which should discipline and educate them to labor which would not only maintain themselves, but be serviceable to the commonwealth. The question is simply this—we *must* feed the drunkard, vagabond, and thief—but shall we do so by letting them steal their food, and do no work for it? or shall we give them their food in appointed quantity, and enforce their doing work which shall be worth it? and which in process of time, will redeem their own characters, and make them happy and serviceable members of society?

I find by me a violent little fragment of undelivered lecture, which puts this, perhaps, still more clearly. Your idle people (it says), as they are now, are not merely waste coal-beds. They are explosive coal-beds, which you pay a high annual rent for. You are keeping all these idle persons, remember, at far greater cost than if they were busy. Do you think a vicious person eats less than an honest one? or that it is cheaper to keep a bad man drunk, than a good man sober? There is, I suppose, a dim idea in the mind of the public, that they don't pay for the maintenance of

people they don't employ. Those staggering rascals
at the street corner, grouped around its splendid angle
of public-house, we fancy they are no servants of
ours? that we pay them no wages? that no cash out of
our pockets is spent over that beer-stained counter!

Whose cash is it then they are spending? It is not
got honestly by work. You know that much. Where
do they get it from? Who has paid for their dinner
and their pot? Those fellows can only live in one of
two ways—by pillage or beggary. Their annual income by thieving comes out of the public pocket, you
will admit. They are not cheaply fed, so far as they
are fed by theft. But the rest of their living—all
that they don't steal—they must beg. Not with success from you, you think. Wise as benevolent, you
never gave a penny in "indiscriminate charity."
Well, I congratulate you on the freedom of your conscience from that sin, mine being bitterly burdened
with the memory of many a sixpence given to beggars
of whom I knew nothing, but that they had pale faces
and thin waists. But it is not that kind of street
beggary that the vagabonds of our people chiefly
practice. It is home beggary that is the worst beggars' trade. Home alms which it is their worst degradation to receive. Those scamps know well enough
that you and your wisdom are worth nothing to them.
They won't beg of you. They will beg of their
sisters, and mothers, and wives, and children, and of

any one else who is enough ashamed of being of the same blood with them to pay to keep them out of sight. Every one of those blackguards is the bane of a family. *That* is the deadly " indiscriminate charity "—the charity which each household pays to maintain its own private curse.

133. And you think that is no affair of yours? and that every family ought to watch over and subdue its own living plague? Put it to yourselves this way, then: suppose you knew every one of those families kept an idol in an inner room—a big-bellied bronze figure to which daily sacrifice and oblation was made; at whose feet so much beer and brandy was poured out every morning on the ground; and before which, every night, good meat, enough for two men's keep, was set and left, till it was putrid and then carried out and thrown on the dunghill; you would put an end to that form of idolatry with your best diligence, I suppose. You would understand then that the beer and brandy and meat were wasted; and that the burden imposed by each household on itself lay heavily through them on the whole community? But, suppose farther, that this idol were not of silent and quiet bronze only; but an ingenious mechanism, wound up every morning, to run itself down in automatic blasphemies; that it struck and tore with its hands the people who set food before it; that it was anointed with poisonous unguents and infected the air for miles

round. You would interfere with the idolatry then,
straightway? Will you not interfere with it now,
when the infection that the venomous idol spreads is
not merely death—but sin?

134. So far the old lecture. Returning to cool
English, the end of the matter is, that sooner or later,
we shall have to register our people; and to know
how they live; and to make sure, if they are capable
of work, that right work is given them to do.

The different classes of work for which bodies of
men could be consistently organized, might ultimately
become numerous; these following divisions of occupation may at once be suggested:

1. *Road-making.*—Good roads to be made, wherever needed, and kept in repair; and the annual loss
on unfrequented roads, in spoiled horses, strained
wheels, and time, done away with.

2. *Bringing in of waste land.*—All waste lands
not necessary for public health, to be made accessible
and gradually reclaimed; chiefly our wide and waste
seashores. Not our mountains nor moorland. Our
life depends on them, more than on the best arable we
have.

3. *Harbor-making.*—The deficiencies of safe or
convenient harborage in our smaller ports to be rem-
edied; other harbors built at dangerous points of
coast, and a disciplined body of men always kept in
connection with the pilot and life-boat services.   There

is room for every order of intelligence in this work, and for a large body of superior officers.

4. *Porterage.*—All heavy goods, not requiring speed in transit, to be carried (under preventive duty on transit by railroad) by canal-boats, employing men for draught; and the merchant-shipping service extended by sea; so that no ships may be wrecked for want of hands, while there are idle ones in mischief on shore.

5. *Repair of buildings.*—A body of men in various trades to be kept at the disposal of the authorities in every large town, for repair of buildings, especially the houses of the poorer orders, who, if no such provision were made, could not employ workmen on their own houses, but would simply live with rent walls and roofs.

6. *Dressmaking.*—Substantial dress, of standard material and kind, strong shoes and stout bedding, to be manufactured for the poor, so as to render it unnecessary for them, unless by extremity of improvidence, to wear cast-off clothes, or be without sufficiency of clothing.

7. *Works of Art.*—Schools to be established on thoroughly sound principles of manufacture, and use of materials, and with sample and, for given periods, unalterable modes of work; first in pottery, and embracing gradually metal work, sculpture, and decorative painting; the two points insisted upon, in dis-

tinction from ordinary commercial establishments, being perfectness of material to the utmost attainable degree, and the production of everything by hand-work, for the special purpose of developing personal power and skill in the workman.

The two last departments, and some subordinate branches of the others, would include the service of women and children.

I give now, for such farther illustration as they contain of the points I desire most to insist upon with respect both to education and employment, a portion of the series of notes published some time ago in the *Art Journal*, on the opposition of Modesty and Liberty, and the unescapable law of wise restraint. I am sorry that they are written obscurely, and it may be thought affectedly: but the fact is, I have always had three different ways of writing; one, with the single view of making myself understood, in which I necessarily omit a great deal of what comes into my head: another, in which I say what I think ought to be said, in what I suppose to be the best words I can find for it (which is in reality an affected style —be it good or bad); and my third way of writing is to say all that comes into my head for my own pleasure, in the first words that come, retouching them afterward into (approximate) grammar. These notes for the *Art Journal* were so written: and I like them myself, of course; but ask the reader's pardon for their confusedness

135. " Sir, it cannot be better done."

We will insist, with the reader's permission, on this comfortful saying of Albert Dürer's in order to find out, if we may, what Modesty is; which it will be well for painters, readers, and especially critics, to know before going farther. What it is; or, rather, who she is; her fingers being among the deftest in laying the ground-threads of Aglaia's Cestus.

For this same opinion of Albert's is entertained by many other people respecting their own doings—a very prevalent opinion, indeed, I find it; and the answer itself, though rarely made with the Nuremberger's crushing decision, is nevertheless often enough intimated, with delicacy, by artists of all countries, in their various dialects. Neither can it always be held an entirely modest one, as it assuredly was in the man who would sometimes estimate a piece of his unconquerable work at only the worth of a plate of fruit, or a flask of wine—would have taken even one "fig for it," kindly offered; or given it royally for nothing, to show his hand to a fellow-king of his own, or any other craft—as Gainsborough gave the "Boy at the Stile" for a solo on the violin. An entirely modest saying, I repeat, in him—not always in us. For Modesty is " the measuring virtue " of *modes* or limits. She is, indeed, said to be only the third or youngest of the children of the cardinal virtue, Temperance; and apt to be despised, being more given to arithmetic,

and other vulgar studies (Cinderella-like) than her
elder sisters : but she is useful in the household, and
arrives at great results with her yard-measure and
slate-pencil—a pretty little Marchande des Modes
cutting her dress always according to the silk (if this
be the proper feminine reading of "coat according to
the cloth"), so that, consulting with her carefully of
a morning, men get to know not only their income,
but their inbeing—to know *themselves,* that is, in a
gauger's manner, round, and up and down—surface
and contents; what is in them, and what may be got
out of them; and, in fine, their entire canon of weight
and capacity. That yard-measure of Modesty's, lent
to those who will use it, is a curious musical reed, and
will go round and round waists that are slender
enough, with latent melody in every joint of it, the
dark root only being soundless, moist from the wave
wherein

> " Null' altra pianta che facesse fronda
> O indurasse, puote aver vita." *

But when the little sister herself takes it in hand, to
measure things outside of us with, the joints shoot out
in an amazing manner; the four-square walls even of
celestial cities being measurable enough by that reed;
and the way pointed to them, though only to be followed, or even seen, in the dim starlight shed down

---

* *Purgatorio,* i. 103.

from worlds amid which there is no name of Measure any more, though the reality of it always. For, indeed, to all true modesty the necessary business is not inlook, but outlook, and especially *up*look; it is only her sister Shamefacedness who is known by the drooping lashes—Modesty, quite otherwise, by her large eyes full of wonder; for she never contemns herself, nor is ashamed of herself, but forgets herself—at least until she has done something worth memory. It is easy to peep and potter about one's own deficiencies in a quite immodest discontent; but Modesty is so pleased with other people's doings, that she has no leisure to lament her own: and thus, knowing the fresh feeling of contentment, unstained with thought of self, she does not fear being pleased, when there is cause, with her own rightness, as with another's, saying calmly, "Be it mine or yours, or whose else's it may it is no matter—this also is well." But the right to say such a thing depends on continual reverence, and manifold sense of failure. If you have known yourself to have failed, you may trust, when it comes, the strange consciousness of success: if you have faithfully loved the noble work of others, you need not fear to speak with respect of things duly done, of your own.

136. But the principal good that comes of art's being followed in this reverent feeling, is vitally manifest in the associative conditions of it. Men who

know their place, can take it and keep it, be it low or high, contentedly and firmly, neither yielding nor grasping; and the harmony of hand and thought follows, rendering all great deeds of art possible— deeds in which the souls of men meet like the jewels in the windows of Aladdin's palace, the little gems and the large all equally pure, needing no cement but the fitting of facets; while the associative work of immodest men is all jointless and astir with wormy ambition; putridly dissolute and forever on the crawl: so that if it come together for a time, it can only be by metamorphosis through flash of volcanic fire out of the vale of Siddim, vitrifying the clay of it, and fastening the slime, only to end in wilder scattering; according to the fate of those oldest, mightiest, immodestest of builders, of whom it is told in scorn, "They had brick for stone, and slime had they for mortar."

137. The first function of modesty, then, being this recognition of place, her second is the recognition of law, and delight in it, for the sake of law itself whether her part be to assert it, or obey. For as it belongs to all immodesty to defy or deny law, and assert privilege and license, according to its own pleasure (it being therefore rightly called "in*solent*," that is, "custom-breaking," violating some usual and appointed order to attain for itself greater forwardness or power), so it is the habit of all modesty to love the

constancy and "*solem*nity," or, literally, "accustomed-ness," of law, seeking first what are the solemn, appointed, inviolable customs and general orders of nature and of the master of nature, touching the matter in hand; and striving to put itself, as habitually and inviolably in compliance with them. Out of which habit, once established, arises what is rightly called "conscience," not "science" merely, but "with-science," a science "with us," such as only modest creatures can have—with or within them—and within all creation besides, every member of it, strong or weak, witnessing together, and joining in the happy consciousness that each one's work is good; the bee also being profoundly of that opinion; and the lark, and the swallow, in that noisy, but modestly upside-down Babel of hers, under the eaves, with its unvolcanic slime for mortar; and the two ants who are asking of each other at the turn of that little ant's foot-worn path through the moss, "*lor via e lor fortuna ;*" and the builders also, who built yonder pile of cloud-marble in the west, and the gilder who gilded it, and is gone down behind it.

138. But I think we shall better understand what we ought of the nature of modesty and of her opposite, by taking a simple instance of both, in the practice of that art of music which the wisest have agreed in thinking the first element of education; only I must ask the reader's patience with me through a parenthesis.

Among the foremost men whose power has had to assert itself, though with conquest, yet with countless loss, through peculiarly English disadvantages of circumstance, are assuredly to be ranked together, both for honor and for mourning, Thomas Bewick and George Cruikshank. There is, however, less cause for regret in the instance of Bewick. We may understand that it was well for us once to see what an entirely powerful painter's genius, and an entirely keen and true man's temper, could achieve, together, unhelped, but also unharmed, among the black banks and wolds of Tyne. But the genius of Cruikshank has been cast away in an utterly ghastly and lamentable manner: his superb linework, worthy of any class of subject, and his powers of conception and composition, of which I cannot venture to estimate the range in their degraded application, having been condemned by his fate, to be spent either in rude jesting or in vain war with conditions of vice too low alike for record or rebuke, among the dregs of the British populace. Yet perhaps I am wrong in regretting even this: it may be an appointed lesson for futurity, that the art of the best English etcher in the nineteenth century, spent on illustrations of the lives of burglars and drunkards, should one day be seen in museums beneath Greek vases fretted with drawings of the wars of Troy, or side by side with Dürer's "Knight and Death."

139. Be that as it may, I am at present glad to be able to refer to one of these perpetuations, by his strong hand, of such human character as our faultless British constitution ocasionally produces, in out-of-the-way corners. It is among his illustrations of the Irish rebellion, and represents the pillage and destruction of a gentleman's house by the mob. They have made a heap in the drawing-room of the furniture and books, to set first fire to, and are tearing up the floor for its more easily kindled planks : the less busily-disposed meanwhile hacking round in rage, with axes, and smashing what they can with butt-ends of guns. I do not care to follow with words the ghastly truth of the picture into its detail ; but the most expressive incident of the whole, and the one immediately to my purpose, is this, that one fellow has sat himself at the piano, on which, hitting down fiercely with his clinched fists, he plays, grinning, such tune as may be so producible, to which melody two of his companions, flourishing knotted sticks, dance, after their manner, on the top of the instrument.

140. I think we have in this conception as perfect an instance as we require of the lowest supposable phase of immodest or licentious art in music ; the " inner consciousness of good " being dim, even in the musician and his audience ; and wholly unsympathized with, and unacknowledged, by the Delphian, vestal, and all other prophetic and cosmic powers. This repre-

sented scene came into my mind suddenly one evening, a few weeks ago, in contrast with another which
I was watching in its reality ; namely, a group of gentle school-girls, leaning over Mr. Charles Hallè as he
was playing a variation on "Home Sweet Home."
They had sustained with unwonted courage the glance
of subdued indignation with which, having just closed
a rippling melody of Sebastian Bach's (much like what
one might fancy the singing of nightingales would be
if they fed on honey instead of flies), he turned to the
slight, popular air.　But they had their own associations with it, and besought for, and obtained it ; and
pressed close, at first, in vain, to see what no glance
could follow, the traversing of the fingers.　They soon
thought no more of seeing.　The wet eyes, round-open,
and the little scarlet upper lips, lifted, and drawn
slightly together, in passionate glow of utter wonder,
became picture-like—porcelain-like—in motionless joy,
as the sweet multitude of low notes fell in their timely
infinities, like summer rain.　Only La Robbia himself
(nor even he, unless with tenderer use of color than is
usual in his work) could have rendered some image of
that listening.

141.　But if the reader can give due vitality in his
fancy to these two scenes, he will have in them representative types, clear enough for all future purpose,
of the several agencies of debased and perfect art.
And the interval may easily and continuously be

filled by meditate gradations. Between the entirely immodest, unmeasured, and (in evil sense) unmannered, execution with the fist; and the entirely modest, measured, and (in the noblest sense) mannered, or moral'd execution with the finger; between the impatient and unpracticed doing, containing in itself the witness of lasting impatience and idleness through all previous life, and the patient and practised doing, containing in itself the witness of self-restraint and unwearied toil through all previous life; between the expressed subject of sentiment of home violation, and the expressed subject and sentiment of home love; between the sympathy of audience, given in irreverent and contemptuous rage, joyless as the rabidness of a dog, and the sympathy of audience given in an almost appalled humility of intense, rapturous, and yet entirely reasoning and reasonable pleasure; between these two limits of octave, the reader will find he can class, according to its modesty, usefulness, and grace, or becomingness, all other musical art. For although purity of purpose and fineness of execution by no means go together, degree to degree (since fine, and indeed all but the finest, work is often spent in the most wanton purpose—as in all our modern opera— and the rudest execution is again often joined with purest purpose, as in a mother's song to her child), still the entire accomplishment of music is only in the union of both. For the difference between that "all but " finest and " finest " is an infinite one ; and beside this, however the power of the performer, once attained, may be afterward misdirected, in slavery to popular passion or childishness, and spend itself, at its sweetest, in idle melodies, cold and ephemeral (like Michael Angelo's snow statue in the other art), or else in vicious difficulty and miserable noise—crackling of thorns under the pot of public sensuality—still the attainment of this power, and the maintenance of it, involve always in the executant some virtue or courage of high kind ; the understanding of which, and of the difference between the discipline which develops it and the disorderly efforts of the amateur, it will be one of our first businesses to estimate rightly. And though not indeed by degree to degree, yet in essential relation (as of winds to waves, the one being always the true cause of the other, though they are not necessarily of equal force at the same time), we shall find vice in its varieties, with art-failure—and virtue in its varieties, with art-success—fall and rise together : the peasant girl's song at her spinning-wheel, the peasant-laborer's " to the oaks and rills," domestic music, feebly yet sensitively skillful—music for the multitude, of beneficent, or of traitorous power—dance-melodies, pure and orderly, or foul and frantic—march-music, blatant in mere fever of animal pugnacity, or majestic with force of national duty and memory—song-music reckless, sensual, sickly, slovenly, forgetful even of the foolish words it effaces with foolish noise—or thoughtful, sacred, healthful, artful, forever sanctifying noble thought with separately distinguished loveliness of belonging sound—all these families and gradations of good or evil, however mingled, follow, in so far as they are good, one constant law of virtue (or "life-strength," which is the literal meaning of the word, and its intended one, in wise men's mouths), and in so far as they are evil, are evil by outlawry and unvirtue, or death-weakness. Then passing wholly beyond the domain of death, we may still imagine the ascendant nobleness of the art, through all the concordant life of incorrupt creatures, and a continually deeper harmony of "*puissant* words and murmurs made to bless," until we reach

"The undisturbed song of pure consent,
    Aye sung before the sapphire-colored throne."

142. And so far as the sister arts can be conceived to have place or office, their virtues are subject to a law absolutely the same as that of music, only extending its authority into more various conditions, owing to the introduction of a distinctly representative and historical power, and which acts under logical as well as mathematical restrictions, and is capable of endlessly changeful fault, fallacy, and defeat, as well as of endlessly manifold victory.

143. Next to modesty, and her delight in measures,

let us reflect a little on the character of her adversary, the Goddess of Liberty, and her delight in absence of measures, or in false ones. It is true that there are liberties and liberties. Yonder torrent, crystal-clear, and arrow-swift, with its spray leaping into the air like white troops of fawns, is free enough. Lost, presently, amid bankless, boundless marsh—soaking in slow shallowness, as it will, hither and thither, listless, among the poisonous reeds and unresisting slime—it is free also. We may choose which liberty we like— the restraint of voiceful rock, or the dumb and edgeless shore of darkened sand. Of that evil liberty, which men are now glorifying, and proclaiming as essence of gospel to all the earth, and will presently, I suppose, proclaim also to the stars, with invitation to them out of their courses—and of its opposite continence, which is the clasp and χρυσέη περόνμ of Aglaia's cestus, we must try to find out something true. For no quality of art has been more powerful in its influence on public mind; none is more frequently the subject of popular praise, or the end of vulgar effort, than what we call " Freedom." It is necessary to determine the justice or injustice of this popular praise.

144. I said, a little while ago, that the practical teaching of the masters of art was summed by the O of Giotto. "You may judge my masterhood of craft," Giotto tells us, " by seeing that I can draw a circle un-

erringly." And we may safely believe him, understanding him to mean, that—though more may be necessary to an artist than such a power—at least *this* power is necessary. The qualities of hand and eye needful to do this are the first conditions of artistic craft.

145. Try to draw a circle yourself with the "free" hand, and with a single line. You cannot do it if your hand trembles, nor if it hesitates, nor if it is unmanageable, nor if it is in the common sense of the word "free." So far from being free, it must be under a control as absolute and accurate as if it were fastened to an inflexible bar of steel. And yet it must move, under this necessary control, with perfect untormented serenity of ease.

146. That is the condition of all good work whatsoever. All freedom is error. Every line you lay down is either right or wrong; it may be timidly and awkwardly wrong, or fearlessly and impudently wrong; the aspect of the impudent wrongness is pleasurable to vulgar persons; and is what they commonly call "free" execution: the timid, tottering, hesitating wrongness is rarely so attractive; yet sometimes if accompanied with good qualities, and right aims in other directions, it becomes in a manner charming, like the inarticulateness of a child: but, whatever the charm or manner of the error, there is but one question ultimately to be asked respecting every line

you draw, is it right or wrong? If right, it most assuredly is not a " free " line, but an intensely continent, restrained, and considered line; and the action of the hand in laying it is just as decisive, and just as " free " as the hand of a first-rate surgeon in a critical incision. A great operator told me that his hand could check itself within about the two-hundredth of an inch, in penetrating a membrane; and this, of course, without the help of sight, by sensation only. With help of sight, and in action on a substance which does not quiver nor yield, a fine artist's line is measurable in its proposed direction to considerably less than the thousandth of an inch.

A wide freedom, truly.

147. The conditions of popular art which most foster the common ideas about freedom, are merely results of irregularly energetic effort by men imperfectly educated; these conditions being variously mingled with cruder mannerisms resulting from timidity, or actual imperfection of body. Northern hands and eyes are, of course, never so subtle as southern; and in very cold countries, artistic execution is palsied. The effort to break through this timidity, or to refine the bluntness, may lead to a licentious impetuosity, or an ostentatious minuteness. Every man's manner has this kind of relation to some defect in his physical powers or modes of thought; so that in the greatest work there is no manner visible. It is at first uninteresting

from its quietness; the majesty of restrained power only dawns gradually upon us, as we walk toward its horizon.

There is, indeed, often great delightfulness in the innocent manners of artists who have real power and honesty, and draw, in this way or that, as best they can, under such and such untoward circumstances of life. But the greater part of the looseness, flimsiness, or audacity of modern work is the expression of an inner spirit of license of mind and heart, connected, as I said, with the peculiar folly of this age, its hope of, and trust in "liberty." Of which we must reason a little in more general terms.

148. I believe we can nowhere find a better type of a perfectly free creature than in the common house fly. Nor free only, but brave; and irreverent to a degree which I think no human republican could by any philosophy exalt himself to. There is no courtesy in him; he does not care whether it is king or clown whom he teases; and in every step of his swift mechanical march, and in every pause of his resolute observation, there is one and the same expression of perfect egotism, perfect independence and self-confidence, and conviction of the world's having been made for flies. Strike at him with your hand; and to him, the mechanical fact and external aspect of the matter is, what to you it would be if an acre of red clay, ten feet thick, tore itself up from the ground in one mas-

sive field, hovered over you in the air for a second, and came crashing down with an aim. That is the external aspect of it; the inner aspect, to his fly's mind, is of a quite natural and unimportant occurrence —one of the momentary conditions of his active life. He steps out of the way of your hand, and alights on the back of it. You cannot terrify him, nor govern him, nor persuade him, nor convince him. He has his own positive opinion on all matters; not an unwise one, usually, for his own ends; and will ask no advice of yours. He has no work to do—no tyrannical instinct to obey. The earthworm has his digging; the bee her gathering and building; the spider her cunning net-nork; the ant her treasury and accounts. All these are comparatively slaves, or people of vulgar business. But your fly, free in the air, free in the chamber—a black incarnation of caprice—wandering, investigating, flitting, flirting, feasting at his will, with rich variety of choice in feast, from the heaped sweets in the grocer's window to those of the butcher's back-yard, and from the galled place on your cab-horse's back, to the brown spot in the road, from which, as the hoof disturbs him, he rises with angry republican buzz—what freedom is like his?

149. For captivity, again, perhaps your poor watch-dog is as sorrowful a type as you will easily find. Mine certainly is. The day is lovely, but I must write this, and cannot go out with him. He is chained in

the yard, because I do not like dogs in rooms, and the garden does not like dogs in gardens. He has no books —nothing but his own weary thoughts for company, and a group of those free flies, whom he snaps at, with sullen ill success. Such dim hope as he may have that I may yet take him out with me, will be, hour by hour, wearily disappointed ; or, worse, darkened at once into a leaden despair by an authoritative "No"—too well understood. His fidelity only seals his fate; if he would not watch for me, he would be sent away, and go hunting with some happier master : but he watches, and is wise, and faithful, and miserable; and his high animal intellect only gives him the wistful powers of wonder, and sorrow, and desire, and affection, which embitter his captivity. Yet of the two, would we rather be watch-dog, or fly ?

150. Indeed the first point we have all to determine is not how free we are, but what kind of creatures we are. It is of small importance to any of us whether we get liberty ; but of the greatest that we deserve it. Whether we can win it, fate must determine; but that we will be worthy of it, we may ourselves determine ; and the sorrowfullest fate, of all that we can suffer, is to have it, *without* deserving it.

151. I have hardly patience to hold my pen and go on writing, as I remember (I would that it were possible for a few consecutive instants to forget) the infinite follies of modern thought in this matter, centered

in the notion that liberty is good for a man, irrespectively of the use he is likely to make of it. Folly unfathomable! unspeakable! unendurable to look in the full face of, as the laugh of a cretin. You will send your child, will you, into a room where the table is loaded with sweet wine and fruit—some poisoned, some not—you will say to him, "Choose freely, my little child! It is so good for you to have freedom of choice: it forms your character—your individuality! If you take the wrong cup, or the wrong berry, you will die before the day is over, but you will have acquired the dignity of a free child!"

152. You think that puts the case too sharply? I tell you, lover of liberty, there is no choice offered to you, but it is similarly between life and death. There is no act, nor option of act possible, but the wrong deed or option has poison in it which will stay in your veins thereafter forever. Never more to all eternity can you be as you might have been, had you not done that—chosen that. You have "formed your character," forsooth! No; if you have chosen ill, you have de-formed it, and that forever! In some choices, it had been better for you that a red-hot iron bar struck you aside, scarred and helpless, than that you had so chosen. "You will know better next time!" No. Next time will never come. Next time the choice will be in quite another aspect—between quite different things—you, weaker than you were by the evil

into which you have fallen; it, more doubtful than it was, by the increased dimness of your sight. No one ever gets wiser by doing wrong, nor stronger. You will get wiser and stronger only by doing right, whether forced or not; the prime, the one need is to do *that*, under whatever compulsion, until you can do it without compulsion. And then you are a man.

153. "What!" a wayward youth might perhaps answer incredulously; "no one ever gets wiser by doing wrong? Shall I not know the world best by trying the wrong of it and repenting? Have I not, even as it is, learned much by many of my errors?" Indeed, the effort by which partially you recovered yourself was precious; that part of your thought by which you discerned the error was precious. What wisdom and strength you kept and rightly used, are rewarded; and in the pain and the repentance, and in the acquaintance with the aspects of folly and sin, you have learned *something;* how much less than you would have learned in right paths, can never be told, but that it *is* less is certain. Your liberty of choice has simply destroyed for you so much life and strength, never regainable. It is true you now know the habits of swine, and the taste of husks: do you think your father could not have taught you to know better habits and pleasanter tastes, if you had stayed in his house; and that the knowledge you have lost would not have been more, as well as sweeter, than that you have

gained? But "it so forms my individuality to be free!" Your individuality was given you by God, and in your race; and if you have any to speak of, you will want no liberty. You will want a den to work in, and peace and light—no more—in absolute need; if more, in anywise, it will still not be liberty, but direction, instruction, reproof and sympathy. But if you have no individuality, if there is no true character nor true desire in you, then you will indeed want to be free. You will begin early; and, as a boy, desire to be a man; and, as a man, think yourself as good as every other. You will choose freely to eat, freely to drink, freely to stagger and fall, freely, at last, to curse yourself and die. Death is the only real freedom possible to us: and that is consummate freedom—permission for every particle in the rotting body to leave its neighbor particle and shift for itself. You call it "corruption" in the flesh; but before it comes to that, all liberty is an equal corruption in mind. You ask for freedom of thought; but if you have not sufficient grounds for thought, you have no business to think; and if you have sufficient grounds, you have no business to think wrong. Only one thought is possible to you, if you are wise—your liberty is geometrically proportionate to your folly.

154. "But all this glory and activity of our age; what are they owing to, but to our freedom of thought?" In a measure they are owing—what good

is in them—to the discovery of many lies and the escape from the power of evil. Not to liberty but to the deliverance from evil or cruel masters. Brave men have dared to examine lies which had long been taught, not because they were *free*-thinkers, but because they were such stern and close thinkers that the lie could no longer escape them. Of course the restriction of thought, or of its expression by persecution, is merely a form of violence, justifiable or not, as other violence is, according to the character of the persons against whom it is exercised, and the divine and eternal laws which it vindicates or violates. We must not burn a man alive for saying that the Athanasian creed is ungrammatical, nor stop a bishop's salary because we are getting the worst of an argument with him; neither must we let drunken men howl in the public streets at night. There is much that is true in the part of Mr. Mill's essay on liberty which treats of freedom of thought; some important truths are there beautifully expressed, but many, quite vital, are omitted; and the balance, therefore, is wrongly struck. The liberty of expression, with a great nation, would become like that in a well-educated company, in which there is indeed freedom of speech, but not of clamor; or like that in an orderly senate, in which men who deserve to be heard, are heard in due time and under determined restrictions. The degree of liberty you can rightly grant to a number of men is in the inverse ratio of their desire for it; and a general hush, or call to order, would be often very desirable in this England of ours. For the rest, of any good or evil extent, it is impossible to say what measure is owing to restraint and what to license where the right is balanced between them. I was not a little provoked one day, a summer or two since, in Scotland, because the Duke of Athol hindered me from examining the gneiss and slate junctions in Glen Tilt, at the hour convenient to me; but I saw them at last, and in quietness; and to the very restriction that annoyed me, owed, probably, the fact of their being in existence, instead of being blasted away by a mob-company; while the " free " paths and inlets of Loch Katrine and the Lake of Geneva are forever trampled down and destroyed, not by one duke, but by tens of thousands of ignorant tyrants.

155. So a Dean and Chapter may, perhaps, unjustifiably charge me twopence for seeing a cathedral; but your free mob pulls spire and all down about my ears and I can see it no more forever. And even if I cannot get up to the granite junctions in the glen, the stream comes down from them pure to the Garry; but in Beddington Park I am stopped by the newly-erected fence of a building speculator; and the bright Wandel, divine of waters as Castaly, is filled by the free public with old shoes, obscene crockery and ashes.

156. In fine, the arguments for liberty may in general be summed in a few very simple forms as follows:

Misguiding is mischievous: therefore guiding is.

If the blind lead the blind, both fall into the ditch: therefore, nobody should lead anybody.

Lambs and fawns should be left free in the fields; much more bears and wolves.

If a man's gun and shot are his own, he may fire in any direction he pleases.

A fence across a road is inconvenient; much more one at the side of it.

Babes should not be swaddled with their hands bound down to their sides: therefore they should be thrown out to roll in the kennels naked.

None of these arguments are good, and the practical issues of them are worse. For there are certain eternal laws for human conduct which are quite clearly discernible by human reason. So far as these are discovered and obeyed, by whatever machinery or authority the obedience is procured, there follow life and strength. So far as they are disobeyed, by whatever good intention the disobedience is brought about, there follow ruin and sorrow. And the first duty of every man in the world is to find his true master, and, for his own good, submit to him; and to find his true inferior, and, for that inferior's good, conquer him. The punishment is sure, if we either refuse the reverence, or are too cowardly and indolent to enforce the compulsion. A base nation crucifies or poisons its wise men, and lets its fools rave and rot in its streets. A wise nation obeys the one, restrains the other, and cherishes all.

157. The best examples of the results of wise normal discipline in art will be found in whatever evidence remains respecting the lives of great Italian painters, though, unhappily, in eras of progress, but just in proportion to the admirableness and efficiency of the life, will be usually the scantiness of its history. The individualities and liberties which are causes of destruction may be recorded; but the loyal conditions of daily breath are never told. Because Leonardo made models of machines, dug canals, built fortifications, and dissipated half his art-power in capricious ingenuities, we have many anecdotes of him—but no picture of importance on canvas, and only a few withered stains of one upon a wall. But because his pupil, or reputed pupil, Luini, labored in constant and successful simplicity, we have no anecdotes of him—only hundreds of noble works. Luini is, perhaps, the best central type of the highly-trained Italian painter. He is the only man who entirely united the religious temper which was the spirit-life of art, with the physical power which was its bodily life. He joins the purity and passion of Angelico to the strength of Veronese: the two elements, poised in perfect balance, are so

calmed and restrained, each by the other, that most of
us lose the sense of both. The artist does not see the
strength, by reason of the chastened spirit in which it
is used: and the religious visionary does not recognize
the passion, by reason of the frank human truth with
which it is rendered. He is a man ten times greater
than Leonardo—a mighty colorist, while Leonardo
was only a fine draughtsman in black, staining the
chiaroscuro drawing, like a colored print: he perceived
and rendered the delicatest types of human beauty
that have been painted since the days of the Greeks,
while Leonardo depraved his finer instincts by carica-
ture, and remained to the end of his days the slave of
an archaic smile: and he is a designer as frank, instinctive, and exhaustless as Tintoret, while Leonardo's
design is only an agony of science, admired chiefly because it is painful, and capable of analysis in its best
accomplishment. Luini has left nothing behind him
that is not lovely; but of his life I believe hardly anything is known beyond remnants of tradition which
murmur about Lugano and Saronno, and which remain
ungleaned. This only is certain, that he was born in
the loveliest district of north Italy, where hills, and
streams, and air, meet in softest harmonies. Child of
the Alps, and of their divinest lake, he is taught, without doubt or dismay, a lofty religious creed, and a sufficient law of life, and of its mechanical arts. Whether
lessoned by Leonardo himself, or merely one of many

disciplined in the system of the Milanese school, he
learns unerringly to draw, unerringly and enduringly
to paint. His tasks are set him without question day
by day, by men who are justly satisfied with his work,
and who accept it without any harmful praise, or senseless blame. Place, scale, and subject are determined
for him on the cloister wall or the church dome ; as he
is required, and for sufficient daily bread, and little
more, he paints what he has been taught to design
wisely, and has passion to realize gloriously : every
touch he lays is eternal, every thought he conceives is
beautiful and pure : his hand moves always in radiance
of blessing ; from day to day his life enlarges in power
and peace ; it passes away cloudlessly, the starry twilight remaining arched far against the night.

158.   Oppose to such a life as this that of a great
painter amid the elements of modern English liberty.
Take the life of Turner, in whom the artistic energy
and inherent love of beauty were at least as strong as
in Luini : but, amid the disorder and ghastliness of
the lower streets of London, his instincts in early
infancy were warped into toleration of evil, or even
into delight in it. He gathers what he can of instruction by questioning and prying among half-informed
masters ; spells out some knowledge of classical fable ;
educates himself, by an admirable force, to the production of wildly majestic or pathetically tender and pure
pictures, by which he cannot live. There is no one

to judge them, or to command him : only some of the English upper classes hire him to paint their houses and parks, and destroy the drawings afterward by the mast wanton neglect. Tired of laboring carefully, without either reward or praise, he dashes out into various experimental and popular works—makes himself the servant of the lower public, and is dragged hither and thither at their will; while yet, helpless and guideless, he indulges his idiosyncrasies till they change into insanities; the strength of his soul increasing its sufferings, and giving force to its errors; all the purpose of life degenerating into instinct; and the web of his work wrought, at last, of beauties too subtle to be understood, his liberty, with vices too singular to be forgiven—all useless, because magnificent idiosyncrasy had become solitude, or contention, in the midst of a reckless populace, instead of submitting itself in loyal harmony to the art-laws of an understanding nation. And the life passed away in darkness; and its final work, in all the best beauty of it, has already perished, only enough remaining to teach us what we have lost.

159. These are the opposite effects of law and of liberty on men of the highest powers. In the case of inferiors the contrast is still more fatal : under strict law, they become the subordinate workers in great schools, healthily aiding, echoing, or supplying, with multitudinous force of hand, the mind of the leading

masters : they are the nameless carvers of great architecture—stainers of glass—hammerers of iron—helpful scholars, whose work ranks round, if not with
their master's, and never disgraces it. But the inferiors under a system of license for the most part perish
in miserable effort ; * a few struggle into pernicious
eminence—harmful alike to themselves and to all who
admire them ; many die of starvation ; many insane,
either in weakness of insolent egotism, like Haydon,

---

* As I correct this sheet for press, my *Pall Mall Gazette* of last
Saturday, April 17th, is lying on the table by me. I print a few
lines out of it :

" AN ARTIST'S DEATH : A sad story was told at an inquest held
in St. Pancras last night by Dr. Lankester on the body of * * *,
aged fifty-nine, a French artist, who was found dead in his bed at
his rooms in * * *, street. M. * * *, also an artist, said he had
known the deceased for fifteen years. He once held a high position,
and being anxious to make a name in the world, he five years ago
commenced a large picture, which he hoped, when completed, to
have in the gallery at Versailles ; and with that view he sent a
photograph of it to the French emperor. He also had an idea of
sending it to the English Royal Academy. He labored on this
picture, neglecting other work which would have paid him well
and gradually sank lower and lower into poverty. His friends assisted him, but being absorbed in his great work, he did not heed
their advice, and they left him. He was, however, assisted by the
the French ambassador, and last Saturday he (the witness) saw
deceased, who was much depressed in spirits, as he expected the
brokers to be put in possession for rent. He said his troubles were so
great that he feared his brain would give way. The witness gave him
a shilling, for which he appeared very thankful. On Monday the
witness called upon him, but received no answer to his knock. He
went again on Tuesday, and entered the deceased's bedroom and
found him dead. Dr. George Ross said that when called in to the
deceased he had been dead at least two days. The room was in
a filthy dirty condition, and the picture referred to—certainly a
very fine one—was in that room. The post-mortem examination
showed that the cause of death was fatty degeneration of the heart,
the latter probably having ceased its action through the mental excitement of the deceased."

or in a conscientious agony of beautiful purpose and warped power, like Blake. There is no probability of the persistence of a licentious school in any good accidentally discovered by them ; there is an approximate certainty of their gathering, with acclaim, round any shadow of evil, and following *it* to whatever quarter of destruction it may lead.

160. Thus far the notes on freedom. Now, lastly, here is some talk which I tried at the time to make intelligible : and with which I close this volume, because it will serve sufficiently to express the pratical relation in which I think the art and imagination of the Greeks stand to our own ; and will show the reader that my view of that relation is unchanged, from the first day on which I began to write, until now.

THE HERCULES OF CAMARINA.

Address to the Students of the Art School of South Lambert, March 15th, 1869.

161. AMONG the photographs of Greek coins which present so many admirable subjects for your study, I must speak for the present of one only : the Hercules of Camarina. You have, represented by a Greek workman, in that coin, the face of a man, and the skin of a lion's head. And the man's face is like a man's face, but the lion's skin is not like a lion's skin.

162. Now there are some people who will tell you that Greek art is fine, because it is true; and because it carves men's faces as like men's as it can.

And there are other people who will tell you that Greek art is fine because it is not true : and carves a a lion's skin so as to look not at all like a lion's skin.

And you fancy that one or other of these sets of people must be wrong, and are perhaps much puzzled to find out which you should believe.

But neither of them are wrong, and you will have eventually to believe, or rather to understand and know, in reconciliation, the truths taught by each—but

for the present, the teachers of the first group are those
you must follow.

It is they who tell you the deepest and usefullest
truth, which involves all others in time. *Greek art,
and all other art, is fine when it makes a man's face
as like a man's face as it can.* Hold to that. All
kinds of nonsense are talked to you, now-a-days, in-
geniously and irrelevantly about art. Therefore, for
the most part of the day, shut your ears, and keep
your eyes open; and understand primarily, what you
may, I fancy, understand easily, that the greatest masters of all greatest schools—Phidias, Donatello, Titian,
Velasquez, or Sir Joshua Reynolds—all tried to make
human creatures as like human creatures as they could;
and that anything less like humanity than their work,
is not so good as theirs.

Get that well driven into your heads; and don't let
it out again, at your peril.

163. Having got it well in, you may then farther
understand, safely, that there is a great deal of secondary work in pots, and pans, and floors, and carpets,
and shawls, and architectural ornament, which ought
essentially, to be *unlike* reality, and to depend for its
charm on quite other qualities than imitative ones.
But all such art is inferior and secondary—much of it
more or less instinctive and animal, and a civilized
human creature can only learn its principles rightly,
by knowing those of great civilized art first—which is

always the representation, to the utmost of its power, of whatever it has got to show—made to look as like the thing as possible. Go into the National Gallery, and look at the foot of Correggio's Venus there. Correggio made it as like a foot as he could, and you won't easily find anything liker. Now, you will find on any Greek vase something meant for a foot, or a hand, which is not at all like one. The Greek vase is a good thing in its way, but Correggio's picture is the best work.

164. So, again, go into the Turner room of the National Gallery, and look at Turner's drawing of "Ivy Bridge." You will find the water in it is like real water, and the ducks in it are like real ducks. Then go into the British Museum, and look for an Egyptian landscape, and you will find the water in that constituted of blue zig-zags, not at all like water; and ducks in the middle of it made of red lines, looking not in the least as if they could stand stuffing with sage and onions. They are very good in their way, but Turner's are better.

165. I will not pause to fence my general principle against what you perfectly well know of the due contradiction—that a thing may be painted very like, yet painted ill. Rest content with knowing that it *must* be like, if it is painted well; and take this farther general law: Imitation is like charity. When it is done for love it is lovely; when it is done for show, hateful.

166. Well, then, this Greek coin is fine, first because the face is like a face. Perhaps you think there is something particularly handsome in the face, which you can't see in the photograph, or can't at present appreciate. But there is nothing of the kind. It is a very regular, quiet, commonplace sort of face; and any average English gentleman's, of good descent, would be far handsomer.

167. Fix that in your heads also, therefore, that Greek faces are not particularly beautiful. Of the much nonsense against which you are to keep your ears shut, that which is talked to you of the Greek ideal of beauty, is among the absolutest. There is not a single instance of a very beautiful head left by the highest school of Greek art. On coins, there is even no approximately beautiful one. The Juno of Argos is a virago; the Athena of Athens, grotesque, the Athena of Corinth is insipid; and of Thurium, sensual. The Siren Ligeia, and fountain of Arethusa, on the coins of Terina and Syracuse, are prettier, but totally without expression, and chiefly set off by their well-curled hair. You might have expected something subtle in Mercuries; but the Mercury of Ænus is a very stupid-looking fellow, in a cap like a bowl with a knob on the top of it. The Bacchus of Thasos is a drayman with his hair pomatumed. The Jupiter of Syracuse is, however, calm and refined; and the Apollo of Clazomenæ would have been impressive, if he had

not come down to us much flattened by friction. But on the whole, the merit of Greek coins does not primarily depend on beauty of features, nor even, in the period of highest art, that of the statues. You may take the Venus of Melos as a standard of beauty of the central Greek type. She has tranquil, regular, and lofty features; but could not hold her own for a moment against the beauty of a simple English girl of pure race and kind heart.

168. And the reason that Greek art, on the whole, bores you (and you know it does), is that you are always forced to look in it for something that is not there; but which may be seen every day, in real life, all round you; and which you are naturally disposed to delight in, and ought to delight in. For the Greek race was not all one of exalted beauty, but only of general and healthy completeness of form. They were only, and could be only, beautiful in body to the degree that they were beautiful in soul (for you will find, when you read deeply into the matter, that the body is only the soul made visible). And the Greeks were indeed very good people, much better people than most of us think, or than many of us are; but there are better people alive now than the best of them, and lovelier people to be seen now, than the lovliest of them.

169. Then what *are* the merits of this Greek art, which make it so exemplary for you? Well, not that

it is beautiful, but that it is right.* All that it desires to do, it does, and all that it does, does well. You will find, as you advance in the knowledge of art, that its laws of self-restraint are very marvelous; that its peace of heart, and contentment in doing a simple thing, with only one or two qualities, restrictedly desired, and sufficiently attained, are a most wholesome element of education for you, as opposed to the wild writhing, and wrestling, and longing for the moon, and tilting at windmills, and agony of eyes, and torturing of fingers, and general spinning out of one's soul into fiddlestrings, which constitute the ideal life of a modern artist.

Also observe, there is entire masterhood of its business up to the required point. A Greek does not reach after other people's strength, nor out-reach his own. He never tries to paint before he can draw; he never tries to lay on flesh where there are no bones; and he never expects to find the bones of anything in his inner consciousness. Those are his first merits—sincere and innocent purpose, strong common sense and principle, and all the strength that comes of these, and all the grace that follows on that strength.

170. But, secondly, Greek art is always exemplary in disposition of masses, which is a thing that in modern days students rarely look for, artists not enough, and the public never. But, whatever else Greek work

---

* Compare above, § 101.

may fail of, you may be always sure its masses are
well placed, and their placing has been the object of
the most subtle care. Look, for instance, at the inscription in front of this Hercules of the name of the
town—Camarina. You can't read it, even though you
may know Greek, without some pains; for the sculptor knew well enough that it mattered very little
whether you read it or not, for the Camarina Hercules
could tell his own story; but what did above all things
matter was, that no K or A or M should come in a wrong
place with respect to the outline of the head, and di-
vert the eye from it, or spoil any of its lines. So the
whole inscription is thrown into a sweeping curve of
gradually diminishing size, continuing from the lion's
paws, round the neck, up to the forehead, and answering a decorative purpose as completely as the curls of
the mane opposite. Of these, again, you cannot
change or displace one without mischief; they are almost as even in reticulation as a piece of basket-work;
but each has a different form and a due relation to the
rest, and if you set to work to draw that mane rightly,
you will find that, whatever time you give to it, you
can't get the tresses quite into their places, and that
every tress out of its place does an injury. If you
want to test your powers of accurate drawing, you
may make that lion's mane your *pons asinorum.* I
have never yet met with a student who didn't make
an ass in a lion's skin of himself, when he tried it.

171. Granted, however, that these tresses may be finely placed, still they are not like a lion's mane. So we come back to the question, if the face is to be like a man's face, why is not the lion's mane to be like a lion's mane? Well, because it can't be like a lion's mane without too much trouble; and inconvenience after that, and poor success, after all. Too much trouble in cutting the die into fine fringes and jags; inconvenience after that—because fringes and jags would spoil the surface of a coin; poor success after all—because, though you can easily stamp cheeks and foreheads smooth at a blow, you can't stamp projecting tresses fine at a blow, whatever pains you take with your die.

So your Greek uses his common sense, wastes no time, loses no skill and says to you, " Here are beautifully set tresses, which I have carefully designed and easily stamped. Enjoy them, and if you cannot understand that they mean lion's mane, heaven mend your wits."

172. See then, you have in this work, well-founded knowledge, simple and right aims, thorough mastery of handicraft, splendid invention in arrangement, unerring common sense in treatment—merits these, I think, exemplary enough to justfy our tormenting you a little with Greek art. But it has one merit more than these, the greatest of all. It always means something worth saying. Not merely worth saying

for that time only, but for all time. What do you think this helmet of lion's hide is always given to Hercules for? You can't suppose it means only that he once killed a lion and always carried its skin afterward to show that he had, as Indian sportsmen send home stuffed rugs, with claws at the corners and a lump in the middle which one tumbles over every time one stirs the fire. What *was* this Nemean lion, whose spoils were evermore to cover Hercules from the cold? Not merely a large specimen of *Felis Leo*, ranging the fields of Nemea, be sure of that. This Nemean cub was one of a bad litter. Born of Typhon and Echidna—of the whirlwind and the snake—Cerberus his brother, the Hydra of Lerna his sister—it must have been difficult to get his hide off him. He had to be found in darkness too, and dealt upon without weapons, by grip at the throat—arrows and club of no avail against him. What does all that mean?

173. It means that the Nemean lion is the first great adversary of life, whatever that may be—to Hercules, or to any of us, then or now. The first monster we have to strangle, or be destroyed by, fighting in the dark, and with none to help us, only Athena standing by, to encourage with her smile. Every man's Nemean lion lies in wait for him somewhere. The slothful man says, there is a lion in the path. He says well. The quiet unslothful man says the same, and knows it too. But they differ in their

farther reading of the text. The slothful man says I shall be slain, and the unslothful, IT shall be. It is the first ugly and strong enemy that rises against us, all future victory depending on victory over that. Kill it; and through all the rest of life, what was once dreadful is your armor and you are clothed with that conquest for every other, and helmed with its crest of fortitude for evermore.

Alas, we have most of us to walk bare-headed; but that is the meaning of the story of Nemea—worth laying to heart and thinking of, sometimes, when you see a dish garnished with parsley, which was the crown at the Nemean games.

174. How far, then, have we got, in our list of the merits of Greek art now?

Sound knowledge.

Simple aims.

Mastered craft.

Vivid invention.

Strong common sense.

And eternally true and wise meaning.

Are these not enough? Here is one more then, which will find favor, I should think, with the British lion. Greek art is never frightened at anything, it is always cool.

175. It differs essentially from all other art, past or present, in this incapability of being frightened. Half the power and imagination of every other school

depend on a certain feverish terror mingling with their sense of beauty—the feeling that a child has in a dark room, or a sick person in seeing ugly dreams. But the Greeks never have ugly dreams. They cannot draw anything ugly when they try. Sometimes they put themselves to their wits'-end to draw an ugly thing—the Medusa's head, for instance—but they can't do it—not they—because nothing frightens them. They widen the mouth, and grind the teeth, and puff the cheeks, and set the eyes a goggling: and the thing is only ridiculous after all, not the least dreadful, for there is no dread in their hearts. Pensiveness; amazement; often deepest grief and desolateness. All these; but terror never. Everlasting calm in the presence of all fate; and joy such as they could win, not indeed in a perfect beauty, but in beauty at perfect rest! A kind of art this, surely, to be looked at, and thought upon sometimes with profit, even in these latter days.

176. To be looked at sometimes. Not continually, and never as a model for imitation. For you are not Greeks; but, for better or worse, English creatures; and cannot do, even if it were a thousand times better worth doing, anything well, except what your English hearts shall prompt, and your English skies teach you. For all good art is the natural utterance of its own people in its own day.

But also, your own art is a better and brighter one

than ever this Greek art was. Many motives, powers, and insights have been added to those elder ones. The very corruptions into which we have fallen are signs of a subtle life, higher than theirs was, and therefore more fearful in its faults and death. Christianity has neither superseded, nor, by itself, excelled heathenism: but it has added its own good, won also by many a Nemean contest in dark valleys, to all that was good and noble in heathenism: and our present thoughts and work, when they are right, are nobler than the heathen's. And we are not reverent enough to them, because we possess too much of them. That sketch of four cherub heads from an English girl, by Sir Joshua Reynolds, at Kensington, is an incomparably finer thing than ever the Greeks did. Ineffably tender in the touch, yet Herculean in power; innocent, yet exalted in feeling; pure in color as a pearl; reserved and decisive in design, as this lion crest—if *it* alone existed of such—if it were a picture by Zeuxis, the only one left in the world, and you build a shrine for it, and were allowed to see it only seven days in a year, it alone would teach you all of art that you ever needed to know. But you do not learn from this or any other such work, because you have not reverence enough for them, and are trying to learn from all at once, and from a hundred other masters besides.

177. Here, then is the practical advice which I would venture to deduce from what I have tried

to show you. Use Greek art as a first, not a final teacher. Learn to draw carefully from Greek work; above all, to place forms correctly and to use light and shade tenderly. Never allow yourselves black shadows. It is easy to make things look round and projecting; but the things to exercise yourselves in are the placing of the masses and the modeling of the lights. It is an admirable exercise to take a pale wash of color for all the shadows, never reinforcing it everywhere, but drawing the statue as if it were in far distance, making all the darks one flat pale tint. Then model from those into the lights, rounding as well as you can, on those subtle conditions. In your chalk drawings, separate the lights from the darks at once all over; then reinforce the darks slightly where absolutely necessary and put your whole strength on the lights and their limits. Then, when you have learned to draw thoroughly, take one master for your painting, as you would have done necessarily in old times by being put into his school (were I to choose for you, it should be among six men only— Titian, Correggio, Paul Veronese, Velasquez, Reynolds or Holbein). If you are a landscapist, Turner must be your only guide (for no other great landscape painter has yet lived); and having chosen, do your best to understand your own chosen master and obey *him*, and no one else, till you have strength to deal with the nature itself round you, and then, be your own master and see with your own eyes. If you have got masterhood or sight in you, that is the way to make the most of them; and if you have neither, you will at least be sound in your work, prevented from immodest and useless effort and protected from vulgar and fantastic error.

And so I wish you all, good speed, and the favor of Hercules and of the Muses; and to those who shall best deserve them, the crown of parsley first and then of the laurel.

THE END.

POPULAR LITERATURE FOR THE MASSES, COMPRISING CHOICE SELECTIONS FROM THE TREASURES OF THE WORLD'S KNOWLEDGE, ISSUED IN A SUBSTANTIAL AND ATTRACTIVE CLOTH BINDING, AT A POPULAR PRICE

BURT'S HOME LIBRARY is a series which includes the standard works of the world's best literature, bound in uniform cloth binding, gilt tops, embracing chiefly selections from writers of the most notable English, American and Foreign Fiction, together with many important works in the domains of History, Biography, Philosophy, Travel, Poetry and the Essays.

A glance at the following annexed list of titles and authors will endorse the claim that the publishers make for it—that it is the most comprehensive, choice, interesting, and by far the most carefully selected series of standard authors for world-wide reading that has been produced by any publishing house in any country, and that at prices so cheap, and in a style so substantial and pleasing, as to win for it millions of readers and the approval and commendation, not only of the book trade throughout the American continent, but of hundreds of thousands of librarians, clergymen, educators and men of letters interested in the dissemination of instructive, entertaining and thoroughly wholesome reading matter for the masses.

⌐SEE FOLLOWING PAGES⌐

Abbe Constantin. By LUDOVIC HALEVY.
Abbott. By SIR WALTER SCOTT.
Adam Bede. By GEORGE ELIOT.
Addison's Essays. EDITED BY JOHN RICHARD GREEN.
Aeneid of Virgil. TRANSLATED BY JOHN CONNINGTON.
Aesop's Fables.
Alexander, the Great, Life of. By JOHN WILLIAMS.
Alfred, the Great, Life of. By THOMAS HUGHES.
Alhambra. By WASHINGTON IRVING.
Alice in Wonderland, and Through the Looking-Glass. By LEWIS CARROLL
Alice Lorraine. By R. D. BLACKMORE
All Sorts and Conditions of Men. By WALTER BESANT.
Alton Locke. By CHARLES KINGSLEY.
Amiel's Journal. TRANSLATED BY MRS. HUMPHREY WARD.
Andersen's Fairy Tales.
Anne of Geirstein. By SIR WALTER SCOTT.
Antiquary. By SIR WALTER SCOTT.
Arabian Nights' Entertainments.
Ardath. By MARIE CORELLI.
Arnold, Benedict, Life of. By GEORGE CANNING HILL.
Arnold's Poems. By MATTHEW ARNOLD.
Around the World in the Yacht Sunbeam. By MRS. BRASSEY.
Arundel Motto. By MARY CECIL HAY.
At the Back of the North Wind. By GEORGE MACDONALD.
Attic Philosopher. By EMILE SOUVESTRE.
Auld Licht Idylls. By JAMES M. BARRIE.
Aunt Diana. By ROSA N. CAREY.
Autobiography of Benjamin Franklin.
Autocrat of the Breakfast Table. By O. W. HOLMES.
Averil. By ROSA N. CAREY.
Bacon's Essays. By FRANCIS BACON.
Barbara Heathcote's Trial. By ROSA N. CAREY.
Barnaby Rudge. By CHARLES DICKENS.
Barrack Room Ballads. By RUDYARD KIPLING.
Betrothed. By SIR WALTER SCOTT.
Beulah. By AUGUSTA J. EVANS.
Black Beauty. By ANNA SEWALL.
Black Dwarf. By SIR WALTER SCOTT.
Black Rock. By RALPH CONNOR.
Black Tulip. By ALEXANDRE DUMAS.
Bleak House. By CHARLES DICKENS.
Blithedale Romance. By NATHANIEL HAWTHORNE.
Bondman. By HALL CAINE.
Book of Golden Deeds. By CHARLOTTE M. YONGE.
Boone, Daniel, Life of. By CECIL B. HARTLEY.

Bride of Lammermoor. By SIR WALTER SCOTT.
Bride of the Nile. By GEORGE EBERS.
Browning's Poems. By ELIZABETH BARRETT BROWNING.
Browning's Poems. (SELECTIONS.) By ROBERT BROWNING.
Bryant's Poems. (EARLY.) By WILLIAM CULLEN BRYANT.
Burgomaster's Wife. By GEORGE EBERS.
Burn's Poems. By ROBERT BURNS.
By Order of the King. By VICTOR HUGO.
Byron's Poems. By LORD BYRON.
Caesar, Julius, Life of. By JAMES ANTHONY FROUDE.
Carson, Kit, Life of. By CHARLES BURDETT.
Cary's Poems. By ALICE AND PHOEBE CARY.
Cast Up by the Sea. By SIR SAMUEL BAKER.
Charlemagne (Charles the Great), Life of. By THOMAS HODGKIN, D. C. L.
Charles Auchester. By E. BERGER.
Character. By SAMUEL SMILES.
Charles O'Malley. By CHARLES LEVER.
Chesterfield's Letters. By LORD CHESTERFIELD.
Chevalier de Maison Rouge. By ALEXANDRE DUMAS.
Chicot the Jester. By ALEXANDRE DUMAS.
Children of the Abbey. By REGINA MARIA ROCHE.
Child's History of England. By CHARLES. DICKENS.
Christmas Stories. By CHARLES DICKENS.
Cloister and the Hearth. By CHARLES READE.
Coleridge's Poems. By SAMUEL TAYLOR COLERIDGE.
Columbus, Christopher, Life of. By WASHINGTON IRVING.
Companions of Jehu. By ALEXANDRE DUMAS.
Complete Angler. By WALTON AND COTTON.
Conduct of Life. By RALPH WALDO EMERSON.
Confessions of an Opium Eater. By THOMAS DE QUINCEY.
Conquest of Granada. By WASHINGTON IRVING.
Conscript. By ERCKMANN-CHATRIAN.
Conspiracy of Pontiac. By FRANCIS PARKMAN, JR.
Conspirators. By ALEXANDRE DUMAS.
Consuelo. By GEORGE SAND.
Cook's Voyages. By CAPTAIN JAMES COOK.
Corinne. By MADAME DE STAEL.
Countess de Charney. By ALEXANDRE DUMAS.
Countess Gisela. By E. MARLITT.

Countess of Rudolstadt. By George Sand.

Count Robert of Paris. By Sir Walter Scott.

Country Doctor. By Honore de Balzac.

Courtship of Miles Standish. By H. W. Longfellow.

Cousin Maude. By Mary J. Holmes.

Cranford. By Mrs. Gaskell.

Crockett, David, Life of. An Autobiography.

Cromwell, Oliver, Life of. By Edwin Paxton Hood.

Crown of Wild Olive. By John Ruskin'

Crusades. By Geo. W. Cox, M. A.

Daniel Deronda. By George Eliot.

Darkness and Daylight. By Mary J. Holmes.

Data of Ethics. By Herbert Spencer.

Daughter of an Empress, The. By Louisa Muhlbach.

David Copperfield. By Charles Dickens.

Days of Bruce. By Grace Aguilar.

Deemster, The. By Hall Caine.

Deerslayer, The. By James Fenimore Cooper.

Descent of Man. By Charles Darwin.

Discourses of Epictetus. Translated by George Long.

Divine Comedy. (Dante.) Translated by Rev. H. F. Carey.

Dombey & Son. By Charles Dickens.

Donal Grant. By George Macdonald.

Donovan. By Edna Lyall.

Dora Deane. By Mary J. Holmes.

Dove in the Eagle's Nest. By Charlotte M. Yonge.

Dream Life. By Ik Marvel.

Dr. Jekyll and Mr. Hyde. By R. L. Stevenson.

Duty. By Samuel Smiles.

Early Days of Christianity. By F. W. Farrar.

East Lynne. By Mrs. Henry Wood.

Edith Lyle's Secret. By Mary J. Holmes.

Education. By Herbert Spencer.

Egoist. By George Meredith.

Egyptian Princess. By George Ebers.

Eight Hundred Leagues on the Amazon. By Jules Verne.

Eliot's Poems. By George Eliot.

Elizabeth and her German Garden.

Elizabeth (Queen of England), Life of. By Edward Spencer Beesly, M.A.

Elsie Venner. By Oliver Wendell Holmes.

Emerson's Essays. (complete.) By Ralph Waldo Emerson.

Emerson's Poems. By Ralph Waldo Emerson.

English Orphans. By Mary J. Holmes.

English Traits. By R. W. Emerson.

Essays in Criticism. (First and Second Series.) By Matthew Arnold.

Essays of Elia. By Charles Lamb.

Esther. By Rosa N. Carey.

Ethelyn's Mistake. By Mary J. Holmes.

Evangeline. (with notes.) By H. W. Longfellow.

Evelina. By Frances Burney.

Fair Maid of Perth. By Sir Walter Scott.

Fairy Land of Science. By Arabella B. Buckley.

Faust. (Goethe.) Translated by Anna Swanwick.

Felix Holt. By George Eliot.

Fifteen Decisive Battles of the World. By E. S. Creasy.

File No. 113. By Emile Gaboriau.

Firm of Girdlestone. By A. Conan Doyle.

First Principles. By Herbert Spencer.

First Violin. By Jessie Fothergill.

For Lilias. By Rosa N. Carey.

Fortunes of Nigel. By Sir Walter Scott.

Forty-Five Guardsmen. By Alexandre Dumas.

Foul Play. By Charles Reade.

Fragments of Science. By John Tyndall.

Frederick, the Great, Life of. By Francis Kugler.

Frederick the Great and His Court. By Louisa Muhlbach.

French Revolution. By Thomas Carlyle.

From the Earth to the Moon. By Jules Verne.

Garibaldi, General, Life of. By Theodore Dwight.

Gil Blas, Adventures of. By A. R. Le Sage.

Gold Bug and Other Tales. By Edgar A. Poe.

Gold Elsie. By E. Marlitt.

Golden Treasury. By Francis T. Palgrave.

Goldsmith's Poems. By Oliver Goldsmith.

Grandfather's Chair. By Nathaniel Hawthorne.

Grant, Ulysses S., Life of. By J. T. Headley.

Gray's Poems. By Thomas Gray.

Great Expectations. By Charles Dickens.

Greek Heroes. Fairy Tales for My Children. By Charles Kingsley.

Green Mountain Boys, The. By D. P. Thompson.

Grimm's Household Tales. By the Brothers Grimm.

Grimm's Popular Tales. By the Brothers Grimm.

Gulliver's Travels. By Dean Swift.

Guy Mannering. By Sir Walter Scott.

Hale, Nathan, the Martyr Spy. By CHARLOTTE MOLYNEUX HOLLOWAY.

Handy Andy. By SAMUEL LOVER.

Hans of Iceland. By VICTOR HUGO.

Hannibal, the Carthaginian, Life of By THOMAS ARNOLD, M. A.

Hardy Norseman, A. By EDNA LYALL.

Harold. By BULWER-LYTTON.

Harry Lorrequer. By CHARLES LEVER.

Heart of Midlothian. By SIR WALTER SCOTT.

Heir of Redclyffe. By CHARLETTE M. YONGE.

Hemans' Poems. By MRS. FELICIA HEMANS.

Henry Esmond. By WM. M. THACKERAY.

Henry, Patrick, Life of. By WILLIAM WIRT.

Her Dearest Foe. By MRS. ALEXANDER.

Hereward. By CHARLES KINGSLEY.

Heriot's Choice. By ROSA N. CAREY.

Heroes and Hero-Worship. By THOMAS CARLYLE.

Hiawatha. (WITH NOTES.) By H. W. LONGFELLOW.

Hidden Hand, The. (COMPLETE.) By MRS. E. D. E. N. SOUTHWORTH.

History of a Crime. By VICTOR HUGO.

History of Civilization in Europe. By M. GUIZOT.

Holmes' Poems. (EARLY) By OLIVER WENDELL HOLMES.

Holy Roman Empire. By JAMES BRYCE.

Homestead on the Hillside. By MARY J. HOLMES.

Hood's Poems. By THOMAS HOOD.

House of the Seven Gables. By NATHANIEL HAWTHORNE.

Hunchback of Notre Dame. By VICTOR HUGO.

Hypatia. By CHARLES KINGSLEY.

Hyperion. By HENRY WADSWORTH LONGFELLOW.

Iceland Fisherman, By PIERRE LOTI.

Idle Thoughts of an Idle Fellow. By JEROME K. JEROME.

Iliad, POPE'S TRANSLATION.

Inez. By AUGUSTA J. EVANS.

Ingelow's Poems By JEAN INGELOW.

Initials By THE BARONESS TAUTPHOEUS.

Intellectual Life. By PHILIP G. HAMERTON.

In the Counsellor's House. By E. MARLITT.

In the Golden Days. By EDNA LYALL.

In the Heart of the Storm. By MAXWELL GRAY.

In the Schillingscourt. By E. MARLITT.

Ishmael. (COMPLETE.) By MRS. E. D. E. N. SOUTHWORTH.

It Is Never Too Late to Mend. By CHARLES READE.

Ivanhoe. By SIR WALTER SCOTT.

Jane Eyre. By CHARLOTTE BRONTE.

Jefferson, Thomas, Life of. By SAMUEL M. SCHMUCKER, LL.D.

Joan of Arc, Life of. By JULES MICHELET.

John Halifax, Gentleman. By MISS MULOCK.

Jones, John Paul, Life of. By JAMES OTIS.

Joseph Balsamo. By ALEXANDRE DUMAS.

Josephine, Empress of France, Life of. By FREDERICK A. OBER.

Keats' Poems. By JOHN KEATS.

Kenilworth. By SIR WALTER SCOTT.

Kidnapped. By R. L. STEVENSON.

King Arthur and His Noble Knights. By MARY MACLEOD.

Knickerbocker's History of New York. By WASHINGTON IRVING.

Knight Errant. By EDNA LYALL.

Koran. TRANSLATED BY GEORGE SALE.

Lady of the Lake. (WITH NOTES.) By SIR WALTER SCOTT.

Lady with the Rubies. By E. MARLITT.

Lafayette, Marquis de, Life of. By P. C. HEADLEY.

Lalla Rookh. (WITH NOTES.) By THOMAS MOORE.

Lamplighter. By MARIA S. CUMMINS.

Last Days of Pompeii. By BULWER-LYTTON.

Last of the Barons. By BULWER-LYTTON.

Last of the Mohicans. By JAMES FENIMORE COOPER.

Lay of the Last Minstrel. (WITH NOTES.) By SIR WALTER SCOTT.

Lee, General Robert E., Life of. By G. MERCER ADAM.

Lena Rivers. By MARY J. HOLMES.

Life of Christ. By FREDERICK W. FARRAR.

Life of Jesus. By ERNEST RENAN.

Light of Asia. By SIR EDWIN ARNOLD.

Light That Failed. By RUDYARD KIPLING.

Lincoln, Abraham, Life of. By HENRY KETCHAM.

Lincoln's Speeches. SELECTED AND EDITED BY G. MERCER ADAM.

Literature and Dogma. By MATTHEW ARNOLD.

Little Dorrit. By CHARLES DICKENS.

Little Minister. By JAMES M. BARRIE.

Livingstone, David, Life of. By THOMAS HUGHES.

Longfellow's Poems. (EARLY.) By HENRY W. LONGFELLOW.

Lorna Doone. By R. D. BLACKMORE.

Louise de la Valliere. By ALEXANDRE DUMAS.

Love Me Little, Love Me Long. By CHARLES READE.

Lowell's Poems. (EARLY.) BY JAMES RUSSELL LOWELL.
Lucile. BY OWEN MEREDITH.
Macaria. BY AUGUSTA J. EVANS.
Macaulay's Literary Essays. BY T. B. MACAULAY.
Macaulay's Poems. BY THOMAS BABINGTON MACAULAY.
Madame Therese. BY ERCKMANN-CHATRIAN.
Maggie Miller. BY MARY J. HOLMES.
Magic Skin. BY HONORE DE BALZAC.
Mahomet, Life of. BY WASHINGTON IRVING.
Makers of Florence. BY MRS. OLIPHANT.
Makers of Venice. BY MRS. OLIPHANT.
Man and Wife. BY WILKIE COLLINS.
Man in the Iron Mask. BY ALEXANDRE DUMAS.
Marble Faun. BY NATHANIEL HAWTHORNE.
Marguerite de la Valois. BY ALEXANDRE DUMAS.
Marian Grey. BY MARY J. HOLMES.
Marius, The Epicurian. BY WALTER PATER.
Marmion. (WITH NOTES.) BY SIR WALTER SCOTT.
Marquis of Lossie. BY GEORGE MACDONALD.
Martin Chuzzlewit. BY CHARLES DICKENS.
Mary, Queen of Scots, Life of. BY P. C. HEADLEY.
Mary St. John. BY ROSA N. CAREY.
Master of Ballantrae, The. BY. R. L. STEVENSON.
Masterman Ready. BY CAPTAIN MARRYATT.
Meadow Brook. BY MARY J. HOLMES.
Meditations of Marcus Aurelius. TRANSLATED BY GEORGE LONG.
Memoirs of a Physician. BY ALEXANDRE DUMAS.
Merle's Crusade. BY ROSA N. CAREY.
Micah Clarke. BY A. CONAN DOYLE.
Michael Strogoff. BY JULES VERNE.
Middlemarch. BY GEORGE ELIOT.
Midshipman Easy. BY CAPTAIN MARRYATT
Mildred. BY MARY J. HOLMES.
Millbank. BY MARY J. HOLMES.
Mill on the Floss. BY GEORGE ELIOT.
Milton's Poems. BY JOHN MILTON.
Mine Own People. BY RUDYARD KIPLING.
Minister's Wooing, The. BY HARRIET BEECHER STOWE.
Monastery. BY SIR WALTER SCOTT.
Moonstone. BY WILKIE COLLINS.
Moore's Poems. BY THOMAS MOORE
Mosses from an Old Manse. BY NATHANIEL HAWTHORNE.
Murders in the Rue Morgue. BY EDGAR ALLEN POE.
Mysterious Island. BY JULES VERNE.
Napoleon Bonaparte, Life of. BY P. C. HEADLEY.

Napoleon and His Marshals. BY J. T. HEADLEY.
Natural Law in the Spiritual World. BY HENRY DRUMMOND.
Narrative of Arthur Gordon Pym. BY EDGAR ALLAN POE.
Nature, Addresses and Lectures. BY R. W. EMERSON.
Nellie's Memories. BY ROSA N. CAREY.
Nelson, Admiral Horatio, Life of. BY ROBERT SOUTHEY.
Newcomes. BY WILLIAM M. THACKERAY.
Nicholas Nickleby. BY CHAS. DICKENS.
Ninety-Three. BY VICTOR HUGO.
Not Like Other Girls. BY ROSA N. CAREY.
Odyssey. POPE'S TRANSLATION.
Old Curiosity Shop. BY CHARLES DICKENS.
Old Mam'selle's Secret. BY E. MARLITT.
Old Mortality. BY SIR WALTER SCOTT.
Old Myddleton's Money. BY MARY CECIL HAY.
Oliver Twist. BY CHAS. DICKENS.
Only the Governess. BY ROSA N. CAREY.
On the Heights. BY BERTHOLD AUERBACH.
Oregon Trail. BY FRANCIS PARKMAN.
Origin of Species. BY CHARLES DARWIN.
Other Worlds than Ours. BY RICHARD PROCTOR.
Our Bessie. BY ROSA N. CAREY.
Our Mutual Friend. BY CHARLES DICKENS.
Outre-Mer. BY H. W. LONGFELLOW.
Owl's Nest. BY E. MARLITT.
Page of the Duke of Savoy. BY ALEXANDRE DUMAS.
Pair of Blue Eyes. BY THOMAS HARDY.
Pan Michael. BY HENRYK SIENKIEWICZ.
Past and Present. BY THOS. CARLYLE.
Pathfinder. BY JAMES FENIMORE COOPER.
Paul and Virginia. BY B. DE ST. PIERRE.
Pendennis. History of. BY WM. M. THACKERAY.
Penn, William, Life of. BY W. HEPWORTH DIXON.
Pere Goriot. BY HONORE DE BALZAC.
Peter, the Great, Life of. BY JOHN BARROW.
Peveril of the Peak. BY SIR WALTER SCOTT.
Phantom Rickshaw, The. BY RUDYARD KIPLING.
Philip II. of Spain, Life of. BY MARTIN A. S. HUME.
Gloriela. BY X. B. SAINTINE.

Pickwick Papers. By CHARLES DICKENS.

Pilgrim's Progress. By JOHN BUNYAN.

Pillar of Fire. By REV. J. H. INGRAHAM.

Pilot. By JAMES FENIMORE COOPER.

Pioneers. By JAMES FENIMORE COOPER.

Pirate. By SIR WALTER SCOTT.

Plain Tales from the Hills. By RUDYARD KIPLING.

Plato's Dialogues. TRANSLATED BY J. WRIGHT, M. A.

Pleasures of Life. By SIR JOHN LUBBOCK.

Poe's Poems. By EDGAR A. POE.

Pope's Poems. By ALEXANDER POPE.

Prairie. By JAMES F. COOPER.

Pride and Prejudice. By JANE AUSTEN.

Prince of the House of David. By REV. J. H. INGRAHAM.

Princess of the Moor. By E. MARLITT.

Princess of Thule. By WILLIAM BLACK.

Procter's Poems. By ADELAIDE PROCTOR.

Professor at the Breakfast Table. By OLIVER WENDELL HOLMES.

Professor. By CHARLOTTE BRONTE.

Prue and I. By GEORGE WILLIAM CURTIS.

Put Yourself in His Place. By CHAS. READE.

Putnam, General Israel, Life of By GEORGE CANNING HILL.

Queen Hortense. By LOUISA MUHLBACH.

Queenie's Whim. By ROSA N. CAREY.

Queen's Necklace. By ALEXANDRE DUMAS.

Quentin Durward. By SIR WALTER SCOTT.

Rasselas, History of. By SAMUEL JOHNSON.

Redgauntlet. By SIR WALTER SCOTT.

Red Rover. By JAMES FENIMORE COOPER.

Regent's Daughter. By ALEXANDRE DUMAS.

Reign of Law. By DUKE OF ARGYLE.

Representative Men. By RALPH WALDO EMERSON.

Republic of Plato. TRANSLATED BY DAVIES AND VAUGHAN.

Return of the Native. By THOMAS HARDY.

Reveries of a Bachelor. By IK MARVEL.

Reynard the Fox. EDITED BY JOSEPH JACOBS

Rienzi. By BULWER-LYTTON.

Richelieu, Cardinal, Life of. By RICHARD LODGE.

Robinson Crusoe. By DANIEL DEFOE.

Rob Roy. By SIR WALTER SCOTT.

Romance of Natural History. By P. H. GOSSE.

Romance of Two Worlds. By MARIE CORELLI.

Romola. By GEORGE ELIOT.

Rory O'More. By SAMUEL LOVER.

Rose Mather. By MARY J. HOLMES.

Rossetti's Poems. By GABRIEL DANTE ROSSETTI.

Royal Edinburgh. By MRS. OLIPHANT.

Rutledge. By MIRIAN COLES HARRIS.

Saint Michael. By E. WERNER.

Samantha at Saratoga. By JOSIAH ALLER'S WIFE. (MARIETTA HOLLEY.)

Sartor Resartus. By THOMAS CARLYLE.

Scarlet Letter. By NATHANIEL HAWHORNE.

Schonberg-Cotta Family. By MRS. ANDREW CHARLES.

Schopenhauer's Essays. TRANSLATED BY T. B. SAUNDERS.

Scottish Chiefs. By JANE PORTER.

Scott's Poems. By SIR WALTER SCOTT.

Search for Basil Lyndhurst. By ROSA N. CAREY.

Second Wife. By E. MARLITT.

Seekers After God. By F. W. FARRAR.

Self-Help. By SAMUEL SMILES.

Self-Raised. (COMPLETE.) By MRS. E. D. E. N. SOUTHWORTH.

Seneca's Morals.

Sense and Sensibility. By JANE AUSTEN.

Sentimental Journey. By LAWRENCE STERNE.

Sesame and Lilies. By JOHN RUSKIN.

Shakespeare's Heroines. By ANNA JAMESON.

Shelley's Poems. By PERCY BYSSHE SHELLEY.

Shirley. By CHARLOTTE BRONTE.

Sign of the Four. By A. CONAN DOYLE.

Silas Marner. By GEORGE ELIOT.

Silence of Dean Maitland. By MAXWELL GRAY.

Sir Gibbie. By GEORGE MACDONALD

Sketch Book. By WASHINGTON IRVING.

Smith, Captain John, Life of. By W. GILMORE SIMMS.

Socrates, Trial and Death of. TRANSLATED BY F. J. CHURCH, M. A.

Soldiers Three. By RUDYARD KIPLING.

Springhaven. By R. D. BLACKMORE.

Spy. By JAMES FENIMORE COOPER.

Stanley, Henry M., African Explorer, Life of. By A. MONTEFIORE.

Story of an African Farm. By OLIVE SCHREINER.

Story of John G. Paton. TOLD FOR YOUNG FOLKS. By REV. JAS. PATON.

St. Ronan's Well. By SIR WALTER SCOTT.

Study in Scarlet. By A. CONAN

Surgeon's Daughter. By SIR WALTER SCOTT.

Swinburne's Poems. By A. C. SWINBURNE.

Swiss Family Robinson. By JEAN RUDOLPH WYSS.

Taking the Bastile. By ALEXANDRE DUMAS.

Tale of Two Cities. By CHAS. DICKENS.

Tales from Shakespeare. By CHAS. AND MARY LAMB.

Tales of a Traveller. By WASHINGTON IRVING.

Talisman. By SIR WALTER SCOTT.

Tanglewood Tales. By NATHANIEL HAWTHORNE.

Tempest and Sunshine. By MARY J. HOLMES.

Ten Nights in a Bar Room. By T. S. ARTHUR.

Tennyson's Poems. By ALFRED TENNYSON.

Ten Years Later. By ALEXANDER DUMAS.

Terrible Temptation. By CHARLES READE.

Thaddeus of Warsaw. By JANE PORTER.

Thelma. By MARIE CORELLI.

Thirty Years' War. By FREDERICK SCHILLER.

Thousand Miles Up the Nile. By AMELIA B. EDWARDS.

Three Guardsmen. By ALEXANDER DUMAS.

Three Men in a Boat. By JEROME K. JEROME.

Thrift. By SAMUEL SMILES.

Throne of David. By REV. J. H. INGRAHAM.

Toilers of the Sea. By VICTOR HUGO

Tom Brown at Oxford. By THOMAS HUGHES.

Tom Brown's School Days. By THOS. HUGHES.

Tom Burke of "Ours." By CHARLES LEVER.

Tour of the World in Eighty Days. By JULES VERNE.

Treasure Island. By ROBERT LOUIS STEVENSON.

Twenty Thousand Leagues Under the Sea. By JULES VERNE.

Twenty Years After. By ALEXANDRE DUMAS.

Twice Told Tales. By NATHANIEL HAWTHORNE.

Two Admirals. By JAMES FENIMORE COOPER.

Two Dianas. By ALEXANDRE DUMAS.

Two Years Before the Mast. By R. H. DANA, Jr.

Uarda. By GEORGE EBERS.

Uncle Max. By ROSA N. CAREY.

Uncle Tom's Cabin. By HARRIET BEECHER STOWE.

Under Two Flags. By "OUIDA."

Utopia. By SIR THOMAS MORE.

Vanity Fair. By WM. M. THACKERAY.

Vendetta. By MARIE CORELLI.

Vespucius, Americus, Life and Voyages. By C. EDWARDS LESTER.

Vicar of Wakefield. By OLIVER GOLDSMITH.

Vicomte de Bragelonne. By ALEXANDRE DUMAS.

Views A-Foot. By BAYARD TAYLOR.

Villette. By CHARLOTTE BRONTE.

Virginians. By WM. M. THACKERAY.

Walden. By HENRY D. THOREAU.

Washington, George, Life of. By JARED SPARKS.

Washington and His Generals. By J. T. HEADLEY.

Water Babies. By CHARLES KINGSLEY.

Water Witch. By JAMES FENIMORE COOPER.

Waverly. By SIR WALTER SCOTT.

Webster, Daniel, Life of. By SAMUEL M. SCHMUCKER, LL.D.

Webster's Speeches. (SELECTED.) By DANIEL WEBSTER.

Wee Wifie. By ROSA N. CAREY.

Westward Ho! By CHARLES KINGSLEY.

We Two. By EDNA LYALL.

What's Mine's Mine. By GEORGE MACDONALD.

When a Man's Single. By J. M. BARRIE.

White Company. By A. CONAN DOYLE.

Whites and the Blues. By ALEXANDRE DUMAS.

Whittier's Poems. (EARLY.) By JOHN G. WHITTIER.

Wide, Wide World. By SUSAN WARNER.

William, the Conqueror, Life of. By EDWARD A. FREEMAN, LL.D.

William, the Silent, Life of. By FREDERICK HARRISON.

Willy Reilly. By WILLIAM CARLETON.

Window in Thrums. By J. M. BARRIE

Wing and Wing. By JAMES FENIMORE COOPER.

Wolsey, Cardinal, Life of. By MANDELL CREIGHTON.

Woman in White. By WILKIE COLLINS.

Won by Waiting. By EDNA LYALL.

Wonder Book. For BOYS AND GIRLS. By NATHANIEL HAWTHORNE.

Woodstock. By SIR WALTER SCOTT.

Wooed and Married. By ROSA N. CAREY.

Wooing O't. By MRS. ALEXANDER.

Wordsworth's Poems. By WILLIAM WORDSWORTH.

Wormwood. By MARIE CORELLI.

Wreck of the Grosvenor. By W. CLARK RUSSELL.